FOLLOWING THE FRONT

FOLLOWING THE FRONT

The Dispatches of World War II Correspondent
Sidney A. Olson

EDITED BY MARGOT CLARK-JUNKINS

ROWMAN & LITTLEFIELD
Lanham • Boulder • New York • London

Published by Rowman & Littlefield
An imprint of The Rowman & Littlefield Publishing Group, Inc.
4501 Forbes Boulevard, Suite 200, Lanham, Maryland 20706
www.rowman.com

86-90 Paul Street, London EC2A 4NE, United Kingdom

British Library Cataloguing in Publication Information Available

Library of Congress Cataloging-in-Publication Data available
ISBN 978-1-5381-9208-5 (cloth: alk. paper)
ISBN 978-1-5381-9209-2 (electronic)

♾️™ The paper used in this publication meets the minimum requirements of American National Standard for Information Sciences—Permanence of Paper for Printed Library Materials, ANSI/ NISO Z39.48-1992.

For Sid

How could an entire nation lose every trace of gentleness and humility, the common property of all men under the stars? Every morning brought home to me again the enormity and the dangers of an entire people lost in darkness.

—O. M. MAGNUSSEN
*THE LONG NORWEGIAN NIGHT:
A WWII RESISTANCE FIGHTER'S LIFE IN NAZI CAMPS*

Contents

ACKNOWLEDGMENTS

This book was brought to life by Sidney Olson's daughter—my mother—Whitney O. Clark. We worked in tandem on this project for over five years. Every question I had, she answered. Every e-mail I exchanged with an expert, she read their responses. There was a daily give-and-take, by phone, text, and e-mail and often in person, since we lived just five minutes apart until 2021. She read the manuscript over and over again with the eyes of an eagle. Every idea we had for the book was bounced back and forth until a decision was made. The call and response we developed was proof of a sound partnership, but more than that, it was evidence of the love between a mother and daughter. She died before she could hold the book in her hands, but it pleased her beyond measure that it would soon be held by students of history and, hopefully, read for generations to come.

Thank you for supporting us with your advice, feedback, ideas, and encouragement: Laney Ackley, Rowman & Littlefield Publishers; Merilee Bostock; Gemma R. Birnbaum, American Jewish Historical Society; Debbie Bloom, The Dead Librarian; Deb Brown; Josh Caster, Archives & Special Collections, Love Library, University of Nebraska–Lincoln; Rachael Cerrotti, *We Share the Same Sky: A Memoir of Memory & Migration*; Julia Kennedy, *Ed Kennedy's War: V-E Day, Censorship, and the Associated Press*; Joshua Cochrane, American History & Diplomacy, Beinecke Rare Book and Manuscript Library, Yale University; Joelle Delbourgo, Joelle Delbourgo Associates Literary Agency; Ashley Dodge, Rowman & Littlefield Publishers; Dan Dougherty, U.S. 7th Army, 45th Division, 157th Regiment, C Company; Colonel Kevin W. Farrell, PhD, U.S. Army Retired, Battlefield Leadership, LLC; Lori Inglis

Hall, The Lee Miller Archives, Farleys House & Gallery; Ann Godoff, Penguin Press; Bill Hooper, New-York Historical Society; Kay Grigsby, Wartburg College Archives & Archives of Iowa Broadcasting; Mark A. Huddle, *Roi Ottley's World War II: The Lost Diary of an African American Journalist*; Sara Ickow, International Center for Photography; Samuel Kassow, *Who Will Write Our History? Rediscovering a Hidden Archive from the Warsaw Ghetto*; Hilbert Margol, Battery B, 392nd Field Artillery Battalion, 42 Infantry (Rainbow) Division; Suellen R. McDaniel, Rainbow Reveille and Rainbow Trail History Newsletters, Rainbow Division Veterans Foundation; Deena R. Merlen, Esq., Reavis Page Jump LLP; Julie Metz, *Eva and Eve: A Search for My Mother's Lost Childhood and What a War Left Behind*; Francesca Pitaro, Associated Press Archives; Noel Ragsdale; Heidi Reavis, Esq., Reavis Page Jump LLP; Lily Rothman, *Time* magazine; Holly Rubino, Holly Rubino Editorial; Kyra Schuster, National Institute for Holocaust Documentation, United States Holocaust Memorial Museum; Gretchen Shoemaker, National Archives at St. Louis; Victoria Skurnick, Levine Greenberg Rostan Literary Agency; Anatole Steck, National Institute for Holocaust Documentation, United States Holocaust Memorial Museum; Jane Leventhal Valentine; Alberto Vitale, Random House; Jacqueline Wachholz, John W. Hartman Center for Sales, Advertising, and Marketing History, David M. Rubenstein Rare Book & Manuscript Library, Duke University; Olivia B. Waxman, *Time* magazine; Ronald Weber, *Dateline—Liberated Paris: The Hotel Scribe and the Invasion of the Press*; and Mark S. Zaid, P.C.

Special and deepest thanks to my family—Allen M. Clark, Theodore Junkins, Madeleine Junkins, Guy Junkins, Robinson Clark, Tony Clark, Mardie Luppold, and John and Linwood Olson—and to my friends—Jackie Berner, Caroll Claps, Mary Fitzgibbons, Paula Fung, Sara Girard, Jamie Jensen, Aviva Kamander, Sonali Laschever, Ann Magalhaes, Julia McCartney, Carin Mehler, Emi Meulbroek, Maria Nowak, Alison Cupp Relyea, Sian Roath, and Amy Vijayanagar.

Thanks, too, to the many archives that proved instrumental to the success of this project: Beinecke Rare Book and Manuscript Library, Yale University; Benson Ford Research Center, The Henry Ford; John W. Hartman Center for Sales, Advertising, and Marketing History,

David M. Rubenstein Rare Book & Manuscript Library, Duke University; Margaret Herrick Library, Academy of Motion Picture Arts and Sciences; Houghton Library, Harvard University; Archives & Special Collections, Love Library, University of Nebraska–Lincoln; Patricia D. Klingenstein Library, New-York Historical Society; New York Public Library; South Caroliniana Library, University of South Carolina; and Harry S. Truman Library.

PREFACE

This book is a compilation of World War II dispatches written by Sidney A. Olson while serving as a correspondent for *Time* and *Life* magazines during the final months of the war in Europe.

Plenty of World War II correspondents went on to publish their memoirs, but for some reason, Olson chose not to write his own. After his death in 1995, his daughter Whitney (my mother) preserved his personal papers, which included war dispatches along with correspondence, diary pages, clippings, and ephemera from the 1920s through the 1980s.

In 2019, my mother and I began the painstaking process of transcribing the war dispatches, which were known to the family in a limited sort of way. No one was terribly sure what Olson had seen during the war; the only thing we knew for certain was that he had published an article in *Time* about the liberation of Dachau concentration camp. As we began to place the dispatches in chronological order, two things became apparent: his writing was exquisite and often heartbreaking, and some of his dispatches were missing entirely.

As we stitched together a timeline, we began to understand the startling scope of his experiences while overseas. He catapulted from one scene of destruction to another, eloquently describing the human toll and the growing population of displaced persons ("DPs"). Like the buildings around him, civilization appeared to be collapsing before his eyes. He did what all journalists are expected to do: he recorded what he saw, doing his best to mute his personal beliefs and emotional reactions. Few of us can understand the magnitude of this expectation. He risked his life on more than one occasion. Years later, he wrote in his diary, "A question to ask myself repeatedly: where did I get my courage?"[1]

A fair amount of what Olson typed up and cabled back to Time Inc.'s New York office was never published. Some of his dispatches were passed over for practical reasons: *Time* and *Life* were weekly publications, and due to the number of events taking place at the tumultuous close of the war, news from the front changed hourly. Often, his dispatches were carved up by his editors, and in keeping with Time Inc.'s practice of pooling information, portions were folded into large articles with multiple contributors.

Thankfully, Olson saved some of his dispatches, and we were able to track down more at the New-York Historical Society and Harvard University. This was challenging in the midst of a global pandemic.

As we progressed in our research, we were pleasantly surprised to discover that Olson had in fact received a "byline" for some of his reporting. We also developed a profound respect for the dispatches themselves, fragile primary source documents that could have easily been lost or discarded. In fact, seven years after the war ended, much of the World War II–related material at Time Inc. may have been discarded, according to a memo written by a vice president there: "This will confirm our telephone conversation of a few minutes ago in which I said that Mr. Luce, Mr. Billings and myself all agree that our full collection of foreign cables received in the years 1939–1946 (and now occupying 34 filing cabinets) can be destroyed. As Mr. Luce remarked, 'History will not lack for volumes of material on World War II.'"[2]

As a body of work, Olson's dispatches contain fascinating and sometimes little-known details about the war. They provide dramatic glimpses of the front, the shifting nature of battle strategy, and alternately colorful and tragic snippets of information about generals, soldiers, refugees, prisoners, and civilians, all of whom were operating under extreme duress.

His accounts of men and women at their best and worst under dreadful circumstances help put today's complex world in perspective, especially at a time when democratic ideals are being tested and the threat of rising nationalism calls to mind the Nazi regime. For more than 70 years, Olson's dispatches sat mutely inside archival boxes; now they will inform future generations about the horrors of war. If we expect to strive for a better world, we must all become—and remain—students of history.

—Margot Clark-Junkins

NOTE

In the dispatches, any parenthetical remarks were made by Olson. All bracketed comments were made by the editor of this book.

The words "dispatch" and "cable" are used interchangeably.

Unless otherwise indicated with a footnote, all archival material is from Sidney A. Olson Papers, currently in a private collection but intended for future scholars to access at the Beinecke Rare Book and Manuscript Library, Yale University.

Chapter I

Prewar

On the evening of January 31, 1942, Sid Olson received a telegram at the Cadillac Hotel in Detroit. "Dear Sidney," it read. "You are herewith offered a job as *Time* correspondent, any place anywhere, at practically any salary."

In fact, Olson already worked for *Time*. He had just turned in an elegantly written and insightful article, full of granular detail about defense production, autoworkers, and assembly lines, to David Hulburd, *Time's* chief of the News Bureau.[1] Hulburd was only joking, but he added on a more serious note, "That is really superb stuff you've been turning out this week and I think you are wasting your time writing those little *Time* stories."

Seven weeks earlier, on December 7, 1941, the Japanese had attacked Pearl Harbor. On December 8, the United States declared war on Japan. On December 11, the United States declared war on Germany and Italy. The nation's defenses needed ramping up in a hurry. Olson had gone to Michigan to cover the "conversion" from automobile manufacturing to weapons production. It made one hell of a story.

In his article about the conversion, Olson described the colossal waste that was about to take place: most of the machinery used to make America's cars could not possibly be repurposed. "The whole argument of conversion," he explained, "hinges on what percentage of auto-making tools are general-purpose tools suitable for arms production." He watched as "the big presses and special spot-welding machines and great dies and fixtures—all of which were single-purpose, special-purpose tools doing one little operation in a production-line, and fit for nothing else—were loaded one by one on flat cars and hauled out into the plant yard."

Olson moved on to the good news: defense production. "I have now been to these plants. . . . Ford's Willow Run bombers; his River Rouge Pratt and Whitney engine plant, and the Rouge plant generally; the Chrysler tank arsenal; the Chrysler Bofors gun plant; the Fisher tank design in Detroit, and tank plant in Flint; Chevrolet in Flint; AG spark plugs in Flint, who are making about 85 Browning machine guns a day; the General Motors Pontiac plant making Oerlikon guns; the Pontiac plant where they are beginning to make air torpedoes."

In touring the various plants, he saw sights difficult to describe. "The biggest story out here—and they're all big—is welded tanks. This has to be seen to be appreciated." Of Ford's Willow Run, he wrote, "The size of the plant is beyond belief. The size of the operation is incredible. Somebody in a month or two could do a magnificent story merely by starting at one end of the plant with a piece of aluminum and flying in a heavy bomber out of the other end hours later. . . . There are eleven miles of airplane run ways alone, and at least 11 miles of statistics which all boil down to the words: the biggest, the best, the fastest, and the most."

After receiving Hulburd's telegram with its glowing praise, Olson must have felt a wave of gratitude wash over him; such encouragement was rare. He had been with Time Inc. for almost three years, starting out as a contributing editor covering national affairs.[2] It couldn't have been easy for the son of Swedish immigrants and a Mormon from Salt Lake City, Utah; he was a fish out of water in Manhattan, surrounded by East Coast intellectuals from Yale and Harvard. And working at Time Inc. was something of a blood sport: writers battled for approval from founder Henry Luce (cofounder Briton Hadden died in 1929) by hunting down and filing the best stories possible while tiptoeing around their boss's staunchly Republican political agenda.

Olson's article about the conversion appears to have earned him a promotion because shortly after his return to New York, his former employer, the *Washington Post*, ran this announcement: "Made a Senior Editor of *Time*—Sid Olson, former city editor of *The Post*, whose elevation to senior editor for national affairs, Army and Navy, was announced by *Time*."[3]

Hulburd's telegram, the *Post* announcement, and the promotion itself were welcome forms of validation. He could sit back for a moment, take stock, and revel in his success. In earlier days, his course had been less clear; he had groped his way forward with little guidance and few mentors. But a keen intellect and raw ambition had sustained him, always.

Sidney Alexander Olson was born in Salt Lake City on April 30, 1908. It is unlikely that either of Sid's parents received more than a rudimentary education, but it can be said that they achieved the American dream: Alex Olson worked for the Union Pacific Railroad, and Sigrid kept house. They owned a modest home on Girard Avenue where they raised three boys: Sid was the eldest, followed by Clifford, and then Stanley.

Olson entered the University of Utah in the fall of 1925. He was an editor of the university's newspaper as well as its literary and humor magazines. His diary entries reflect an earnest young man in love with learning who sought a more cerebral life than his parents could provide. He followed news and politics avidly. He loved to read and kept a book log, always including the total number of pages and a short review.

After his junior year, he left college and began working at Stevens & Wallis (S&W), an advertising and printing company in Salt Lake City.[4] Money may have been a factor: he came of age during the height of the Depression. From 1929 to 1933, banks collapsed, farms went into foreclosure, and jobs vanished weekly.[5] Sometimes, S&W could not afford to pay their staff, and Olson frequently noted in his diary that he was short on cash.

In January 1932, Sid met a beautiful young woman named Zembra, who was the daughter of State Senator Albert Holmgren and his wife, Nancy. The family had a farm in nearby Bear River City. Zembra had already completed a two-year teaching program at the University of Utah and was teaching grammar school.[6] Sid was enchanted by her, and they became quite serious about each other in spite of the fact that Zembra was engaged to a young man from Salt Lake City who happened to be away on the East Coast, studying to become a doctor.

Sid frequently bemoaned the fact that he could not afford to take Zembra out for the evening. Meanwhile, her parents made it clear that they were unhappy about Olson's appearance on the scene; he had no obvious career prospects and no income to support a wife. Although she was in love with Sid, Zembra felt intense pressure to honor her engagement and told him she planned to meet her parents' expectations. Sid wrote with frustration in his diary in June 1933,

> Can she not rise above that . . . narrow way of thinking, and imagine how things are in the great world? Here she does not even stop to appreciate this fine breadth and tolerance of my mind—and I'm not boasting. . . . Once in New York, she would soon see who was right, and how acceptable my mind, habits and ways of thinking would be. . . . It's impossible for her, or anyone else, after all, to understand what I am working toward, until it is done. Or to know how hard I have worked and am working. Geez, no one but me will *ever* know! But what a rich background I've got! It'll pay me yet, and plenty, too.

Whenever he could afford it, Sid invited Zembra to see a show at one of Salt Lake City's theaters, which featured films, musical acts, and even live broadcasts of the news. He participated in "radio tryouts" and had begun to write some of the news programs for KSL.[7] Radio was still something of a novelty, and its popularity as a source of news and culture was growing rapidly. While he was still a full-time student, an area newspaper had reported, "Leading men in all various departments of the University of Utah have been engaged to speak from station KSL and station KFUT . . . within a short time a large supply of radio equipment is expected to arrive at the university for the use of the campus radio station."[8] In 1932, KSL joined the CBS Radio Network and moved to the top floor of the Union Pacific building.[9] In February 1933, he wrote, "More steady work at KSL stuff. We are getting established there more solidly every day."[10]

In addition to writing the news for KSL, Olson had begun contributing book reviews to the *Deseret News*. It is clear from these small victories that he was cobbling together experiences—and money—as best he could in an effort to propel himself forward. His friends were beginning to leave him behind, setting off for new cities in search of employment.

On March 20, 1933, Olson left S&W. He wrote in his diary, "I was with S&W for 4 years, 9 months, 6 days . . . Jesus Christ, what a relief!" Meanwhile, he had convinced Zembra to break off her engagement. While his joy was great, it was now imperative that he find a steady job. By October, he was writing articles for the *Deseret News*. He noted proudly, "Inside of three weeks I had an article on the front page with a byline." He often stood at the airport late at night, waiting for planes that stopped to refuel en route to Los Angeles, hoping to snag a good interview. That winter, when a plane carrying eight people crashed in the mountains north of Salt Lake City and killed all on board, Olson raced to the scene and was pictured among the rescuers in a photo picked up by the *New York Times*.[11]

One night at the airport, Olson met "a tall, thin Colonel named H. H. ('Hap') Arnold [who] advised me to go to Washington."[12] Olson was intrigued with this idea. In January 1934, his friend Harold Rhoden-baugh, a photographer at the *Washington Post*, alerted him to an open position there. Although Sid was not yet ready to leave Zembra, the idea of moving to Washington, D.C., gave him hope for a brighter future. In early August, when offered "the last free pass ever issued by United Airlines," Olson grabbed it. He flew to Cleveland and from there took a bus to Washington, D.C.[13] He arrived with less than $100 in his wallet and a letter of reference from editor Joseph J. Cannon: "During the year you have been with *The Deseret News*, I have looked on you not only as one of the keenest and best trained minds on our staff, but as having unusual future possibilities from which the paper would benefit. If you have a change of heart and come back to us, you know how sincere the welcome will be."[14]

Olson dropped off his portfolio with Ralph Renaud, the managing editor at the *Washington Post*. In a letter to Zembra dated August 10, 1934, Sid assured her that his prospects looked good: "Very definite chance that I will land a job interviewing people, as *Post* interview man, handling airport and hotel beat."[15]

Days later, Mark F. Ethridge, the assistant managing editor at the *Washington Post*, hired him. His job of clipping and filing news items was not glamorous, but he found that he enjoyed it: "I do love it and work at it for one solid reason—I learn daily. Hundreds and hundreds of facts—national backgrounds, etc. It keeps me very well-informed and that I like."[16]

In December 1934, he was given the opportunity to cover the National Conference on Crime, working with Ed Folliard, "our ace man," at the *Post*. In a letter to Zembra, he breathlessly cataloged the many political figures whom he was encountering and might soon be permitted to interview: "I'm so happy now . . . this arrangement is tentative, but it's my chance and I'm going to make the best of it . . . it's a bigger thing to happen to me than moving to Washington. . . . Now I'm getting a chance to be a top man, and make lots of money . . . *this* is the break you've been waiting for, and it's up to me now more than ever."[17]

Because he had written book and film reviews for the *Deseret News*, the *Post* gave him that chance, too. Within half a year, he had gotten his name on a handful of reviews. Next, he pitched the idea of creating a brand-new section in the newspaper, one that would give him an opportunity to cover current events. He wrote in his diary, "Last day in city-room of *Washington Post* as Monday I begin in Sunday dept on 'News Review of Week' idea."[18] As for his airport and hotel beat: "Told all hotels I was leaving the run."[19]

His dream of writing for a living was now a reality. He received a steady paycheck signed by Eugene Meyer, who had purchased the *Washington Post* just a year earlier. Meyer was known to be both hard-driving and thoughtful when it came to his staff.[20] It was not unusual for Olson and his colleagues to show up at the office late at night and remain there, working straight into the next day. To his delight, keeping up with the news had become his raison d'être.

In October 1935, Zembra joined Sid in Washington, finding rooms to share with several other young women. By November 1, she had secured a job as a junior stenographer, working for the U.S. government's Procurement Division, Branch of Supply.

On Sunday, December 29, 1935, Olson's headline stretched across the first page of the *Post*'s "Weekly News Review": "A Year of Violent Struggle at Home and Turmoil Abroad." That his byline sat squarely beneath the title was perhaps the best Christmas gift he had ever received. He wrote,

> The year to come, shadowed by war and the promises of violence, with a national election that is more and more significant with every passing month, with the stand of the Supreme Court on the rest of the New Deal soon to be announced, and with the threat of inflation in this country, from the excess reserves that have piled up month by month, as one of the chief dangers—the year to come will make the newspapers more exciting than ever to the thoughtful public, as day by day the fresh black ink will tell which way the spinning world is going.[21]

He continued to receive new assignments. On February 20, 1936, he wrote in his diary that he had "cleaned up straggling ends of narcotics bureau story, whipped it into shape and planted it firmly. Will crack open in final edition tomorrow morning." He added proudly, "I get my first byline on the front page since coming to the National Bureau and first since January of last year, due to anonymity of the News Review set-up. Should bust things open plenty."[22] On March 8, he wrote, "Offer from *News-Week* to go to New York, about $65 or $70." Then, almost as an afterthought, he added, "To White House Correspondents Ball last night."[23]

Franklin D. Roosevelt (FDR), who was known for his close relationship with the press, often took time to converse with journalists. White House Press Secretary Stephen Early acted as gatekeeper, allowing only those who were card-carrying members of the House and Senate press galleries and the White House Correspondents' Association.[24] Olson carried both.

The year 1936 proved to be a pivotal one for him. He began covering complex news stories, such as the New Deal, the National Recovery Administration, the Tennessee Valley Authority, and the economic and social implications of severe drought, flooding, food shortages, farm relief, and labor disputes. His pieces often landed on the newspaper's front page.

His success at work spilled over pleasantly into his personal life. On May 14, 1936, Zembra received an invitation from the White House to accompany Sid to a formal "At Home" for correspondents. "The people I met," she wrote, "like Sir Willmott Lewis (correspondent for the *London Times*) . . . the Washington representatives of the *N.Y. Times*, the *N.Y. Herald Tribune*, the *Chicago Tribune*, the *Baltimore Sun*, the *United Press* and the *Associated Press*."[25] She mentioned that the president's secretary, Marvin H. McIntyre, had tapped Sid on the shoulder to say hello, and she listed some of the other important people she met that night, including Roosevelt's secretary of state, Cordell Hull, and the secretary of commerce, Daniel C. Roper. She added, "I almost skipped saying about Eleanor. She's very charming too and flutters and stutters about just like a butterfly. . . . I met her and shook hands with her too . . . she smiles so much and is so sweet and has so much poise that she makes herself look almost beautiful."

President Roosevelt's physical condition surprised her: "The President is quite a pathetic sight when he stands up. At 11 o'clock the music stopped and he said goodnight to everyone and then was helped out by Mr. McIntyre and one of the Secret Service men. He is so big and jolly from the waist up, but his legs are almost useless. Oh he can walk but it's more of a drag. He has so much jolly fun about him and is so charming."

Olson proved to be especially adept at covering politics. In early June 1936, he was sent to cover the Republican convention in Cleveland. The newspaper ran a photograph of Olson as he interviewed Republican Senator William E. Borah of Idaho.[26] Ten days later, in anticipation of the Democratic convention in Philadelphia, the *Post* ran another photograph of Olson, this time interviewing Democratic Senator Alben W. Barkley of Kentucky on the steps of the Capitol in Washington, D.C.[27]

His reporting at both conventions reflected a comfortable understanding of the political sphere; his articles had a certain style—they tended to be acerbic and sometimes glib and were often peppered with references to popular culture. He knew how to set the scene and create drama. On the final day of the convention in Philadelphia, FDR accepted the nomination for president, uttering the famous phrase "rendezvous with destiny." Olson's recap of the speech ran on the front page of the *Post*: "As the President said 'I accept—,' the gathering, sensing the conclusion of the address, tore loose its vocal chords and scattered noise to the hazy skies. His final sentence was lost in the din."[28] In his career as a journalist, Olson would go on to cover three more cycles of party conventions and presidential elections.

In October, he was one of 26 journalists selected to travel with the president. On this particular trip, FDR moved north by train from Washington, D.C., to New Jersey, New York, Pennsylvania, and Delaware, stopping to preside at ceremonies and give public addresses.[29] CBS broadcaster Harry Butcher was also on board; during World War II, he would become General Eisenhower's aide and was one of the few to witness the German surrender at Reims in May 1945.[30]

On January 16, 1937—on the anniversary of their first meeting five years earlier—Sid and Zembra were married at last in Washington, D.C. A few days later, the *Salt Lake Telegram* ran their wedding announcement.[31] Immediately after the ceremony, Sid and Zembra took a cab to Union Station and boarded a train to New York City. They had dinner and danced at the Rainbow Room atop Rockefeller Center and spent the night at the Waldorf Astoria. What an astonishing change he had managed to make in his life.

A few days later, on January 20, 1937, Olson attended Roosevelt's inauguration as an invited member of the press. The same-day headline of his full-page article in the *Post* read, "'The Boss' Has Matured during Four Years in White House."[32]

Olson had hit his stride, finding success and happiness on all fronts. In June, he wrote in his diary, "The end of the half-year finds me: married 5 1/2 months and even more in love with my wife than before. . . . My job is apparently as secure as any newspaper job not under contract could be. I have really gained in prestige since January." Soon after that, he wrote, "I am soon to be a father, something I have long looked forward to with the keenest anticipation."

Their daughter Whitney was born on October 26, 1937. As Christmas approached, Sid made a list of resolutions for the coming year, concluding humbly, "To be patient, to work hard, and to amount to something for my wife and my daughter."[33]

He was appointed city editor in 1938.[34] On March 12, he attended the White House Correspondents' 17th Annual Dinner at the Mayflower Hotel. On April 9, he dined with his colleagues at the Gridiron Club's Spring Dinner at the Willard Hotel. He was a true Washingtonian now: the seating plan placed him closer to FDR than his future boss, *Time*'s founder, Henry Luce.[35]

One year later, Olson found himself face-to-face with Luce at the Mayflower Hotel in Washington, D.C. Luce was a towering figure in American publishing, politics, and society who oversaw a lucrative and expanding media empire that included *Time*, *Life*, and *Fortune* magazines. He wanted Olson to join *Time*; the magazine needed his political acumen and D.C. contacts. But Olson, who had advanced at breakneck speed from clipping stories to White House correspondent to city editor, was reluctant to make a change.

"I have just come from an hour's chat with Henry Luce at the Mayflower hotel," he wrote to Zembra, who had taken the baby to visit her family in Utah.[36] "You know, the *Time-Life-Fortune-March of Time* tycoon. He is very hot to get me." The letter reflects his characteristic resolve and confidence: "I want to be with something that's going somewhere. And I seriously think the *Post* will one day be the greatest newspaper in the world. It's well on its way now. What's more, Casey has told me twice in the last week, quite apart from this proposition, that I am the next managing editor—when he becomes general manager."[37] He continued,

> *Time* writing is formulized, stereotyped, patterned. I don't want to write like that. I told Luce that. I told him about my wanting to grow, about that fact that I want to be with something that is moving and not static—not to be associated with a past success but with a future success, in whose glory I will have some part in shaping. What I'm saying in brief is that I don't have the old college feeling about *Time*. The offer doesn't kill me as it perhaps should. I don't know who I am that I should talk back to the most successful magazine publisher of our times, but after all I am me, and I know in a vague and fumbling way (and yet in

a clear, hard and cold way) exactly what I want and where I want to go. I want to leave an imprint, and I won't do it in becoming one of the Slaves in the cells at *Time*, which has become so much like a factory.

Strong words, perhaps, for a 31-year-old reporter who had arrived in Washington, D.C., just five years earlier without money or a job, but in that time he had gained traction in his chosen field and written more than 700 articles with a byline.[38] Given his successes thus far, his hesitation was understandable.

He accepted the job. It is likely that the salary offered by Luce was too good to pass up. Time Inc. was turning an enormous profit, and Luce was in a position to offer his editors fairly high salaries as well as steady contracts and perks, such as profit sharing.[39] It would also be fair to surmise that Olson could not resist the allure of Luce and *Time*—the prestige that came from being associated with both. With their one-and-a-half year-old daughter in tow, Sid and Zembra moved to New York City and rented an apartment on Fort Washington Avenue. In July, Olson reported for work at the 36-story Time & Life Building at 9 Rockefeller Plaza.[40]

Now he was one of Luce's "slaves." Like all the other Time "Inc-ers," he worked 10 to 14 hours a day, Thursday through Monday (with Tuesdays and Wednesdays as their "weekend"). At first, he served as an editor of national affairs.[41]

In June 1940, Luce's deputy, John Shaw Billings, wrote in his diary, "New Time Inc. set-up in Washington—with Olson in charge."[42] In July, a small news item announced Olson's presence in D.C., where he was "centralizing *Time*, *Life*, *Fortune*, and the *March of Time* into one office."[43]

On July 16, 1940, Olson was in Chicago covering the Democratic convention. The president had not yet accepted the nomination for an unprecedented third term. Olson fed a page of Western Union "Press Message" stationery into a typewriter and typed, "Franklin Roosevelt is still optimistic that England will hold out, that the United States will have time to arm, that the British fleet will remain throughout the winter a barrier to Hitler and a defense for the U.S. In short, Franklin Roosevelt will probably accept the nomination because he thinks he, the U.S. and perhaps England will still be around to cash in on the defense program when the first new tanks roll through the streets, when the U.S. Army is on the march." FDR accepted the nomination and was reelected in November, defeating Wendell Willkie.

On the night of December 29, 1940, in one of his "fireside chats," the president addressed the nation in a radio broadcast, announcing the end of America's nonintervention policy. The United States would get involved indirectly through a "Lend-Lease" arrangement, which is best explained by the historian Doris Kearns Goodwin as an "unconventional idea that the United States could send Britain weapons and supplies without charge and then, after the war, be repaid not in dollars but in kind."[44] This particular fireside chat came to be known as FDR's "arsenal of democracy" speech.

A number of writers and other public figures have been credited with the invention of this phrase, including the playwright Robert Sherwood, who was one of FDR's speechwriters; Harry Hopkins, FDR's liaison to Winston Churchill and the administrator of the Lend-Lease program; and William S. Knudsen, a Detroit auto executive. It is therefore quite extraordinary to read what Olson wrote 11 years later to a colleague at the advertising agency J. Walter Thompson:

> I will tell you a true short story. Luce hired me away from the Washington Post, where I had become city editor, in 1939; but I still returned many times a month to Washington, often to go to press conferences at the White House. Once, when I lingered, Mr. Roosevelt was grumbling about the lend-lease problem. He said he needed "a line." I told him I had written a line in *Time*'s National Affairs section that week which might help; in it I had said that the U.S. might become "the arsenal of democracy." He kept *Time* in a rack on the back of his office lavatory-door; now he shook several more hands and then waved to me, shouting: "I'll go read it now!"[45]

Sherwood himself speculated about the phrase's origin, writing that "in preparation of the Fireside Chat (delivered December 29) Hopkins provided the key phrase which had already been used in some newspaper editorial: 'We must be the great arsenal of democracy.' I have been told that the phrase was originated by William S. Knudsen and also by Jean Monnet, but whoever originated it, Roosevelt was the one who proclaimed it."[46]

With the official passage of the Lend-Lease Act in March 1941, Detroit (and other Michigan manufacturing towns, such as Flint and Dearborn) entered the national spotlight, taking on a central role in the production of planes, tanks, and munitions. Meanwhile, FDR's assistant secretary of war, John McCloy, issued a secret memorandum about the state of the nation's defenses, and the news was not good: the United States was lacking in war readiness.

In September, a "digest" of this secret memo was shared with Luce and a handful of editors at Time Inc., including Olson. It stated ominously, "Present production schedules show that the existing program for several of the very important ordnance and aircraft items will not be completed until well into the fiscal year 1944."[47]

The United States was not yet officially engaged in World War II, but all indications seemed to point to the country's future involvement. Luce believed that his three magazines had the ability, perhaps even the duty, to influence the course of events. Time Inc. editors feverishly tracked— and debated—the shifting geopolitical landscape.

On December 7, 1941, Olson tore a stunning announcement from the teletype machine announcing, "Japs attack Pearl Harbor." He scrawled in red pen, "John Hersey got the other half of this flash."[48] In January 1942, he headed to Detroit. His article about the conversion of factories in preparation for war was a big story, and he was glad for the opportunity to cover it.

In March, he was named "senior editor for National Affairs, Army and Navy."[49] That summer, he was given two plum temporary assignments: that of executive editor, followed by assistant managing editor.[50] He worked constantly, researching and writing his own articles but primarily acting as editor and manager. He stayed up very late most nights, reading, writing, smoking, and drinking coffee.

His career and home life were full and rewarding. On July 1, 1942, their son John was born. The previous fall, Sid and Zembra had purchased their first home, a grand Georgian-style brick house at 21 Pryer

Lane in Larchmont, New York.[51] They were permanently situated at last, tending to house and garden, happily raising their two children, and playing bridge with neighborhood friends.

In his work life, Olson could be counted as part of Luce's inner circle. On July 12, 1943, *Time*'s "A Letter from the Publisher" highlighted his role at the magazine: "This is Sidney Olson, at 35 a veteran newspaper man, former City Editor of the *Washington Post*, for three years top political writer for *Time*, now Senior Editor for U.S. at War, Business & Finance, Press."[52]

As a senior editor, he regularly crossed paths with powerful figures who interested Luce in one way or another. His diary entries from 1943 describe meetings and business dinners with politicians, economists, and other influential thinkers as well as interoffice relationships that either pleased him or caused frustration. On October 28, he wrote in his diary about "Tom Matthews' increasingly bewildered—and at times really execrable—management of *Time*" as well as a dinner with Lord Keynes at the Union Club with 15 other editors.[53] He mentioned that he had lunch with Beardsley Ruml and that the office had "acquired Willi Schlamm from *Fortune* via HRL for 3 months to try as writer."[54]

In early May 1944, a memo was handed to the senior-most members of Time Inc. containing confidential information relating to "plans and preparations for coverage of impending events in the European war theater."[55] D-Day was at hand. *Time* and *Life* raced to get their correspondents accredited and placed. Once Olson was sent overseas to cover the war—an assignment for which he waited impatiently—he would need to familiarize himself with the latest version of the guidelines set forth in this memo.

In August 1944, Luce began thinking ahead. A postwar world was coming into view. He wrote to his editors, requesting "a personal letter to me stating what job or jobs he would like to have during the next four or five years—indicating first and second choice. Each editor is also required to indicate how much in need he thinks he is of a long vacation or other 'rehabilitation' measures."[56]

Olson sent him a long reply, campaigning to be sent to the front. It was not too late. He underscored his appreciation for Luce's mentorship.

They had gotten to know each other quite well; their "bull sessions" over coffee at Kaufman-Bedrick Pharmacy on West 49th Street had become something of a tradition and were mutually beneficial. Their discussions ran the gamut from literature to politics and from economics to philosophy. Over time, Olson had gained Luce's confidence by playing a supporting role; what he got in return was a mentor—and not just any mentor but the high-flying, legendary, erudite, and exacting Henry Luce.

After outlining all his merits and accomplishments, Olson finally cut to the chase: he wanted Luce's permission to cover the war in Europe. For the past few years, the most ambitious of *Time*'s writers had been vying for this privilege. As early as 1943, management at Time Inc. had been forced to remind those writers who were chomping at the bit that it was "more than [a] *Life* matter or *Time* matter—it's [a] matter involving company policy and our relations with War and State Departments, both of whom pass on all correspondents to London, accredited or not."[57] Olson understood all too well that there were limited openings and, ultimately, that it was the military that controlled who and how many could go as well as where they went and when.

Years later, in a letter to a colleague, Olson described how he had asked Luce for an overseas assignment many times, with mounting frustration: "During all of 1939, all of 1940, all of 1941, all of 1942, all of 1943 and through most of 1944, I fought almost daily, and certainly weekly, with Luce for permission to go abroad as a war correspondent. Twice I was almost set. Once I even had my shots and my uniforms; each time Luce, over my dead body, prevailed on me to stay to help handle the journalistic problems at *Time*."[58]

This time Luce agreed. On December 9, 1944, Olson received "invitational travel orders" from the War Department. The contract contains one surprising stipulation: "the travel herein authorized is directed as necessary for the accomplishment of an emergency war mission. Travel expenses are to be borne by *Time* Magazine."

On December 11, he signed a contract drafted by the War Department's Bureau of Public Relations, which recognized him as a civilian "accredited to the Army of the United States." The document stipulated that "for the purpose of securing news or story material," he would agree to

> govern my movements and actions in accordance with the instructions of the War Department and the commanding officer of the Army or Navy unit to which I am accredited, which includes the submitting for the purposes of U.S. military censorship all statements, written material, and all photography intended for publication or release either while with the Army or Navy or after my return, if the interviews, written matter, or photography are based on my observations made during the period or pertain to the places visited under this authority.

On December 14, Olson was issued a card identifying him as a civilian noncombatant with the armed forces. He was now part of an elite group of more than 500 correspondents who reported to the Press Division of the Supreme Headquarters Allied Expeditionary Force (SHAEF). According to the military historian Forrest Pogue, the arrangement was unusual enough that membership came with its own set of rules:

> On May 1, 1944, SHAEF issued its plans for control of the press during the Overlord operations. It was to accredit correspondents, radiomen, photographers, and newsreel men and assign them to lower units in accordance with a block system by which a specified number was to be accepted by each unit. Correspondents from the various Allied countries were to be treated on a basis of equality in regard to communications, transportation, and the like. During the next month, the Public Relations Division worked at the task of compiling a list of accredited photographers, press correspondents, and radiomen. The list on 7 June 1944 numbered 530.[59]

Public relations officers (or PROs) oversaw all accredited journalists and were tasked with disseminating information approved by the military. The journalists had to agree that they would omit any unsanctioned information. All dispatches were reviewed by censors before being cabled to news outlets; the censors had the authority—and often wielded it—to draw a line through or even slice out typed copy.[60] Journalists quickly learned to censor themselves by avoiding taboo subjects, such as place-names and any references to American suffering.

In his letter to Luce, Olson also asked for permission to go as far as China and Japan and to take a full year to cover all of that ground. No doubt he hoped to make the most of what might be his only chance to travel the world. Again, Luce agreed.

It was nearing Christmas 1944, so Sid and Zembra formed a hasty plan. They decided to rent out the Larchmont house; Zembra would take the children to Bear River to live with her parents, arriving in time for Christmas. Sid kissed them good-bye on a train platform, then he boarded the *Queen Elizabeth*, which was filled with soldiers bound for Gourock, Scotland.[61]

While crossing the Atlantic, he wrote on the cover of his datebook, "Sidney Olson. Correspondent: *Time* & *Life* magazines. If lost, finder please try to return to Time Inc. office: London, Paris, New York, Cairo, Rome, Chungking." He was 36 years old and a long way from Salt Lake City.

MAY 20 [1939] [LETTER TO ZEMBRA]

Darling baby:

The die is cast. I'm going to New York and be a great man for you. The money makes a big difference, after all.

I've seen Casey. He said he could give me my immediate raise to $100, and in six months more to $125. Then, he said if he gets rid of Deac [*sic*] Leake in a year, I'd go to $150. That would be tops, and any other arrangements would throw the whole thing out of line. I agreed with him.

In this thing he's been perfectly swell, as near to a father as any man not your father could be. I couldn't part from an organization with better feeling.

But he advised me, for my own good, to take it. He thinks it will be a swell thing for me, and it was all the tougher for him to say, as he added, because there is absolutely no one to take my place. There are plenty of routine Riselings and deadwood DeVores, but they need someone with vision, as he put it, and he said he'd never seen anyone come along faster than I.

So I've told him that I'm going to New York. He thinks I'll do swell there. Of course, it's up to me.

Here is what Gottfried, the m.e. of *Time*, said in a note confirming his wire:

> Confirming my telegram of this morning I just wanted to say that after talking matters over with Harry Luce, we agreed that if you would like to come on with us at $10,000 a year, that will be fine. Of course it is a gamble on both sides but we think it is a good one and we would like to take it. If you decide that you're for it, will you let me know about when you will be able to take on the job. With best regards, sincerely yours, etc., etc.

That's the word-for-word on it.

Of course it's a gamble. But I'll go in and win for you and Whitney.

First job for you is to get well. Then, after six–eight weeks, I'll quit the *Post*, drive out and get you, bring you back here. Then I'll take a little rest for myself.

I really will need it.

Then I'll go up there and live in a hotel-room or something until you're ready to start house-hunting in New Jersey, Connecticut, Long Island, etc. We'll rent something reasonable, with a yard and plenty of room, and try not to go over $125 a month. That's about the best we can do, I suppose.

I'll have to work like hell. I won't get any time for sports. But I'll be making money at last, money that should give us a margin of something over, so that we can get a nest egg at last.

I think we're going to be very happy now, darl. I only hope you like all this change and stuff, although I know you're just as loyal to me as a wife could be. I had only a five minute chat with Butch today. He wants to see me Monday. I'll give him a sendoff chat then.

So you can well see that your first problem is to accept your present thyroid situation, knock it off quickly, and get well and lusty and then we'll make love and save money and work hard.

The letter I wrote you last night came after I was terribly terribly pooped. After I'd slept on the thing and had talked to Casey it all straightened out swiftly enough and now I haven't a doubt.

Today I loafed, got two books at Brentano's, called up Jan and Wayne, found Esther and Mrs. S there, showed them the letter from Gottfried, and let them drink some of my Scotch. Then we played bridge for a long time and Wayne and I killed them consistently. I just drove Esther home. Jan and Mrs. S. went with me. Very hot here today. Don't think Esther is serious about Bryson at all. News note, very minor—I now squeeze all the oranges at once and put the juice in a bottle, from which I pour every morning. Why didn't I think of that months ago? Good gosh.

I love you millions, and I'll be working Sunday—tomorrow, and I'll write you another letter. Millions of love to you, little feathered mother bird, and get well quick and come back to your new mansion in Long Island, or wherever. I dream of you all the time and say good night to you each night. Come back to me in sweet health soon.

Love love and love love, S.

April 30, 1944 [Diary]

It's a little after midnight, so I'm not 36 yet—I was born at 4:30 a.m. of a Thursday, April 30, 1908.

Today was almost a May Day. It's Saturday (29th). I played my war game (the Eleventh War); rolled the front lawn, very hard work; talked to Junie Sachs, on furlough after his 5 wks boot training in the Navy; made martinis for Darl, Tenney, Phyllis; and it was the first day this year it was comfortable enough to drink on the sunporch. (Day I first noticed purple color of apple tree trunk near stone bench.)

I am over the feeling I had about going to England.[62] (Nearly everybody was more excited about it than I was—I never really saw myself there; the way one senses such things and knows they'll come true.) But I had some feeling about it, naturally.

Tonight Tenney, Darl & I had dinner, then I played chess with Bill, and lost as usual, through an oversight. I find in chess I play too much a predetermined game; I can work many moves ahead mentally, and this is often a defect against such an audacious opportunist as Bill Hayden, as my finely-conceived long-range logistics and strategy often break down against tough, hit-&-miss, grab-&-run tactics. I must work on this.

This past year was a year of Promise and Promises for me. My 36th year will be a year of Decision (and Decisions), I feel sure. Well—I must work hard and lace up.

MAY 6, 1944
To: Grover, Matthews, Alexander, Osborne, Kay, Billings, Longwell, Hicks, Calhoun, Miss Robinson, Miss Burrell
From: W. W. Johnson

The following confidential memo from Alan Gould, Assistant General Manager of the AP, re. Invasion coverage is passed along for your information.[63]

"The following confidential information relates to plans and preparations for coverage of impending events in the European war theater:

"At the outset of operation Allied Command information and guidance facilities for war correspondents will be concentrated at our central point in England. Communiques will be issued simultaneously in London, Washington and Army Group Headquarters. The Army has agreed in principle to the issuance of two communiques daily, whenever possible. Special communiques also will likely be issued as special events warrant. Correspondents covering SHAEF (Supreme Headquarters Allied Expeditionary Forces) will be briefed at conferences after communiques are issued.

"Plans for a single unified censorship expansion of communications facilities for both name and picture transmissions, and pooling of news dispatches during early phases of assaults have been made public. Approximately 200 places ultimately will be available for American correspondents to cover the various headquarters, as well as field operations of the ground, sea and air forces. Seventeen photographers have been assigned to ground, sea and air forces as representatives of the U.S. Wartime Still Photo Pool. Correspondents in the field will have maximum freedom of movement, with conducting officers serving mainly as guides and liaison with headquarters. Army authorities are supporting the correspondents' request for assurance of combined facilities capable of handling the equivalent of 500,000 words daily for press, radio and picture file."

There follows excerpts from a letter written to a managing editor expressing concern that every precaution to be taken to guard against anything misleading in connection with Western Front operations.

"From a military standpoint, of course, we all have to recognize that the shots are not going to be called in any way or detail that would tip off the Allies' operational hand. When a given landing or series of landings is announced, such announcements presumably would not at once indicate the scope or objectives.

"While we are reasonably assured announcements of the first or any major invasion strikes are going to come initially from Allied sources, there can be no absolute guarantee of this. First reports conceivably could come from enemy or neutral broadcasts. We are exercising extreme care now in the assessment and handling of information from all sources, knowing that both sides are all out in the war of nerves. We intend that the same basic caution and objectivity apply to coverage throughout.

"As respects identification of the first actual operation—and referring here to the use of the word 'invasion'—we shall rely basically, of course, on what Allied communiques say. If the first communique reports actual landings were effected by sea or air, it becomes automatically the first invasion strike and will be so labelled, even though we may not be able to determine or say at once whether it is diversionary or an all-out phase of the attack.

"We realize that the heaviest kind of responsibility devolves upon us to be objective as well as fast and clear and effective. Our main purpose must be, throughout, to keep our balance and perspective, primarily by calling appropriate attention to all salient possibilities in any move, by awaiting exact information before saying exactly what took place, and by refraining from jumping at any premature or unjustified conclusions. Our motto, these days, is 'Be prepared, keep cool, and be concise.'"

[SEPTEMBER–OCTOBER 1944]
To: H. R. Luce
From: Sidney Olson

I. I suppose my reaction to your memo was typical: I began to dream enormous dreams, pretty much along the lines of taking a year's seminar of travel and study, with maybe just a touch of work in the Antibes branch of the Paris office.[64]

After some furious thinking, much like the man who had three wishes and settled finally for three aspirin tablets, I decided that what I really want more than anything else is a couple of weeks off.

But when the election is over, I think I want a change of venue. In five years at very much the same stand, I've "had it."

I am not physically tired or enfeebled in any way that I know of— although my left eye seems to need more sleep then it's been getting. I am momently fed up with Washington and all its synonyms. I say "momently" unless, by any chance, Roosevelt wins another term. Then I'm not so sure.

In general my zest has not flagged in that long unremitting grind, but when it has flagged, the repercussions have been notably loud, particularly after a disastrous two weeks after I returned from vacation this May, Harry, and you sent me a deservedly sharp toe-the-mark memo.

I mention this only because, try as I might, with all the will I have, I cannot guarantee to maintain my fading zest for politics after the election. Not now I can't. Maybe I'll feel different after the Dewey inaugural.[65]

I do not plead for any special treatment, however. But not many *Time* men, I suppose, have been so committed to one particular area for so long, without trips or change of scene or something. (On *Time* I have had two trips, as you know, one for one week to Detroit, in January, 1942; and one for one week to Groton school. I except the trips to conventions for obvious reasons.)

II. Time Inc. owes me nothing, of course. Here I have had a great opportunity, subject mainly to my own limitations, to develop as a journalist, in the direction I preferred. I am very grateful for this opportunity.

To make my meaning clear, if I had studied medicine I would have still been paying for this training.

But with the elections over, I feel that in general—again subject to my limitations of background and education—that I have completed my internship, and am ready to practice as a journalist.

III. When I wrote advertising, I could see my way clearly ahead to a very comfortable future. I deliberately broke off, and went into the newspaper business as the lowliest of $15-a-week cubs, because I thought a career in journalism would give me the realler satisfactions I sought.

I did this for two closely-related reasons. In journalism I would be a ringside spectator of history; and as such, as a critic of the course of events, I could participate, at the very least vicariously in that history as it was made. Sometimes I could participate actively, as a journalist influences events through forming public opinion.

And I felt that if I proved fit, as an editor, I could gradually make some vital contribution to the American attitude as we went about making the American destiny. I am afraid this is put poorly or fragmentarily, but I mean to say that I have faith in the American destiny and I would like to add my faith actively to the total.

The other motive was, in a way, egoistic. But it is this: I believe I am a good teacher of writing. This is really in line with my first motive, in the way of passing on the torch. For I felt that if I failed in my journalistic mission, I could at least help train the young ones, the better journalists to come, to do the great, never-ending journalistic work that should be done.

You may remember, Harry, our very first session in your office in the mid-May, 1939, with Gott, when you decided to hire me. One of my worries about leaving the *Washington Post* was that as a city editor there, I had in my hands the molding of as smart a young crew of 30-odd reporters as could be found, and that I hated to leave off that work for the somewhat more selfish—as I then thought—work of improving myself. Of course, what really decided me was my feeling of ignorance—that if I could become even a reasonable success at *Time* I could become a better torch-passer. Perhaps I am not as good a young professor of journalism as I should be, but I tell you this because such work, the choosing and developing of young journalists, is a main concern of mine, and I would never like to be very far from it.

In short, I do not aspire to be our correspondent in Paris, or Moscow, or wherever—no matter what kudos attached thereto—because it would take me away from a part of my work that I like very much, and about which I have definite ideas.

Trying not to sound grandiose, therefore, but in short my two main-springs are: 1) to be as good a journalist as I can, in order thereby to help as only a journalist can in making a better world; and 2) to help the journalists-to-be to get a sound start.

IV. I should say that I still feel a vast ignorance, less books than of the world—although I cannot see myself plain, and perhaps you would reverse the two.

I wish from my very bones that I had gotten a chance to see the U.S. at War, for myself; luckily for my work I had been up and down and through and through some 43 states, and I still remembered the square turns in the highways down in the heel of Missouri, and the look of the woods in western Massachusetts, which is so much like the look of the woods in southern Idaho and north Utah; and the purple quilts for sale along the roads in Georgia; and the old people in St. Petersburg and the smell of a field of wheat in Kansas; and what mountains mean.

Perhaps, when gas-rationing is over, it might be a good investment for *Time* to send me around the country, not in a hurry, and not on a mission, but just to see what has happened to the U.S. For until I came to *Time* I certainly knew what the country looked like. (I am not carping; I blame Hitler.)

Perhaps it would be a better investment eventually for *Time* if I saw some of the world instead. I hesitate to put it any other way than as an investment; in the sense in which I put it earlier, *Time* has already spent a lot of money financing my education; and further, I physically don't much like the idea of being out of active production. I have enough of the old fire-horse feeling about our work that I hate to be very long away from the tickers, telephones and headlines; vacations bore me.

Your problem, therefore, is how to have me see something of the world and at the same time be productive. I have no ready proposal.

Certainly I would like to go—practically anywhere, but preferably India and China; but mainly because I hope that I would come back better equipped.

V. With that much said, I wash my hands of the problem of the post-war Olson at *Time*. I would like to make a few more points about *Time* while I have your ear.

VI. I think something definite and sensible should be done to arouse the latent esprit de corps at *Time*. It is only very occasionally that the staff-members, in their incessant, nervous, gnawing shop-talk, stop to realize that this is one of the most brilliant aggregations of journalistic talent ever collected together. True, it might be much better still. But no other organization compares with it in any sense in which it is comparable. Certainly we should be humble about our shortcomings—but no one sees them as clearly as we do.

I don't mean to sound like a cheerleader. But this is a collection of professionals, as able in their lines as surgeons and artists; we help make and break careers week in and out; we are responsible to the people; and we all have a high sense of that responsibility. What I wish, somehow, is that in our daily and weekly meetings we could realize some of the sense of dedication and of dignity that you get from consulting surgeons in the operating-theater; of professionals, gay or solemn, at work on a matter at least as important as life or death.

I suppose that isn't well-put, either; but somehow I often feel that even the weekly USAW[66] conferences should open with the words: "Remember, this is a matter of life and death"; and that when we do not attain, in all good humor, any such high perspective, the week is off to a dim start.

In sum, I think we should often remind ourselves that we are pretty good; and that if we are not, the people suffer.

VII. I would like to call your attention specifically to a darned good rising generation around here. I can best speak of USAW. In Otto Fuerbringer, Hillis Mills, Tom Griffith and Paul O'Neil, I say—and am prepared to state at length—that *Time* has four coming Senior Editors. And they're not very far off, either.

Week in and out, Otto writes the best stories in *Time* magazine, as TSM will testify.[67] A slow grower, he is now well on the way to arriving. And of all the young men I have worked with, he has the best picture ideas. He is marvelously easy to work with. He is tireless, and when my zeal flags, his does not. I think the time is at hand when he can handle USAW—under direction of course—but more creditably than any other young editor around *Time*. To be frank, I think that at this moment he is a much abler editor than say, Messrs. Hobson, Kay and Osborne, and mainly lacks only experience. As a handler of people and of production problems, I would put him above Chambers easily, who is defective in these areas only.

I think Mills could edit half of the back of the book at least as well right now as Messrs. Kay and Hobson. (*The New Yorker*, as you know, tried to hire him for that job.)

Tom Griffith, in many ways, is the most natural *Time* writer I have ever seen. No one that I have seen in five years at *Time* can touch him at the telling of a story concisely. The nearest is Kronenberger; like Louis, Griffith writes all too briefly, and you always wish for more. He needs, in my opinion, only another year's experience, and some steady coaching.

Paul O'Neil is the editor's dream. His flair is narrative. His first tryout story, when he was absolutely green, was "The Invisible Girl," about the Indian princess who walked out into the snowy night, as you'll remember; and requests are still coming in from Stockholm, etc. for permission to reprint. Since then he has not missed. As yet he has no political eye, but once he can begin to do this sort of thing on any subject, from Congress to Donald Nelson, Time Inc. will have a writer any magazine will envy.

VIII. Two recommendations for the future in other areas:

I think Dana Tasker would make a great publisher of *Time* Magazine, for reasons obvious to you.

I think Bob Elson, now our Canada writer—where he is misfitted, as he is a reporter, not a writer—might be a considerable answer to at least part of the Washington problem.[68] If you do not know Elson well, you should, and soonest. My idea in sending him to Quebec was to give him an opportunity to show how such a conference could be covered. Even thus far the results are in no way comparable with Felix's shabby showing at the last Quebec meeting.[69]

Elson has a good mind. His Washington contacts, both for productiveness and for good will, are incomparably superior to Belair's—and I say that most seriously. They are also much more contemporary. He is well and most favorably known to the rest of the Washington press corps. He is a good manager, as attested by his managerial record. I don't believe he is a Krock or Lippman; but he does understand an idea when presented with one; and he has ideas of his own.

IX. I am happy to learn, via the readership charts, that the audience of the Business & Finance section has steadily grown in the last 18 months. That at least means I have done something to make it more readable. And in looking back over the issues for some months, I am struck at the pretty fair quantity and quality of the section.

But with that much said, I cannot claim that I have been a successful editor of the section. My alibi, of course, is that I have been so preoccupied with USAW, etc. But the fact remains that it is still not nearly as good as it might be, and should be, either in staff personnel or in economic outlook. At times Gott has saved the section; at others he has laid a deadening hand on it. But the section really needs a torchbearer in a measure which I have not been able to furnish.

The only nomination I have is Roy Alexander, for whom you doubtless have your own plans. But I do think he might well give the section some of the things which I have failed to give it. [no sign-off, final page may be missing]

NOVEMBER 28, 1944
David Hulburd, chief of Time Inc.'s Newsbureau to:

1. Walter Graebner Time-Life Ltd. 4 Dean St. London

2. Charles Wertenbaker Time & Life 4 Place de la Concorde Paris

Olson who has long asked for chance to travel abroad now gets it stop He's to have foreign tour of duty for at least six months and is to visit London Paris Rome Cairo Chunking as aye senior correspondent without portfolio or specific assignment stop. He will of course travel under aegis of Newsbureau but won't be expected to do any chores except those of his own choosing stop He will warmly welcome cooperation of all of you including arrangements for interviews et other extra curricular needs para

—A. G.[70]

Chapter II

Wartime

During the five days it took to cross the Atlantic, Olson passed the time reading and playing chess, bridge, and a little poker. After one chess game, he wrote in his diary, "Like many players I have found, they know how to break through, but they have no real idea of the end-game." This comment would prove prophetic.

A few days before Christmas, the ship arrived in Scotland, and from there, Olson took a train to Glasgow and another to London. En route, he marveled over the pastoral beauty of the landscape and was shocked to see the destruction wrought by German bombing raids. He checked in at the Dorchester Hotel and visited *Time*'s London office. He spent the last week of December 1944 and the first three weeks of January finalizing his accreditation, conducting research, and picking up the clothing and supplies he would need in his travels. He had shipped out so quickly that he had not had a chance say good-bye to Luce and wrote to him, "I got over here in a hurry, and now am at least partially free of that national guilt-complex all we Americans seem to have, of not really participating in the war."[1]

Having never been abroad, Olson relished his time in London. In his letters home, he sounded confident, chatty. He described famous theaters, churches, pubs and historic sites, dinners out, and meetings with sources who might help him prepare for his coverage of the front. He admired the morale of the people and delighted in their quirky expressions, so different from American slang. He enjoyed the fact that Americans were a novelty to the English. He observed that it was difficult to escape the cold and that rations were quite limited.

Because the entire city went dark each night to prevent targeted bombings by German planes, Olson would go out at night carrying a small flashlight. He described the wrenching sound of an occasional V-bomb as it landed and lamented over the sight of bombed-out sections of London. Although the course of the war was shifting in favor of the Allies, much danger lay ahead. A sense of foreboding crept into his diary entry on Christmas Eve: "by next year, a week hence, a tremendous grind begins for me—with no limits except those of my mind and body."

In those first few weeks, Olson drove out of London several times, once to address a U.S. bomber group and once to visit a RAF fighter group that was taking off on successive bombing missions. He had lunch with one of the most influential men in England, Lord Beaverbrook— Max Aitkin, owner of the *Evening Standard*, a newspaper read by most Londoners—who served as Winston Churchill's minister of aircraft production.

Olson began plotting his course for the coming year, a journey extending east from Rome to the Balkans, from Cairo to Tehran, and on to India, Burma, and Chunking, with "Australia and MacArthur" and the "Navy task force," by September. In letters to Luce, he expressed concerns about what the future might hold for humanity and vowed to avoid the pitfall of biased reporting:

> As a journalist, I will valiantly try to put the stacks of diametrically opposed facts and opinions side by side, and digest them all as best I can. But even more difficult to avoid will be to take a stand on the results. As the mind constantly tests and chooses and moves on, there is an inevitable sediment of belief formed; or better, a coral growth that comes up from under the waters of the mind, a growth of opinion that gradually becomes fixed and almost indestructible.[2]

On January 22, 1945, he crossed the English Channel on a Ministry of War Transport vessel and took a train to Paris, where he stayed two nights with Charles Wertenbaker, the chief of *Time*'s Paris bureau, before moving on to Brussels and Louvain.[3] His January 27 travel orders stipulated that he would be permitted to go with a "conducting officer" to the "Advance Camp" in the Canadian sector for a four- or five-day facility visit. "Mr. Olsen [sic] is particularly anxious to secure information and background regarding flooded areas, winter patrol activities and so forth." And he was in need of more suitable clothing, apparently: "Mr. Olsen's [sic] light-weight American uniform is not considered suitable for his activities on this front and he has had no opportunity of picking up warmer clothes. Please instruct the QM at the Main Press Camp to issue him, if possible, with a Cdn battle-dress and issue sweater."[4]

In Sittard, Holland, on January 28, Olson attempted to record the destruction all around him. "Camouflage fluttering on the helmets. Snow White tarps on tanks. The tapes along minefields. Tanks printing their treads stead[ily] along the snow. The thump and crack of shellfire in the distance. My first hearing of shells." He interviewed Canadian General Harry Crerar and had lunch with Major General Chris Vokes. He interviewed the American port commander in Antwerp. He marveled over the fact that he could cross in and out of three countries—Holland, Belgium, and Germany—within an hour or two.

The tone of Olson's writing changed as his movements quickened and the risks increased, the words growing more staccato. In spite of the fact that he was a seasoned journalist, he faced a steep learning curve. He would need to deliver news of the war, providing context and analysis, at an impossibly fast and unpredictable pace.

Going forward, he would need to spend every waking moment seeking out sources, interviewing them, typing his dispatches, planning his next steps, applying for permission to travel, lining up his transport, and finding his way safely to the next point before doing it all again. Conditions were often harsh. Getting killed was a real possibility. He had to remember to number his dispatches, keep to a limited word count, and navigate the constraints of censorship.[5] He had to consider the timing of each dispatch: how long before the story became obsolete? *Time* and *Life* were not "dailies." Given the lightning speed of events in the European Theater, he faced the constant threat of having his story "bumped" for something for more pressing or more interesting.

One could never assume that the story would even reach New York, let alone the censors in Paris. Courier planes could be shot down. Lines of communication might be broken. The difficulties that all correspondents faced were highlighted in a note from Wertenbaker to the New York office just after D-Day: "Word just came that Press Wireless is closed down so the cables may continue [to] go through London. Let whomever first gets this one send it to the other and let both answer by any available channels. We hope we can keep you adequately covered but transportation is awful and communications now seem to be getting as bad."[6]

Olson's first taste of battle occurred at the end of January 1945 at Kapelsche Veer, a flat marshy area held by the Germans northeast of Antwerp. After days of fighting and terrible losses in brutally cold, muddy conditions, the meager piece of land was finally taken by the Canadian First Army. Olson shared a foxhole with a dead soldier as he watched German tanks go up in flames. It was the first of many harrowing moments, and, if we are to judge from his postwar efforts to describe this battle, he never really recovered from the experience.

He slept in basements and castles, jeeped for hours, and typed when and where he could. Like all correspondents, Olson carried a lightweight manual typewriter, but he was always on the hunt for a heavier, more finely tuned German version, which sometimes turned up in an abandoned house or an office occupied by Americans soldiers. Once completed, his dispatches were issued via cable, or, if he had outrun the line of communications, copies could be sent by courier back to Paris.[7] Surely, some got lost or were ruined. Only a handful of his field notes exist.

Just like the GIs moving swiftly along the front, he was insulated from news of the world. This was frustrating for correspondents in forward positions, who knew everything about one remote outpost where the fiercest fighting might be taking place but little about the larger picture. As Andy Rooney explained in his war memoir, "Neither the communiqués from SHAEF nor the lead stories in my own paper read anything like the firefights I'd seen the day before."[8]

Olson attended few press briefings at the Hotel Scribe in Paris, where some correspondents preferred to remain full-time. He soon developed a proud disdain for those unwilling to risk their own necks. His preference was to follow the action, the true source of all news stories. "The most famous of correspondents," he wrote after the war's conclusion, "still in soft at Paris, others home writing their books, the few at the press camps too anesthetized and tired to [go] to real front—what price the news? and the truth?"[9]

It was true that many correspondents preferred to report the war from the relative comfort of the Hotel Scribe, which served as ground zero for up-to-the-minute press briefings dispensed by SHAEF's public relations officers (called "PROs").[10] When Olson visited Paris, he usually stayed with "Wert" at the Ritz or on his own at the Lancaster. He saw friends, went to nightclubs and parties, rested, and wrote letters. He did stay at the Scribe a few times and certainly enjoyed its famous basement bar. The press briefings, interviews with military personnel and government officials, and even casual conversations with fellow journalists over drinks or while playing poker all provided him with critical information with which to assess the ever-changing situation. It was largely up to him to figure out where he would go next.

Reporters, photographers, press officers, and military figures swirled in and out of his orbit. There was a kind of swashbuckling, whiskey-drinking camaraderie that developed among correspondents, tinged with fierce competition to get the story first and to be the one to tell it best and to push the rules of censorship to their limits. It must have been both fun and comforting, not to mention useful, to cross paths with colleagues from the *Herald Tribune*, the *New York Times*, *Yank*, *Stars and Stripes*, the Associated Press (AP), and *PM* magazine. The collective mindset of war correspondents was captured in Wertenbaker's postwar novel:

> Most of the correspondents and photographers were subject to violent attacks of jealousy or camaraderie, of enthusiasm or depression, of bravery or cowardice; most were angry with their home offices and felt that they were ill-used. It was not simply that they were prima donnas, although to a large degree they were. They were under no discipline except their own. They had no army to blame when they were in discomfort or danger, no system to hate, no officers to revile. Neither did they have the grim satisfaction of knowing that the risks they took could not be avoided. Each risk was a personal, separate decision, the

harder to make because behind the lines they lived in the luxury of civilians with unlimited means. And so they tended to exaggerate both their courage and their fear, and swinging between these extremes to live in an enlargement of all other emotions.[11]

In reading through Olson's dispatches today, one must admire his ability to summon a wide range of facts, not to mention his adaptability in the face of ungovernable events. He had not completed college, had never been to Europe, and, importantly, had few if any books on hand to consult. When it came to fact-checking, the army of *Time* researchers whom he had once relied on in New York were well out of reach. In spite of this, he wrote fluently and knowledgeably about an array of subjects. Only rarely did he specifically ask his editor to check a particular fact.

Another point to consider: most war correspondents filed dispatches for their daily newspapers, whereas Olson had a week between each deadline. In a few of his cables, he mentioned filing a piece on Sunday afternoon in order to meet the New York office's Monday morning deadline.[12]

He rarely mentioned a dead or dying U.S. soldier; censors were quick to remove anything considered bad for U.S. morale. Reporters were also forbidden to reveal where they were located or where they were headed.

In hindsight, we see that most American correspondents did not address the Holocaust adequately for a range of reasons, including but not limited to censorship. In fact, Olson and his fellow correspondents rarely refer to Jews or the Jewish religion, relying on more generic words, such as "Poles" or "DPs" (displaced persons). Their vagueness—and sometimes conscious omission—on this point is both troubling and quite typical for the time. Denial, prejudice, fear, ignorance, and self-censorship—all played a role. For more on this complex and important topic, see Robert H. Abzug's *Inside the Vicious Heart*, Deborah Lipstadt's *Beyond Belief: The American Press & the Coming of the Holocaust 1933–1945*, and Barbie Zelizer's *Remembering to Forget: Holocaust Memory through the Camera's Eye*.[13]

Regarding SHAEF's constraints on journalists, it is notable that the military chose to invite journalists to cover the war. They went so far as to create a handbook with rules about what a journalist could and could not cover. It was a savvy move: they wanted to control the "tone" of war reporting, to garner support and shape the American narrative. Author Paul Fussell, himself a World War II veteran, viewed America's glowing version of the war, both during and after the war, with the deepest cynicism, calling what the military had created in tandem with the press a "morale culture."[14] He and others have argued that the press—and *Time* in particular—fed Americans a heavily patriotic and oddly wholesome view of the U.S. role in the war and in the world. Others would argue that this approach was part of a larger and valiant effort to win a difficult war. Either way, there can be no doubt that the press influenced Americans' view of the war—before, during, and after.

From January to June, Olson would follow the front, jeeping back and forth between press camps and battle sites; interviewing generals (including Patton and Simpson), soldiers, and civilians along the way; and always working his sources—an impressive network of military and press contacts. As soon as he could get set up, he would hammer out his dispatch, run it past the nearest military censor, and send it via cable to *Time's* editors in New York. He wrote personal letters, read books that he picked up and discarded along the way, and plotted his forward movements. Where was the next story to be?

There were many significant moments detailed in his dispatches, but one stands out: on April 29, 1945, Olson was among the first wave of American soldiers to enter Dachau's concentration camp at the very moment of its liberation.[15] He toured the camp for several hours, then jeeped back to press camp in the darkness to type up his report. He filed his 18-page dispatch at 3 a.m. on Sunday, April 30, begging the censors, "Please do not hold this copy up or refer it! If it must be cut, cut it and send it on as it must reach *Time* Magazine as early as possible Monday in order to make this week."

He saw parts of the camp with Walter Ridder of the *St. Paul Pioneer Press-Dispatch*, AP reporter Howard Cowan, General Henning Linden, and several unnamed GIs. Scott Corbett—a soldier reporter for the 42nd Infantry Division's *Rainbow Reveille* newspaper—must have been with Olson at some point, too, because he wrote to his wife, "Don't worry about its effect on me, because surprisingly enough, the effect on a person of any stability is not to give him the shakes or unbalance his mind or anything like that. Instead, it's as Sid Olson said, when we first looked at the dead in the boxcars: 'It doesn't make me sick to my stomach or anything like that—it just makes me goddamn mad!'"[16]

Olson and several other soldiers entered the camp through a distant gate and worked their way forward. In a follow-up dispatch, Olson made a point of mentioning *New York Herald Tribune* reporter Marguerite Higgins, who had entered the enclosure at Dachau's main gate.[17]

After describing her as "a smart and pretty young blonde," he credited her for "blitzing many tired old daily paper correspondents along the front with a steady trail of scoops" and suggested that she might be worth a press story. Sadly, most accounts of Higgins's actions at Dachau focus on the fact that she was a good-looking woman rather than a brave correspondent doing her job.

On May 1, 1945, reports of Dachau's liberation filed by Cowan and Higgins made headlines, revealing Dachau's horrors to the world.[18] A portion of Olson's dispatch was published a week later, on May 7, in *Time*. His editors had carved up his dispatch, using about a third of it; another third was used in *Life* on May 14. They bypassed the most disturbing sections altogether. His articles have been cited by a number of historians, but Olson's eyewitness account has never been published in its entirety. The full account provides crucial insights and profoundly disturbing details about what he and the liberators witnessed on that dreadful day, and it merits closer examination by scholars.

The next day, Olson toured Munich and interviewed its citizens. By May 2 or 3, he had arrived at Innsbruck, Austria, where he and two other correspondents searched desperately for comfortable beds and a decent night's sleep. The next morning, he awoke to discover that he had spent the night in a hotel filled with (surrendering) Nazi officers.

It was all too much. He typed up and sent yet another dispatch, then cabled David Hulburd in New York: "I'm completely beaten up emotionally at [the] moment," he wrote. "I only have enough sense left to know I've had enough."

He said that he hoped to get as far as the Brenner Pass in the Tyrol before turning back in order to interview some of the high-profile political prisoners who had been yanked out of Dachau and pushed into the Alps to be used as collateral by escaping Nazis. But news appears to have reached Olson that an official Nazi surrender was suddenly scheduled for May 7 at Reims, outside of Paris. After dining with General Anthony "Nuts" McAuliffe, the commander of the 103rd Division, which was occupying Innsbruck, he requested permission to requisition a vehicle so that he could drive back to Paris.

By May 4, he had made it as far as Dillingen, and on May 5, he reached Sarrebourg. He may have been traveling with another correspondent, Vincent Tubbs, who mentions Olson by name in his description of driving across a defeated Germany:

> Most of the Allied troops had run out of enemy to fight as early as Saturday when I left Austria following the linkup of the Seventh and Fifth Armies and all the German troops in that sector laid down their arms. A few Nazi pockets held out in Bohemia where they fought the Russians fanatically, but 500 miles across Germany there are no evidences of war besides the destruction left behind. Even as Sid Olson of *Time* and *Life* and this correspondent searched for a war to cover, negotiations were under way to end it.[19]

When Olson arrived in Paris late on May 6, he learned that only a handful of reporters had been selected to cover the surrender at Reims; even Wertenbaker—a fixture in Paris with deep contacts—was excluded.[20]

Victory in Europe Day, or V-E Day, was celebrated on May 8, 1945. The streets of Paris were thronged with people wildly rejoicing. In a letter home on May 10, Olson describes the city's happy mayhem, and in his diary, he lists some of his activities—a few night spots, lunches and dinners with friends, time spent writing, and even boating on the Seine.

A controversy broke out in the days that followed. All journalists had been ordered to hold their stories about the surrender at Reims until the Russians had hosted an equivalent surrender and signing in Berlin on

May 8. Throughout the war, American journalists had felt unreasonably constrained by SHAEF rules; the censorship had triggered fierce debates between correspondents and their PROs. The situation reached a boiling point when AP journalist Ed Kennedy went ahead and filed his story early, believing that politics must not dictate the release of such important news. He was condemned for having broken the pact, and his condemnation triggered heated discussions about journalistic integrity.[21] On May 12, Olson cabled *Time* with his take on the whole messy affair.[22]

After May 22, 1945, Olson's paper trail of diary entries, book lists, letters, and dispatches vanishes. He had been exposed to typhus at Dachau, but there is no evidence to suggest that he contracted the dreaded disease. It seems likely that he, like so many others, spent his days celebrating, resting, and enjoying Paris, trying to shed the awful images of war trapped in their memories. Judging from the various club cards and invitations found among his war memorabilia, it appears that he took advantage of Parisian nightlife.

On June 1, he received permission from SHAEF to go home, leaving Paris "on or about" June 3. Transportation would be provided, but he could not be certain whether it would be by plane or boat. "The sorrow at leaving beautiful Paris—" he scrawled in his diary several days later, "eagerness to get home."

On June 4, he caught a night flight to the Azores, where he picked out one of the free pocket-sized books provided by the Special Services Division; interestingly, he selected *Psychology for the Layman*, revealing, perhaps, his state of mind. From there, he flew across the Atlantic, arriving just before midnight on June 5 at Gander Air Base in Newfoundland. The morning of the June 6, he picked out another book from Special Services, *Candles for the Living*, and flew from Gander to the nearby air base at Stephenville and finally onward to New York. Who had set up these flights for him, allowing him to escape an interminable ocean crossing? SHAEF did not do this for every war correspondent.[23] Olson—and certainly Luce—had many powerful connections and may have called in a favor.

He landed late that night and went straight to Larchmont to check on the house and visit with his longtime friends, poet Phyllis McGinley and her husband Charles Hayden, who lived down the street. The next day, he caught a train to Salt Lake City, finally reuniting with his family on June 10. His arduous journey, according to his diary, concludes with a single word: "Sick."

Olson must have felt profoundly relieved to be home. He had followed the front for months, chasing the Nazis across Europe amid death and destruction. His days had been filled with violence, discomfort, chaos, and boredom, with moments of amusement and awe. In Utah, the bucolic scenery and peaceful family life would have stood in stark contrast to the life he had been leading for the past six months.

On June 20, the *Salt Lake Telegram* reported that "*Time* Editor Visits Native Salt Lake": "[Olson] brought back some stories of Dachau and other Nazi horror camps that would tear one's heart out . . . the editor predicted a tough war ahead with the Japs, but reminded that the Japanese have not felt the full strength of America's might."[24] Less than two months later, on August 6 and 9, atom bombs were dropped on Hiroshima and Nagasaki.

Two intriguing clues among Olson's personal papers point to the possibility that by late 1944 or early 1945, Olson may have known about the "Manhattan Project" and the atom bomb. The first clue was written well after the war: "Bio—1944—London—saw Lord Beaverbrook—I had letter from Luce—the Beaver, pink kleenex, apol. for lack of his own *Lares & Penates*. Letter said he (me) knows about THE PROJECT. (That meant Manhattan, the Bomb.)"[25] Perhaps Olson's delivery of this letter was the "emergency war mission" mentioned in his December 9, 1944, travel orders.

The second clue comes in the form of a handwritten letter addressed to Olson and delivered to *Fortune*'s offices by a Colonel James C. Welch on January 15, 1946: "Here is the $50 I have owed you since V-J Day.[26] How did you know the war with Japan would be over before Sept. 15th?" At the bottom of Welch's enclosure note, Olson wrote in pencil, "Outside Dachau on May 1, 1945, I made this bet with this G-2 officer. I'd forgotten it—but he paid the $50, dying with anxiety to find out how I could call this great shot. I didn't tell him; I was still under security about our great secret weapon."[27]

On November 26, 1945, Olson was listed as a recipient, along with many other World War II correspondents, of the European–African–Middle Eastern campaign ribbon for "outstanding and conspicuous service with the armed forces under difficult and hazardous combat conditions," awarded by Headquarters, U.S. Forces, European Theater.[28]

Years later, he scrawled on yet another slip of paper for his "Bio" file, "38 corresp killed in war." A mixture of pride and awe, along with a tinge of sadness, can be discerned in these simple words. He had aimed high. And he had survived.

1. A NEW DARK AGE

DAYBOOK

Sidney Olson, Correspondent *Time* & *Life* magazines
If lost, finder please try to return to Time Inc.
London, Paris, New York, Cairo, Rome, Chunking

December—First Day [1944] [Diary]

The sea—like blue-black marble in the afternoon, veined and flecked with white lines, streaks, blotches and heaving uneasily in great wallows. The wake, cut by the big boat, was like soapy lather, foaming thick then spreading in smeary white circles. The black marble texture of the water was almost greasy.

I saw only one GI sick: at boat drill the sweat popped out of a man near me, and grinning foolishly, he stepped forward and was led away.

The officers' lounge is like a Washington cocktail lounge.

I won a chess game from a Lt. Roth in the lounge after dinner. He had just won four games and was weary.

The food is swell: only twice a day but good and filling. And the people are swell, of course—the wonderful American soldiers, who just don't realize how swell they are. I am in with as fine a set of guys as I could have picked if I'd done the choosing. They're all swell, but don't know how hot they are.

The boat seems damn efficiently run, from all I can see. Everyone is polite; everything goes like clockwork, even the good-natured griping.

I miss Zembra and the kids very much.

I had my first salt water bath tonight. Damn good, though as Hodson said: "It's like scrubbing yourself with Bon-Ami" (meaning the salt-water soap).

I miss the newspapers terribly, after eleven-odd years of reading every edition every day and watching the ticker hour after hour—so I always was on top of the news—and now all hell could be happening everywhere and I would never hear. But it's a disease, and I'll get over it. I watched the sea for hours today, quite at ease, though quite idle. I'm just not used to idleness.

SECOND DAY [DIARY]

Fried liver and bacon for breakfast; cheese crackers for lunch; roast turkey for dinner; the sea a shade rougher but still very pleasant and warm; and the news was a great double rainbow, into which the ship sailed, a little right of center. The vast rainbow, a good omen of course, hooked right around into the water on both sides of the boat.

I stood through emergency muster in the open, on the bow. Then it was cold; and I had a long coughing spell during the one announcement of the muster.

The wake on the sides, when the water is terribly smashed up, often swirls into the most delicate of blues—an Alice-Blue-Gown blue, pale lapis lazuli, like a young girl's evening dress—before subsiding into that soapy lather.

I spent all morning on deck, and as long out in the rain in the afternoon as possible.

I lost a chess game to a Lieut. Sachs tonight.—One misplay cost it—and I almost retrieved it after losing my queen. But it was a good game and well lost.

A Capt. Warren at our table came for his first meal today! Sick all the way! And it hasn't been rough. I expected to go the very first crack, but haven't been bothered yet.

I miss Z. and the kids terribly. Wonder what they did today—and if she will get home for Xmas? I fear not.

THIRD DAY OUT [DIARY]

My cold worse steadily. The water still black, not blue; the white horses of the spray racing up the dark walls of the wake on either side of us endlessly.

Lost two and won one chess game from Lt. Roth—we are now even. I have found his weakness, however—and thus have lost interest. He is mainly concerned with attrition—he tries to get the better of exchanges until he has a real advantage. I changed over from game of position to suit this theory, and beat him handily. I am now confident that unless I were grossly stupid, I could beat him every time, because I can take positional risks fearlessly, as long as I know he is mainly concerned with attacking my pieces and not seeking a checkmate. Too, like many players I have found, they know how to break through, but they have no real idea of the endgame. Bless Capablanca [*sic*]! The endgame is my strongest.

The food good, but weak and wetly cooked, au Britain.

Bob Weir, correspondent for the Fort Worth <u>Star-Telegram</u> and Houston <u>Chronicle</u> is aboard.[29] Nice enough if he'd be natural, but he takes it very big. For instance, when I complimented him on some trifle, he laughed affectedly and said: "Oh, I'm just one of those crazy newspapermen with a photographic memory!" I have thought of that sentence many times since. What a depth of feeble romanticism that is! I honestly pity him; he is a nice enough guy.

Therese Bonney, the woman correspondent, is damned interesting in her way.[30] She lets you know at once that she is a celebrity, but once that is clearly understood, and you are paying proper homage, she is a mine of information about England and France. I have had great luck with her; I even find she is a friend of Raoul Dufy.[31]

FOURTH DAY OUT [DIARY]

Quite sick today—taking medicine—played bridge; won; no money.

FIFTH DAY OUT [DIARY]

Tonight my cold finally broke; am better. Played poker; won about $3.50. Capt. Peterson served us coffee laced with brandy, in paper cups. The "Scientific Society" that meets in our cabin every night is a great laugh.

LONDON, DEC. 23, 1944,[32] 2 A.M. [DIARY]

Things to remember:

The green of the Irish Sea after the black of the ocean. The scenes in the lounge as the soldiers played cards. The GI show, and why they like it better than "name" shows. The Voice: Form your lines; fall in for chow. The FAP's when I was sick with my cold. The silence after jokes were told in our quarters. The short-sheeting and bed-crumbing of the bed of Major Fontz; the pretended sleep-talking of Major Maher—very funny.

Inspecting the negro quarters in the stern over the screws, with Capt. Chas. Hutton.

The morning off Greenock; the dark firth, the misted green hills; the red flashing light; the lighthouse, the ships; the little houses.[33]

The many good omens: the clearing day—the first day's sunshine in many a week. The joke: if you can see the hills, it's going to rain; if you can't see them, it's raining. The lighter: the goodbyes. How they helped me sling my gear. Devlin got me a flashlight. Farewell to the ship.

The floating new Union Jack. Ben Lomond in the mist.[34] The little machine gun a soldier carried. The last two informal meals on ship—and trying the _____ [rations?]; the last card games.

The portholes. The steward: Pavell, 39, 25 years a ship's monkey. His story about the Georgie: "no destination." Salt-water baths. Wonderful to brush teeth in salt-water. Desserts on board—so British. The soldier reporter: Selig Altschul who interviewed me on board[35]—my write-up in the ship's paper. Emergency muster every day. "Action stations." Bunk practice.

The incredible J. Robert Wear of Texas. Neurotic? No. I bet he doesn't last at the front. He'll crack easy. He's not interested in people—only in himself. All his conversation is directed at throwing back a romantic light on his own person. How he could boast, softly and carelessly, gently, modestly, to polite Britons for a solid hour—never once asking them about themselves, or England, but telling them stories in which he, his paper, Texas, his background, etc. figure romantically—except that his notions are all so Grade-B movie, or pulp-magazine, that what sounds glamorous to him about himself et al., merely embarrasses all but the most naive.

Greenock, after the boat ride with Wear and Comdr. Stratton.[36] The long carry up the steps and up the station platform. Into the little offices—what I thought was a light-bulb, but was a gas-lamp. The little officer who issued the tickets. The mug of coffee and a doughnut—free, and how grateful I was to Scotland and the bonny rosy-cheeked girl who gave them to me, as my helmet, mask and musette bag almost cut me in half.

The Scots lounging about as we waited for the commuter train to Glasgow. The begging kids. The last blitz and the distillery, the three kirk steeples. The beauty of the day—a miracle in Greenock, they said.

The train to Glasgow with Bonney and Wear: the little light in the compartment. If I had known what a night we had ahead of us!

The solicitous manner in which the Army freely medicines, feeds, etc. its hosts is very impressive. And it is a thing of high privilege and luck not to be a civilian right now. They are the unlucky ones in so much, in that their suffering is spread through all their days and nights.

Glasgow: the station. The US RTO. Loading the truck. The heavy, weary walk of three blocks through Glasgow to the Central Station. The RTO there. Wear and Bonney—and how each complained to me of the other—and how I loathed them both, but Miss Bonney so much the less, because though she is a whining, fat, affected old maid, she does have a mind, and Wear is a blank.

Our meal together: Wear had a Curaçao after dinner. Haw! I only ate hors d'oeuvres, soup and tea, with a large whiskey & soda before. Glasgow station—the newsstand, the lady announcer, the late-trains sign, the Xmas-travel crowds, the porters, the bobbies, the MPs (one told me to button up).

To the train—our car, with first-class scrawled across the windows— and the beginning, at 9:39 (only 1 minute late) of one of the most damnably torturing rides that could be.

The British Air Ferry captain & his wife. Lt. Rosencrantz of the WAC. Stratton and I sat together. Wear snored. Bonney whined. I learned gin rummy. Rather a dull game, really. The bridge game—Stratton, I, Rosencrantz & a WAC—we lost. The three tortured naps: my tailbone ached all night.

We were due in London at 7:10 a.m. We arrived at 12:30 p.m., after traveling approx 15 hours. The false alarm about Rugby, when we all started to get off. Wear woke me up once, out of a sound sleep, to give me the false news we were at Euston station—he had been taken in by a gagster. . . . "It will never be the thrill of not getting off at Rugby."

The hot tea and cookies at Crewe, which we didn't get, and the hot tea & cookies at Rugby, which we did get. Bless the English. The RR

45

yards at night, in the fog & blackout. The RR men's black shiny caps. The old clothes which the British women so bravely make do.

The first sight of bombed places. The green countryside in the misty dawn morning—the cows and horses on the green-in-winter short cropped fields; the tended, park-like look. The trees are beautifully cared for until you get close to the city. The grassed over air raid shelter in a little backyard.

Arrival at Euston. (Someday perhaps write a story of that night, if it's really worth it.) The casket on a truck—So & So (a woman) aged 80 years. "Got a bony in there?" joked the old pater.

The telephone book that only went A to K, when I needed T for *Time & Life*.

Cab to #2 Dean Street, in Soho. Lunch with Bill Johnson[37] at John (the Greek's) White Tower. Superb lunch after no food in so long. The delivery, finally, of that accursed bagful of Xmas presents to the London office, and of an egg and an orange to Ragsdale whom I was delighted to see.[38]

To the Dorchester, where I slept from 5 to 12, woke, ate a box of K rations and an apple, read a while in *Pride & Prejudice* and the newspapers, and wrote this. Now to bed again. Letters tomorrow.

DEC. 24, 1944, 11:10 P.M. [DIARY]

After a few more days of play and sightseeing and rest, I will organize myself formally, and report herein. In the meantime, rest and play. But by next year, a week hence, a tremendous grind begins for me—with no limits except those of my mind and body.

DEC. 26, 1944 [DIARY]

Looked at Bill's loot from Belgium—a 1939 Iron Cross, some art books by Matisse et al., done during the occupation, damned interesting, and smoked one of his pointed Dutch cigars, borrowed a book and off here, where I sewed a correct insignia on my officer's cap, so that GI's won't be eternally saluting me, and getting depressed because I don't salute well. This took an hour, but now I feel more comfortable with that officer's insignia off my hat.

DEC. 27, 1944 [DIARY]

Got a long letter written to Harry, reporting my fear that the world is possibly on the way to a new Dark Age. Also wrote Z. a long descriptive love letter. Lunched with Dennis Scanlan[39] and Evelyn Irons, a girl reporter on Beaver's *Eve. Standard*, age about 36 and quite plain. But interesting.

Hope to catch Sunday in the country, and next week off to middle England and then Edinburgh; later to Oxford and then to the Thos. Hardy country. Want to stay for Churchill on Jan. 16 or abouts.

DECEMBER 27, 1944

The Dorchester Hotel, Park Lane, Mayfair, London

Darlingest B.G. Zembra darl:

First: my return address will almost certainly be: Sidney Olson, U.S. War Correspondent, P.R. section, U.K. Base, A.P.O. 413, c/o Post Master, New York City.

I say almost certainly because I don't get my APO number until tomorrow. But this is the regular number, apparently. I may get a different one because I'm traveling about so, but in the meantime I could certainly use some quick mail, even V-mail,[40] which is so easy I wonder we don't always use it [*sic*] to the soldiers in the family.

I missed you terribly on all the holidays. I wasn't alone much, so it wasn't actually as bad as last year when I was alone. But I was so lonesome for you and the sight of our little fry rushing to get their presents—this would have been John's first rush, and now I've missed it. But you'll remember that I always was so confident that I'd get off before Christmas, and even get here before Christmas. In things like that I can always trust my instinct.

I had a wonderful crossing. I not only wasn't seasick a second, but didn't even feel inclined that way. Hardly anyone aboard was sick, except those with overheated imaginations. Part of that was because the ship was very steady, and didn't pitch much, and part because the ocean was extraordinarily smooth almost all the way, just as if it had been oiled for us. Old timers vowed it was as smooth as a summer crossing. We were very lucky in quarters, too; there were only seven others in my cabin, a room about as big as our biggest bathroom. All were majors except one naval lt. commander. All were swell guys and we became fast friends. We even had a card-table and two chairs in our cabin, which even the biggest shots on board didn't have, and so we called our place the junior lounge. I played chess eight times on board, and won five games. Played a lot of bridge for fun, and a little cheap poker, finally coming out about $3.50 ahead over all. The Air Corps kids really gambled; I saw one game with $900 on the table for one hand! They have no idea of money at all; they just don't care.

I took a saltwater bath every night, but the best fun was brushing teeth in saltwater. That's really something. We had two meals a day, and if you weren't on time for either breakfast or dinner—too bad. Food not bad, but English-cooked, which is very wet and dank and boiled.

The trip seemed endless, but it was actually fast. One day we sailed through an enormous double rainbow, which curved into the ocean on both sides of the ship, another good omen. And on the day of our arrival, at a place I cannot name, the weather was bright and fair for the first time the natives could remember in the last five months—another break.

I had a terrible cold on board, and still have some of it, in this climate, but I guess it will wear off when I get to the hot countries finally. What almost wrecked me was a 16-hour train ride to London. I thought my crupper was broken forever.

And how I blessed those wonderful people who give soldiers tea or coffee and doughnuts when the train stops at some little place in the depths of the night, in the wet and the fog.

Much of the last three or four hours of the ride, I stood out on the platform watching the parklike English landscape, so neat and tended and pruned and cultivated down to the last blade of grass. Your dad would be fascinated.

I had been practicing my English money on board ship, when we finally got to the station in London I put tuppence (two huge English pennies, about as big as quarters, and worth two cents each) in the big slots, and dialed the *Time-Life* number, and finally got a cab and got there, and they fed me beautifully at an excellent restaurant named The White Tower (the office is in Soho, a kind of Greenwich Village district) and they packed me off here to the Dorchester, which is very swank, ranking with Claridge's and The Savoy as one of the top three hotels in London. There I slept—this was Saturday, Dec. 23—from 5pm until midnight, awoke, ate a box of K-rations in my room, and very good and went back to sleep until 10:30am. Then Ragsdale took me and the Lt. Commander[41] off sightseeing all day Xmas Eve. Saw Lincoln's Inn Fields, and all of the Temple, as they call the old inn section where the lawyers must live before they get their degrees, and Samuel Johnson's house, and where Disraeli died, and a church built by the Normans in the years 1100 and something, now wrecked by a bomb-blast, and Ye Old Cheshire Cheese, where all the literary greats once ate, and Dickens' Old Curiosity Shop, and Fleet Street, where all the newspapers are published, and Oxford Street and Bond street, and Selfridge's Department store, and Regent Street and Hyde Park and Piccadilly Circus and to St. Paul's, which is the Vatican of the English church, and went through it carefully, looking at the crypts, and listening to the Sunday afternoon bells; and ate a buttered bun and cheese and hot tea in a little place, and had a glass of sherry in a pub, and played a pinball machine, and then saw miles of bomb-damage, acres where the famous old houses and fine new ones had been smacked flat and cleared out from several stories high right down through the basements, now overgrown with grass and little weeds. This was sickening, and enough to make you very mad. [At this point, five or six lines were cut out, presumably by censors.]

Saw the Houses of Parliament from the outside—no tourists admitted—and Big Ben and Waterloo Bridge without Vivien Leigh and Westminster bridge and went into Westminster Abbey, but services were on, so after dropping something in the collection box we left, and walked onto Buckingham Palace, a great grey building which looks much like the Department of Commerce in Washington, and so back for high tea. In the evening the Commander and I took our flashlights—it's dark very early here, about 5 p.m. and went to see a wonderful new English movie, Laurence Olivier's production in color of Shakespeare's Henry V—really terrific, darlingest darl dear. Be sure to see it if it ever gets out there. Getting to the theater and back was quite scary, but now I am very confident. It's pitch dark, with only dim flickers of light in the fog, and the streets are the most higgledy-piggledy you could imagine. But Londoners are wonderful, you just ask them and they'll drop everything to take you or show you, the kindest people you could imagine. So rode a British subway, with soft plush cushions and arm-rests, and smoking allowed in some cars, all of them very very deep underground, with the layers of bunks still there for air raids.

Next day, Christmas, up late and went to the Ragsdales for Christmas dinner. Eleanor had just had their first baby, a girl, and was just home from the hospital—three weeks old—and they put on a fine spread of cold roast beef and fried chicken and carrots and little mince pie tarts—the latter round things as big as Schrafft tarts, very tasty, and coffee and madeira wine.[42] The house was very cold as are all English houses—no fuel allowed except for a few hotels, etc., so you sit by little electric or gas heaters, and in this penetrating chill that's something. It's been quite cold here, about 19 degrees, which is about 2 below back there. If you even take off your gloves outdoors for a few minutes the cold soaks in so hard it takes an hour for your whole body to warm up. Home early and very sad at Christmas without you, and went to bed.

The day after Christmas is also a holiday in England. It's called Boxing Day, and gives you an extra day to get over your hangover if you have one. So I haven't been able to get any laundry done yet—and of course cabs and all that were fresh out.

Walked around all day with Bill Johnson of the office here, and beat him at chess. Some of the things I saw I've put in the other list above. After lunch walked some more—on ship we didn't get the slightest exercise for days and so now I crave it—and in the evening went to my first "pantomime," which the British call "the panto." These are like low-grade musical comedies, or high-grade vaudeville. . . . The British around us, noticing our uniforms, were very anxious that we enjoy ourselves, and nudged us to see that we got the jokes, which are very old and threadbare, and so though I always sit through shows very deadpan, I had to laugh and applaud like mad, to please the Britishers, who were delighted that we liked it.

Today the office opened, and I went to work on my red-tape, and doing a little planning for my stay in England, which will probably last until about Jan. 20, near as I figure now.

The package I delivered, at such physical cost of lugging it around that I often swore I'd throw it overboard, was loaded with bobby-pins, hot water bottles, razor blades, lipsticks, nail polish, etc. You should have seen the girls squeal with delight when they saw these poor little treasures. The poor things . . . you'd have thought I'd given them a million dollars each. They called me Father Christmas (which is the British for Santa Claus). On board the boat the majors all called me Father *Time*. The profanest man among them they called The Chaplain.

Back late, 6:30 p.m., to the hotel, and had dinner, and wrote this and will read a little before going to bed. On board I read Jane Austen's *Pride and Prejudice*, and if you liked Thos. Hardy be sure to rush out and get the 25 cent edition of this, because I can now see that we're going to read all of her just [as] we read through Hardy. She's really wonderful, even though Phyllis likes her.[43]

If you get a chance, darl, please write me often. Did you get home for Christmas? I don't even know of course if you're there yet, and maybe this will spoil the surprise. But I'm risking it. Give sweet Whitney and apple butter John a swarm of smackeroos for me, and tell Dad and Mother all you can of what's in this letter and that I'll write them soon.

I worship the ground you walk on, as ever, darling; and miss you. But in this trip I will case the whole world, so that when we four all sail it some sweet day, I'll be able to take you around and show you what's what. In the meantime, it's a dark and miserable world, and there's not much fun anywhere. Watch *Time* & *Life* to see if I write anything. I love you and adore you and worship you, from your heels up. Be so very careful and take good care of your imperial self, and be ready for me when I get back; and take care of the children as only you can. What I would give to be sitting across from you right now in our little breakfast room! (I have broken my vow: I now occasionally drink coffee, when it's all I can get, which is often). Don't worry; I'll be dagnab careful to keep my Swedish pigskin whole. Much love—in fact, all of it, to you, B.G., and please write.

Your s. Sid

DECEMBER 27, 1944

Harry:[44]

Some Notes and first impressions:

After talking to Noel Busch and Bill Johnson, fresh from Belgium and Holland, particularly Holland, I am impressed with a tremendous irony in affairs. They arrive here with the most detailed impressions of the ruin of Holland, of the work of centuries now overthrown almost irretrievably, a land destroyed so that it almost seems more sensible to abandon it than attempt reconstruction, because of the magnitude of the task. Under the Germans the Dutch got 2,000 calories a week, I believe; now, due to the destruction of canals, the traffic can supply the people with at most 1,600 calories. The Americans mainly build low military bridges over the ruined canals, so Dutch traffic, which needs to pass under taller bridges, cannot move. But these are minor points, only illustrative, and Busch's forthcoming Wilhelmina and Holland article for *Life* will develop all this.

Busch particularly is gloomy, as he talks of Europe's "guaranteed chaos" (his phrase). As I remember the little group of fluttery school-teachers that I saw at the Port of Embarkation, who were being sent over here as UNRRA reinforcements in Italy, I am tempted to become as gloomy.[45] With the misery evident everywhere, I am slowly becoming aware of the massiveness of the European Augean Stables. At this distance I already begin to despair of American ingenuity, American force and strength. I think back on Donald Douglas and Roy Grumman in vain; how can the Americans, with all their shiny toys of cargo planes, fingertip radio control from any room in the house, and air conditioning, etc.—how can they, brave and naive as they are, clean this great dirty house? The more so when there is no political organization from above? UNRRA, OWI—all here but the military from the U.S. merely twiddle their thumbs and dream and occasionally get reshuffled or resign in disgust.[46]

The tremendous irony I referred to above, in the first sentence, I can now set forth: here Americans, with the best will in the world, have just committed themselves to participate in international affairs. Now, of all times—the very time when there is no way they can participate very intelligently or forcefully or effectively. How? Busch says that first you must have a plan, as Hitler had, for a New Order in Europe. With full remembrance of Mr. Roosevelt, I suggested that we give up any idea of having a plan; that instead we start at the very bottom with the merest nibbles, that we take a few medium-sized cities and develop them as models of well-run small industrial towns, clean, with sewers; self-sufficient with factories and farms, and then invite the rest of Europe to copy these models. But that is clearly impractical, although it amused Noel, who was instantly reminded of Greenbelt. Well, anyway, here we are, all internationalist and full of beans, and nowhere to go.

Busch's article, by picturing the problem in Holland, should be very important. But for my part I am beginning to feel that perhaps the motif of my tour, the one real question I should ponder, is: Is the world about to enter a New Dark Age?[47] I am going to ask this of the Britishers I meet, anyway, and I'll report to you what they say.

Londoners seemed quite interested in Don Iddon's note from Washington in the *Daily Mail* that it may now be revealed that Mr. Roosevelt spent only 27 weeks out of the 52 last year in the White House.[48] He stresses that many of the 25 missing weeks may have been spent in important secret conferences. As soon as the Fourth Honeymoon is over, this might be a proper subject for study.

The trip here was quite smooth and yet exhausting; a 16-hour train ride hard on it just about gravelled me, but London has been a great tonic. How could anyone help liking this noble old town and its kind people? Every night I set off to the theater, armed only with flashlight and a little nerve, and arrive safely through the dense fogs and the dim-out, usually under escort of bobbies, dogs and citizens, all intensely interested in helping me get wherever I want to get and thence safely home again. The great delight is to ask the most frigid-faced Londoner a direction, confessing absolute helplessness, and watch him thaw out until his glasses get all steamed up with cordiality, as he tells you exhaustively how to get there. The best phrase they use is: "Then you'll come to a turning. Well, deny yourself that, and take the next turn."

At my visit last night, all the audience nearby noted that I was an American. In their solicitude to see that I had a good time, all my neighbors explained all the jokes and nudged me and looked hopefully at me to see if I were properly happy, so that although I usually sit deadpan through all entertainments, I was forced to clap and laugh and nod happily all about me all evening, until I was worn and hoarse. But I couldn't let the good people down, even though the jokes were all the ones I used to throw out of my college humor magazine as too threadbare.

I sight-saw London for the last three days. I am going to try to see the Beaver this week.[49] Then I want to get out of London and see Edinburgh, a Midlands town or two, the Thomas Hardy country, and a bit of South Wales. Oh, and Oxford. I am trying to stay away from the Ministry of Information's beaten track; I want to get into the country where there are no Americans—if possible. I also want to see Parliament in session, and if poss. watch the PM answer questions.[50] They reconvene Jan. 16. Then I will take off for the various fronts, for about a month, and rest up in Paris for a bit.

I was sorry to get off without a goodbye, Harry; but they expedited me, through the really expert work of Jack Manthorp,[51] so very fast that I finally only had a half-hour—honest—in which to pack and say goodbye at home. But the result was good; I got over here in a hurry, and now am at least partially free of that national guilt-complex all we Americans seem to have, of not really participating in the war. The British are lucky in that sense. But don't let your *Time*-sters go too far in denouncing the U.S. homefront. The sins of the people lie on their fathers in Government. And the enormous productivity of a land that can raise its own standard of living when all other peoples are sinking into log-cabin conditions is something never to be ashamed of. (My view only.)

Despite all, the happiest of New Years to you and Clare. Best of luck. —Sid

DEC. 28 [1944] [DIARY]

Up 8:30 a.m., and off to be further accredited.[52] Started the process by being photographed by a Mrs. Laidler, who was kind enough to sew on some of my insignia, on my blouse. Will do the rest myself, as I admire my sewing. . . .

Wrote a digest of a piece by Dean Inge—Passing of the Country House—and sent to HRL & TSM by cable.[53] A good day's work. Also went into my first PX and bought my cigarette ration and candy ration.[54]

DEC. 29, 1944 [DIARY]

Picked up pictures, got new ETO card from Sergeant Rogers, walked about London. Dined with Ragsdales, Johnson, Margot Post (who sent me an egg) at Sandy's (Jack's) where met Col. Eric Ambler, mystery writer and saw Margot Grahame, a bit overripe.[55]

JAN. 2, 1945 [DIARY]

Lunched with Wormser of French embassy at Scanlans' Gargoyles Club.[56] Tea with Rags at Browns Hotel.

JAN. 3, 1945 [DIARY]

. . . to Garter Club for drink with Maj. Clarke Newlin and thence to Dorchester for dinner with *Time* staff.

JAN. 4, 1945 [DIARY]

Once I saw the blast of a V-2,[57] as I came out of the theater—a great lake of light that spread instantly over a wide area of the dark city, much whiter than day, it seemed, a garish light that might cast greenish shadows. The Londoners in the street began to count: one, two, three, but most gave up, and then at 25, the dull crump-crump came, long after the instant light had risen and faded. Then the search lights fingered the sky and blotted out and I took the tube home.

Tomorrow to see the Bbr group.[58] Was accepted by SHAEF today and got fine wire of welcome from Wert.

. . . had wonderful lunch at White Tower with Hans Kahle, the military expert here.[59]

JAN. 5, 1945 [DIARY]

At 2p. to meet Maj. Clarke Newlin at 28 Grosvenor and motored off to US Bomb Group base—over 100 miles; got there at 7:30 to find I was to make speech, which I did for nearly 3 hrs. until I was faint and sweating. Coffee, and stayed up all night but for one hour's nap in a chill Nissen hut, during the briefing etc. At combat mess—two eggs, over easy—perfect, toast, jam, cornflakes, with real creamy milk, and U.S. coffee (& hash brown potatoes!) Watched the liftoffs in the fog. The endless talk & questions about the U.S. The advantages of my technical [?] ignorance. The training _____ [?]. The B-17 insides. The _____ [?]. Talks with Col. Jos. A. Moller.[60] The PRO—Lt. Foster.

Off to Fighter field—Maj. Petersen, 21, & Maj. England, 21. Equipment. The P-51. Inside. Strafing. Bomb escort. Lunch. The long drive back & the gathering fog. The sgt. chauffeur, from La Mesa, Texas. To bed at 9:30p.

Sidney Olson, War Correspondent
P.R.O. U.K. Base

Henry R. Luce
Editor, *Time*

JANUARY 8, 1945

Dear Harry:

Some points which may be useful:

1. In all reports I make to you, bear in mind of course that they have the disadvantage of nearly total ignorance of the course of American news; *Time* is a minimum of two weeks late here, and it is a strange experience for me to read *Time* without the context of the daily newspapers. The advantage is that my mind is freed of the crosscurrents of U.S. opinion; in one sense I can write a journal as would Robinson Crusoe, alone and ignorant, but without either the fertilization or the hindrance of other peoples' thoughts.

2. A foremost thing, and I dare not say more: Time Inc. should never de-emphasize or minimize the V-bombs, no matter what is said officially about them. One thing it is safe to say: recently there have been more of them [remainder of this paragraph was cut out by censors].[61]

3. For your guidance: the London *Economist* editorial titled "Noble Negatives" which I had Johnson cable as excerpted by me, was newsworthy in that it said much better than anyone else what all the dailies were trying to say. Many British seemed to think Crowther had really 'knocked one for six.'"[62]

4. The London *Times* shrewdly asks: "What are powerless politics?" *The Times* asks an end to such catchwords as "power politics" and "spheres of influence," preferring efficient handling of concrete situations as they develop, or a little before. In the absence of a definite U.S. policy, I must say this seems eminently sensible to me.

5. *Life* could most profitably do a picture spread on the "pantomimes."[63] The panto, as you know, is the one totally British form of stage entertainment. I have seen five of them now, the good and the suburban. The stars are either good cheesecake or good fun, and 300 words of text

would be ample. The great pleasure of them is their historicity: many routines and jokes have been kept intact for 100 years or more, giving the pleasure of recognition to generations of children who in turn take their children.

6. Observation: the British newspapers are generally a low form of yellow journalism; the crudest Hearst paper is far more expert and intelligently written. But of course their weekly journals of opinion are in the same degree much better than ours; these are written with an edge, a precision and out of a culture infinitely superior to that of Kirchwey, Bliven et al. The British newspapermen I have met (and women) are shabby drudges, full of pretensions, who write rot. (I'm sure you know this.)

7. No matter what you read, the British themselves take a dim view of General Montgomery. Their hero, in all the fullest senses, is General Alexander. This goes for all classes. I say this so positively because I have used Montgomery as a conversational gambit with bobbies, subway guards, people in pubs, people in clubs, and on up. One phrase you hear from the highest to the lowest about Montgomery. They all say: "Bit of a showman, what?" This, with a significant look. And many of them try this on me; they say, "He's something like your General Patton, don't you think?" Of course, if some frightful criticisms were launched at Montgomery by "outsiders," they would defend him. But Alexander is their boy.

8. Bearing in mind our many past discussions of what the American GI thinks, let me give you some impressions of a trip I made last week to a U.S. Bomb group base and a fighter group base.

The Eighth Air Force asked me to go to bases which had not been visited by anyone but military in ten months, because the men were hungry for news from home.[64] We had a long drive, about 5-1/2 hours. I was shocked to see as I entered the huge main hut, that there were big red posters set up, announcing: "Tonight, at 2000 hours, a speech by Sidney Olson, of *Time* and *Life*." There was no help for it, although I'm no speechmaker. Since we were so late, I had to go right on, as the men had already been waiting in the hall some time. It was jammed with about 450 U.S. soldiers. All but about a dozen were soldiers, ground crewmen, etc., as the pilots, etc. were going out on a mission in the morning, and had been ordered to bed. The dozen or so officers were those who work in the war-room, preparing the maps and weather dope for the briefings, and it was too early for them to be at work.

So I went on, telling them about conditions at home as best I could. I got a great cheer when I opened by saying that I would try to give it to them straight, without any crap. But anyone could have wowed that audience. Now for what will interest you: I talked for about a half an hour, to the most utter and complete attention. Then I asked for questions. They were ready for me. They asked questions from about 8:45 p.m. until 10:30, until I actually was faint and sweating from the lack of dinner, and the heat from the great fire at my back. They got me some water and a stool to sit on, and went on asking questions until 11 o'clock!

And what questions! The first one—you'd never guess—was "What do the people back home think of the Stettinius appointment?"[65] And from then on, with a few exceptions, they were like that. They were all *Time* readers, with gripes because they get *Time* so late.

To cut this down, here are some observations. Within the first hour I suddenly realized that one American generalization about GI's is totally untrue: that they talk about first, girls, second, food, third, girls, and fourth, gripe about the Army, and fifth, when do we go home? It was very obvious that you can only talk about sex for a little while around your hut-stove without repeating yourself, and that you run through food and the other subjects just as rapidly, and that then the GIs got down to the old American habit of arguing about more abstract subjects. And the number one subject, underlined heavily, is U.S. foreign policy. Remember, these were above-average Air Force troops, not infantry GIs; so I am not generalizing, above all. But this should be indicative. All other subjects paled beside that of foreign policy. I told them that two things were obvious: that the election had settled that the U.S. was out in the world to stay, but that the great fact was that we didn't know how to act now that we were out in the world. They took this with great satisfaction: it obviously fitted in with their beliefs. At least a score of times one of them, nudged by his neighbors, would say, "Look, we've been arguing about this for a couple of months . . . now you settle it." "It" would be a question of what should the American stand be on Poland.

To say I was flabbergasted by their acuteness and their depth of interest in this would be a minimum statement. Nothing I have read or heard had prepared me for it. I found them testing me up to and beyond the limits of all I knew of the State Department, and of the possibilities of foreign policy twists in 1945. I did not just get questions from any one clique of troops specially interested; all over the hall some GI would stand up, and wind up a question that reminded me of the Senate, with dignity and knowledge in the question.

I did not satisfy them, I hasten to add, in many respects; but some of that is Mr. Roosevelt's fault. They wanted assurances I could not give them; specifically they wanted to be told that the U.S. was going to take a hand in the world, on its own hook.

They meant definitely that they wanted the U.S. to go ahead and work out things in the world as it saw fit, with a minimum of nods and bows to its Allies, secure in its own power. They didn't know quite how; they agreed that we must carry on with our Allies, without open quarrels, but they wanted the U.S. to dominate the Big Three, not fool around in the rear. They did not think it was at all too late for us to speak up as to how we wanted things in Poland or Greece. They looked to Mr. Roosevelt to do the speaking up, and could not understand why he does not. To a man they would have thrown the British spang out of Greece. To a man they were disgusted with a Russian offensive in Hungary. (I may exaggerate a little on these last two points; they were not unanimous, but close to it.)

From this perhaps you can tell how I was at first taken aback. The foreign policy questions went on for something more than an hour. Then they wanted to hear about reconversion in the sense of what kind of an America they were returning to. I had pin-drop attention when I told them about the difficulties they would encounter as they tried to readjust themselves to civilian life; that they had been maturing in one direction, and the U.S. naturally in another, and that the readjustment of the two sets of views and experiences would inevitably be tough work. You can get some hint of their feelings this way: when I said that in many things the country was waiting for them to come back, so that some grave steps ahead would not be taken without the benefit of their views, someone called out "They'd better wait for us!" and everyone laughed and nodded.

The coldest ground came whenever I mentioned friendship with England. This became so noticeable that once after a pro-British blurb I ventured at random that maybe this wasn't too popular a view, and again someone roared: "You're damned tootin!" So I got after this, with these results: The overwhelming majority regard themselves as anti-British. The British have taken the place of the brass-hats as the main subject of griping. The British are inefficient; it's a miserable country, etc. Later on I discovered that the officers are much worse; boy how anti-British they are! In whole pages I could not over-stress this animosity. But let me make these reservations quickly: many of them had no particular views when they came over here. As nature abhors a vacuum, the prejudices of the most violently prejudiced men were adopted by those without preju-dices, and came to be the popular view. Many of the men merely parrot what they have heard, and are quite amenable to argument. In talking with G-5 officers, and men who have handled Army orientation courses, they say that the anti-British prejudice, while general, is not insuperable at all, and often yields readily to fair argument. But then the officers come in: they do not have to go to orientation classes, and they swiftly undo all the good work done by such classes by preserving their often arrogantly ignorant attitude of scorn and contempt for the British in all things. This is too bad.

In writing this hastily, as it comes to me, I note much bad construc-tion, and the elisions of skipping thought. Please allow for the lack of organization of these notes.

On the same subject: it may well be that these boys will carry their anti-British attitude back home, and add it to whatever percentage is left there, with sour results. On the other hand, perhaps under the pressure of new events, and as memory fades, they may take home kinder impres-sions, and from the superior attitude of much-travelled men, kindly correct American misapprehensions about England. I somewhat incline to this latter view, hopefully. I believe that after they have made it clear to the home-folks how infinitely superior in all things American are to all things British, they may well admit that the British were not too bad, after all. On this line, two more points: one U.S. major, aged 21, an absolute top ace with 35 German planes to his credit, broke off a red-hot denunciation of the British, while showing me his equipment, to say how lucky he was—he had a real British fighter-pilot's helmet, which he said is three times as good as our stuff! And in the map rooms the Bomb group men caroled about their good fortune: they had a full set of the British-made visual-aid bombing maps of Germany, so much better than ours, they said! And so on.

9. One great and main piece of news to me about the U.S. in England is sex. Harry, the situation is unbelievable. The GIs and the British girls up and down the British streets no longer have a lover-like atmosphere—they act like man-&-wife! Most of them I see are obviously past court-ing—they are settled in living together, with ration problems, etc. Some of the dating is innocent: lonely people on both sides who want to go to the movies or a pub together. Some is not innocent. But a great deal of it is love and marriage and happy-ever-after. Item: I am told on all sides that it is an official figure that 15% of all G.I. mail from France comes to British girls they left behind them. Item: the hit song of *Strike It Again* is *I Left My Heart in Piccadilly*, sung by an actor dressed like a GI, to a Brit-ish girl. Wait till the girls back home find out that their boys are coming back home—to England! Wait till the British boys come back and find their wives with babies, their girls engaged to Americans! The extent of it, and its depth, seems to me as much of a story as, in another sense, the English love-affair with the Russians was in *Life* a year or so ago. But it's perhaps an impossible story to do or picture. But maybe some *Life* or *Time* mind can think of a way. All of the London office people agree it's a hell of a story: they don't know how to go about it. British girls I have talked to about it see nothing odd in it at all; they are merely impatient for the war to end so that they can marry their GI and move to the U.S.! I found that with them I have to go very delicately in expressing any surprise at the extent of it—naturally enough.

10. Battlefronts and *Life* should no longer take a hoity-toity view of the scores of aircraft shot up on the ground. The situation has changed very radically. Of course, when a pilot shoots down a plane in the air, that means the elimination of a German pilot, and naturally counts more.

But while that used to be tough work, while strafing grounded planes at airports was easy, the reverse is now true. The American fighters told me that they dearly love to escort U.S. bombers, as they have no trouble potting German fighters. But since the Germans have moved back all their Flak guns from the defense of all of Europe, to concentrate in Germany, our boys go through purest hell every time they are assigned to peel off and go down close to knock off grounded stuff. The Germans often drag around several dummy planes on their airports, to invite the fighters to come down and shoot at them.

11. The jet-planes of the Germans still have not come in close enough. None have been shot down outside Germany, far as I can find out. They are really super: we cannot catch them with anything now in use. We are much in the position the Jap Zeros were; due to our lesser speed, and thereby superior maneuverability, we can turn our planes inside the great loops they must make, and thus get away. Everyone shudders at what the jets will be when the Germans perfect them. German rocket-firing planes are never seen now; though they could plaster our bombers safely from beyond our gun-range, they were soft meat for the fighters, because they were necessarily slow and heavy, to carry the rockets.

12. I expect to have lunch with the Beaver Wednesday. I inspect some British fields later in the week. Next week I want to see Churchill in action at the opening of Parliament, and then off to France: one month along the fronts and then three weeks in Paris before heading for the Italian front and then Rome. I still think I am the luckiest of reporters; and my gratitude to you is still mounting. My best wishes to you and all. —Sid

JANUARY 8, 1945

Dearest Darl, Whitney, John, Mammy & all:

I have been working away steadily at my job, which is merely to see as much as possible, of both places and people. So I have eaten in all kinds of places, from the cheapest little "snack bars" which is the British name for a hash-house, where you can get either a spam sandwich, raw, on the universal utility bread (a wheatish kind of bread that tastes very sawdusty) or a cheese sandwich, and either tea or coffee, all for about seven-pence, which would be 14 cents in U.S. money. And on up to the Savoy and Claridges, the top eating places, and at several of the clubs. There is much fish here, plaice, hake, sole (caught off Dover), and quite good salmon. The good places run out of food very fast. If I want dinner at night in my hotel, the Dorchester, I must order it before 11 a.m., or it will all be gone except for the imitation custard pudding for dessert. The coffee is very very strong and black, almost like drinking thick brown ink, but not rich like Turkish coffee. The tea is superb, even in the poorest places, so I'm quite happy, but oddly enough it's impossible to get at dinner, and hard to get at breakfast, when the British drink coffee instead. Milk is rationed, and very tightly. Butter is scarce. Meat is not at all scarce if you know where to go and get there early. But the British never complain; they go on eating cabbage boiled for three or more hours, brussel sprouts the same. The bacon is very good, but always broiled limp and raw-ish. Eggs, as I've said, are nowhere except with the American troops, and then fairly rare. At a Bombardment Group base I visited last week I ate the combat mess at 3 a.m., and had fresh grapefruit and two eggs over easy in butter, just perfect, with hash-brown potatoes, and real creamy milk over my cornflakes, and real American jam on my toast—toast which I made myself by holding bread against a potbellied stove, so it was hot. The British hold their toast out the window for an hour to be sure it's cold and hard, I believe. I don't dare tell any of my new British friends about the breakfast I've described, because it would ruin Anglo-American relations. Most of them haven't had a fresh egg or any good fresh fruit for more than five years, and that's a heck of a long time. I've been to the theater five times, and had a lot of fun; the English around me always concerned that I get the British jokes, some of which

I frankly say, I don't. Everyone here has been wonderful; we owe a lot of people a lot of hospitality, especially the Ragsdales.

In the carbon I enclose, of another report to Luce, I mention the trip to the Bomb base. What I left out, as not interesting to him, is how wonderfully efficient the Americans are. It was a terrific thrill, after sitting up all night during the preparations of the maps, and the very scientific arrangements for the thousands of bombers to go out, all on a split-second timing, to arrive over the target at a certain exact instant, to watch them go out in the icy, foggy morning. The fog was so thick that visibility was down to 70 yards; we were in the control tower with the colonel, only 125 yards from the big runway, and we couldn't see the bombers take off, although we could hear them roaring past, one after another, a few seconds apart, through the dark dawn, each of them crowded with the finest young men you ever saw, risking their lives miles above Germany. This was their 16th straight night of it, if you can imagine it.

I leave England about Jan. 20, a day or two either way. Write me whenever you can.

—Sid

WED. JAN. 10 [1945] [DIARY]

Lunched Beaverbrook, Arlington House. Drove to inspect RAF group, 100 mi. Snow. The welcome. Grp Capt Haycock, Wg Cmdr Gibb.[66] The dr. The dentist.

THURS. JAN. 11 [1945] [DIARY]

Habbaniya.[67] The sing. The meals. The beds. The inspection. Flight in a Mosquito. Ret. to L. The Scanlans on the drive and at dinner.

From: Sidney Olson
War Correspondent
P.R.O. U.K. Base
A.P.O. 413
c/o Postmaster, New York City

To: Mrs. Sidney Olson
c/o A.E. Holmgren
Bear River City, Utah
U.S.A.

JANUARY 12, 1945

Dearest Darl, B.G.

It is nearly a month now since I left, and due to the mails I haven't had a word from you yet—and perhaps you haven't heard from me. But sooner or later you'll get it all, as I've been pretty diligent, while I don't know when I'll ever get mail, as I'll be leaving here perhaps before I get any, and then it will have to be forwarded. What I now plan is this: a few days before I leave for the trip across I'll cable you through Hulburd my new A.P.O. number, and if you write me immediately by V-mail I'll get my first mail. But it will all catch me somewhere, so keep it up: the bare thought of not knowing anything of you and Whitney and John and the Folks for eight months is more than I can bear. I am still having a continuously pleasant and even exciting time. This week, to compare them with the Americans, I went to a British bomber base, which flies the wonderfully fast Mosquito either as escorts (fighters) with the British bombers, or as lone night intruders that smash up the Germans while hedge-hopping. The RAF people were wonderful to me, fed and slept me well, and as a special treat, one of their Wing-Commanders took me up in one for about an hour. As has been published, they go upwards of 400 miles an hour, and it was a great thrill, as I hadn't been up in any of the hot planes of the war. A wing-commander took me up, and gave me quite a sample of the works in stunt flying; as I found out later, he was trying to make me sick, because I was wearing one of his friends' oxygen-masks and he thought that would be a good joke. But I guess my stomach is too Swedish; the tricky stuff didn't bother me at all, except that upside down the only sensation you have is of terrific pressure on your head, as if someone is sitting on it—to yourself you seem to be flying right-side up except for this weight on our noggin. He dived me as if we were strafing cars on the roads, and took me out over the North Sea for a while, into the fog. It was a wonderful experience, and no real risk, of course. The English countryside, covered with snow, is very beautiful, although the pleasant even regularity of its park-like look often makes me wish for even the careful wildness of Bear Mountain park in Westchester, let alone the real Rockies. I'm staying here a little longer than I expected, as the big war-debate in Commons has been postponed until Jan. 23–24. I'll leave right after to join Wertenbaker for a day or two before I head north for a month in the snow. I feel very well; we're looked after expertly. And the British are really swell, although they don't do things in the good old U.S. way. But sometimes their way is all right, too. Haven't been to the theater for a week; have been too busy at one kind of work or another. Billions of worship, S.

SIDNEY OLSON CABLE[68]
FROM LONDON, TO DAVID HULBURD
SENT JANUARY 13, 1945; REC'D JANUARY 13, 1945

FYI, my itinerary as now planned, subject to the inscrutable fates:

Covering the Churchill war debate January 23–24; then join Wert and move soonest to the fronts for about a five-week tour; then fun and games in Paris and France for three weeks; then the Italian front for two weeks; Rome, three weeks; then Belgrade and Bucharest if possible and Athens in the next three or four weeks; Cairo and Mideast tour, three weeks; Teheran and India tour including the Burma front to Chunking and the Nanning front, three or four weeks; Australia to MacArthur, three weeks; Navy task force, one month; and home the end of September. I plan to see all the fronts and all the available major capitals, ATC and God watching over me.[69]

Tell Alex I made a two-hour speech to 400 Eighth Air Force crewmen a week ago. The next morning they took off in seventy-yard visibility unseeable from the control tower in a fog as thick as my speech. I also inspected the U.S. fighter base which has the best 1944 record. This week I was with the RAF and flew in the newest announced Mosquito over the North Sea with the pilot trying to make me sick as I was wearing his best friend's oxygen mask, but I felt fine except as if someone were sitting on my head. I lunched Beaver last week. Have you had any V-bombs?

Western Union Cablegram

Sidney Olson
Time-Life Ltd.
Dean Street London

JAN. 16, 1945

Your itinerary admirable. I have no influence with ATC but if prayers avail God will watch over you. Don't be too sure about chaos. Man has great powers of recuperation.

Albest,
Harry Luck[70]

Mr. Luce: Mr. Billings & Mr. Grover have read this letter. Also, Mr. Alexander and Mr. Chambers have seen excerpts from it—namely the paragraphs marked by Mr. Grover with a penciled checkmark.[71] —C.T.

JANUARY 17, 1945

Dear Harry:

This is the third of my reports.[72] I hope I'm not too gaseous. I'm sure you'll make sufficient allowance for my newness out in the world. But nearly everything I see delights me or excites me, down to the fact that the British telephone instructions say "listen for the dial-tone (a low purring sound)." The public use of an intimate descriptive adjective like "purring" seems wonderful to me, and very British.

Thanks for your cable approving my itinerary. Let me now set out, as best as I am able, the principles under which I am travelling. The largest possible objective I could have would be to return with some kind of philosophic contribution to make, about the state of the world this year. I am not optimistic about being able to do this, but I shall keep my eyes and ears and wits open, and try hard, with such mind as I have. A personal objective is to return with my own convictions more settled; I am somewhat weary of not knowing what to believe, or rather, little weary of my own long-standing refusal to make up my mind about everything from God to Socialism. I want to settle down a little—not too much—intellectually, if I can do this without using my freedom to be inconsistent, to change my beliefs as I grow and learn.

But on this trip I am, as far as possible, trying to see things plain, without preconceived notions. I am very conscious of the psychological truth that you tend to see what you expect to see, and that the mind unconsciously rejects or forgets those things which do not fit the preconceived notions. I remember Darwin, how he was so aware of this that he used to write down instantly all the objections to his theory, because he knew his mind would unconsciously let slip all disagreeable controverting facts.

So, as a journalist, I will valiantly try to put the stacks of diametrically opposed facts and opinions side by side, and digest them all as best I can.

But even more difficult to avoid will be to take a stand on the results. As the mind constantly tests and chooses and moves on, there is an inevitable sediment of belief formed; or better, a coral growth that comes up from under the waters of the mind, a growth of opinion that gradually becomes fixed and almost indestructible.

Lippmann is a wonderful example.[73] Remember how he wrote, for something like two years, about the "choices" that America must make, the choices that Roosevelt must make, in the field of policy. But he writes no more about choices. He writes as if there is only one choice, that embodied in his last book, a compound of "realism," of "expediency," etc. Why? Because in those two years, as he wrote about choices, he was gradually making his own choice, and he is now committed to it. This is a perfect example of the coral-like growth of a man's belief. This may make Lippmann a very good journalist in his forcefulness, but it inevitably lessens his larger usefulness, because he only knows the world now from his own coral island of opinion, which may be isolated by the current of events. In short, this I intend to avoid, too, if possible. For one thing, in a world moving swiftly, I do not want to go through the pain and destruction of having my coral-island of beliefs suddenly blasted away, as happened to those unfortunates, even around *Time*, who had gradually taken a fixed position on Communism, when suddenly came the Hitler-Stalin pact of 1941. Of course, theirs was a false position in the first place. But how often the same blasting-away has happened throughout the war, to all kinds of views; how many times it will happen again. Consider all the Roosevelt-believers! Look at what is inevitably ahead for them! I set 18 months ahead as the last date for the disappearance of the fixed intellectual pro-Roosevelt position. Then what suffering, hey? I can hardly wait.

So much for some of the philosophic bases from which I have set out.

I lunched with the B. the other day.[74] We got on quite well—at least he laughed alot—but I can't say I did a great job of interviewing him. Or perhaps he just wasn't giving down milk that day.

Anglo-American relations were the main subject. The B. had been at a meeting that morning, some committee or other. He said: "The relations between our countries are like this. If there's one man I can't stand, whom I loathe, despise, abominate from the soles up, it's the ruddy, bloody, f—— Postmaster General. But we're both Conservatives! So we get along. We have to. We march arm-in-arm off together." And he marched up & down the room pantomiming his arm-and-arming it with this loathsome PMG. "That's how it is with America and the British. You may hate our guts. We may hate yours. But we've got to get along. So we will."

The same, he said, went for Russia. He thought Willkie's emotionalism about Russia was all nonsense.[75] "It's a plain matter of sense," he said, snorting. (This happened three days after the Order of Suvorov.)

So, no matter what the papers say, he thinks the windy arguments across the oceans just don't really matter. Greece was another matter. That is on the nerve. The present speech, which I hope to hear tomorrow, by the Prime Minister, has not at all been a matter of approving a few scribbled notes, and trusting to Winston's oratorical glow to carry things through. I got the very strong impression that this has been given the fullest kind of Rosenman-Sherwood treatment, with much testing of the phrases, attitudes, etc.[76] And without stretching this too far, at lunch this week in the Commons several members almost casually assumed that unless the speech is good enough, the present Government might fall. (These were the opinions of only three members, all of them Independents, and so not necessarily representative.)

The one thing he could not tell me about, but which he wanted me to mention to you, *in spades*, are these two words: "jet propulsion." That's all he (or I) can say.

I expect to get a letter off soon to Al Grover about the London office as I have observed it.

I have made one discovery along the lines of wherein the relations of the British and the Americans break down. I can tell it best in personal experience.

When I travelled to see a U.S. Bomber Base and to a U.S. Fighter Base, all preparations were made with routine American efficiency. From the lowest MP at the road-stop all the way up to the base commanders, all the necessary people knew that we were coming and were prepared for it, with a schedule of things to do, etc., adjustable to meet our needs. We were flatteringly welcomed, fed and handled, without interfering with the base routine in any way.

Ah, but when I travelled to an RAF base! In the first place the PRO at the Air Ministry actually did not know exactly where the base was, or how to get there, but advised us to drive to a certain town "and inquire of anyone there." Hmm. After a five-and-one-half hour drive over icy snowy roads we finally found the entrance to the field, being regarded by most of the populace as obviously German spies. The British MPs kept us standing in the snow under guard for about 20 minutes of desultory telephoning. Then we were taken, under guard, to the adjutant's quarters. It took nearly half an hour to satisfy him. No one had warned him to expect us. He said: "I suppose you'll expect to be fed?" in that British tone that has taken centuries of cultivation. But I was grimly determined to be hands-across-the-sea if it killed me, without, however, falling into the cringing servility that distinguishes British reporters up against offi-cialdom. Finally the adjutant got on to the Group-Captain by telephone, and that gentleman's dismay at the calamity that had befallen his base was most audible. I could hear him saying repeatedly "Oh God!" much like Father Day in *Life with Father*. After a bit we were conducted to his quarters, and given a drink, and then to mess, and back to his quarters for an evening's talk. Throughout this time little clusters of higher-ups would observe me narrowly, evidently barely repressing their shudders at this intrusion. The Group-Captain collected a half-dozen of his friends at his quarters to insulate him against the disaster of a completely wasted evening. I admit it got very thick, and it got thicker as every conversational hare I started was slaughtered forthwith. I struggled on against odds which would have killed an Alger boy. On all topics they unanimously took the somewhat impolite you that everything RAF or British was so overwhelmingly superior to anything American that it was too, too tiresome even to discuss.

I had just read Philip Guedalla's new book *Middle East: A Study in Air Power, 1940–1942*, and this finally saved me. The best chapter in the book is about the defense of Habbaniya, in Iraq, by a handful of English training-planes; and it turned out, as I glowed on over this miraculous piece of work by the RAF, that the base-doctor, a decent chap there present, had been at that base at the time. This, and the gradual work of the whiskey on them, finally gave them some manners. Then they took interest; then they got charming, and from that evening on they were all perfectly delightful human beings. Nothing was too much trouble; they saw to our comforts (don't misunderstand—I wasn't asking deluxe accommodations, but just accommodation), and gave me a trip for an hour's stunting in a Mosquito, etc. All next day they were excellent, and practically the whole base saw us off in something like a triumphal parade.

The only point of all this: what if I had stiffened up and gone very firmly American on them, as I was sorely tempted to do, at the start? The provocation was terrific. I could have become curt and contained and hard-to-please, all with perfect right. Then things would have been very stiff and would have ended up foully. I'm not saying that my patience was so very wonderful; but what if I'd started off with less firm resolve to be friends; or, as most often happens, if I had begun with the ill-concealed contempt for the British that so many Americans of the military have? In short, my discovery is merely that it is upon this rock friendships have split; much patience is needed.

All British reporting of the American scene is very poor with the sole exception of Sir Willmott Lewis—when he works at it.[77] USAW editor Alexander should see, as routine, clips of Lewis' pieces. Sir Willmott is excellent.

Time sells Aneurin Bevan too short.[78] I hear on all sides here what a man he is, how sound, how able, etc. Have not met him yet, but this is not just the Socialist belief. Bevan would be a good cover sometime this year—about Election time? No one here really has the faintest idea of which way England will turn in its general election. But most people I've talked to, of all sorts, don't seriously expect a great swing to the left. They believe generally that many of the compulsions formerly existing for a leftward swing have now vanished. But there certainly is a throw-the-rascals-out feeling about all the ind. Labour and the Conservatives, anticipating this, are putting up all sorts of new candidates from the two big parties. RAF candidates are the ones to watch—the British feel almost mystical about the RAF. No member of it can do wrong.

I wish I could get into Spain. But Eisenhower will let no accredited war correspondents in there. I feel the strongest journalistic curiosity about it; Spain is always important. If possible at all, you might most seriously consider establishing a one-man bureau there; some able reporter could make the world wiser from Spain.

From here, Senator Vandenberg looks like a good cover to me.[79] Let some USAW New Dealer seriously ponder his record, and discover how much so-called New Deal social legislation he actually fathered. In all the years I quarrel only with his killing of Passamaquoddy; the U.S. could have used that power most efficiently in New England throughout this war and after.[80]

At lunch, Raimund and I discussed the German prisoner problem,[81] comparing results in the U.S. with those in Britain. Result of comparison: there are no results worth adding up. In short, re-education of Nazis has failed utterly so far. This should interest you: Nazis who desert often give one reason of the whole fabric, but are unable to swear off the whole. To be clear: a Nazi will desert, and will say he is disgusted with Hitler, Nazism, etc. etc. Why? Well, the judicial system is bad; the judges corrupt. Or one of the leaders is wrong. (I am not discussing those who desert because they are afraid or hungry; a meal and safety leaves them ideologically where they were). But when he is interrogated further, the Nazi in question remains unmoved ideologically; he has not lost belief that the persecution of the Jews was correct, or in the *Fuehrer*; it is just that this one phase of the whole was wrong. It is like someone quitting a church because he didn't like the way a sacrament is administered, but still an unshakable believer in God and the religion as a whole. None of this is prepossessing, but it's true. I begin to wonder about that glib phrase "re-educate them."

To France next week. I will report about once every 10 days or so to you; more or less along the lines of our Saturday morning coffee-sessions at the drugstore.

The very best to you.

—Sid

LONDON CABLE 2539[82]
FROM SID OLSON TO DAVID HULBURD
SENT JANUARY 18, 1945; REC'D JANUARY 19, 1945
Churchill Speech:[83]

The day was raw and gray. A cold wind polished shiny-black the tall, plumed statue of Field Marshall Earl Haig, eternally horsed in bronze on broad Whitehall. Past him flicked the quacking little cabs, to swerve to the curb at Westminster, depositing the officialdom of England, of churches, of diplomacy. Most of these men seemed grave as they climbed the steps and went through the rows of tall, silver-buttoned bobbies, past the great empty room where King Charles II was tried and sentenced to the block, and on into the warm, crowded outer lobbies, where several hundred Britons jostled for a better view of the nabobs entering the House.

The Chamber was an oasis of warmth against the day, with the pleasurable advantage of being able to hear plainly from time to time the whistle of the raw wind outside, buffeting the multiplications of Gothic ornament. The question hour dragged on until 12:05 p.m. and then there came a swelling rumble of hear hears from the two opposing rows of red-leather benches, and Winston Churchill came in to sit unobtrusively on the front bench with Clement Attlee on his right and a portlier, greyer Anthony Eden just beyond.

Mr. Churchill was in a black suit, white shirt, black bow tie, with a large white handkerchief flowering out of his breast pocket. But the black and whiteness only accentuated his pinkness. His face and skull veritably shone with a delicate rosy suffusion, a baby's-bottom pinkness as light as face powder. Among all the dark young faces and the pale-ivory old faces and the beef-red middle-aged faces this pinkness stood out healthily.

Now all the scoop-coated, white-tied attendants of the House were at attention. The silken-breached mace bearer, the heavy gold medallion swinging rhythmically from his neck chain, now bowed as he crossed the line into the House, advanced its length over the gray-green carpet, and lowered the massive golden mace from the table which stands before the Speaker and between the rows of facing benches. The question hour was over: now the debate could begin.

Mr. Churchill, rising, disposed a little packet of notes before him, pulled his horn-rimmed glasses well down on his nose, and began with a few mumblings about his having a cold. This must have been more oratorical jockeying from foot to foot before he plunged into the water, because the cold was not noticeable in his voice, and the only time he blew his nose was during a later response by Mr. Greenwood, a blow which seemed time for rhetorical effect rather than anything else.

Then he struck out boldly. The atmosphere was tense. The speech had been the subject of much Cabinet argument and debate; unlike the usual crises, wherein the Cabinet blithely hand the Prime Minister the hot potato, and then lean comfortably back to watch him expertly cool it off. This time many opinions had been taken; many approaches discussed; agreement had been wrought carefully. The reaction to his last speech had been the worst of his war tenure. Failure to overcome this crisis would almost certainly mean the fall of his government.

So the government members were tense, to see if he could overcome the great odds of public opinion, an opinion so massed against the seeming course of policy in Greece that now even the Thunderer, the *London Times*, rumbled every day the wrath of the people. And the Opposition benches were tense; scores of men who once only back-handed their doubts about the government were now most openly and vociferously critical. There were scores of men leaning forward, convinced that there could be no satisfactory answers to the angry questions in their minds. And beyond, the world over perhaps, honest men wanted to know why the British had been fighting the Greeks, the many things that stemmed out of the central question; why had the British been fighting the Greeks?

Against all odds, Mr. Churchill triumphed. Later, as the speech was read closely and flaws picked; as events march badly or well, a new hubbub may arise; new questions will be raised; all may not seem as simple as the Prime Minister made it sound. But for the moment his triumph seemed clear. He laid each doubt by the heels, one by one. The lesser objections he disposed of with the quick wrist twist of the experienced fencer. No executioner could have been surer of his blows. Again and again the tension in the atmosphere was almost palpable; the air seemed thick and hard to breathe; people in the shoulder-to-shoulder jammed galleries would notice a foot or an arm was numb with a cramp, and then forget about it. But the pink little man with the fringe of graying sandy hair, using short, chopping gestures, prowling back and forth before his little packet of notes, grew ever cooler and more adroit as he took his audience of millions through the tragic complexities of the British position in Greece on to a realization of the main facts.

One of the earlier blows was one of the most telling of all, when he said: "Sir, I must admit I underrated them (the ELAS): I judged them on their form against the Germans." This was most shrewd, and most resented by the Leftists, as it carefully smeared ELAS with at least a tincture of Nazism. And by the time he had finished painting this picture, ELAS stood clearly indicated as very like the Michailovich men of Yugoslavia. From his words "the fierce mountaineers who had been so tame and idle against the Germans" on to his quick thrust that they were Trotskyites, "as Trotskyism is a term which has the advantage of being fully as hated in Russia," he so tied up the Opposition that it began to seem a little bit like trading with the enemy to be pro-ELAS.

Mr. Churchill was in very rare form. By the end of the morning session his foes were helpless. He had been speaking then for one hour and fifteen minutes and he had come safely through, to all appearances, the biggest crisis of his career as Prime Minister—and all without really budging any substantial distance from the stated positions taken by the British Government one month ago; the positions which had caused the crisis. At this moment any concessions he has made seem minor, and mainly in tone; perhaps they will seem greater after reflection. But however that may be, this was a triumph, and the further hour he spoke after lunch in his usual masterly review of the war situation, was one long easy procession of rumbles of *hear, hear* from all sides.

This included his solemn and much-applauded tribute to the United States; a tribute that visibly moved many Americans in the galleries, and brought a great glow to the rapt, pale, dark-browned face of Ambassador Winant in his gallery.[84]

Within the hugh [*sic*], cold, rain-wet stones of the historic old building, all the tension had seeped away now. Anthony Eden, who had spent the tensest moments narrowly inspecting the workings of his cufflinks, as if he had never seen them before, now rested his hand somnolently on the back of the bench, apparently comfortably sleepy.[85] And as soon as Mr. Churchill sat down, Major Attlee negligently propped both his feet up on the Speaker's table, near where the Churchill notes had rested.[86] All was harmony, and Arthur Greenwood, standing up for the Opposition for the moment, could only stress that the British Government seemed to be a little more in favor of the Right than the Left in Greece. No doubt he, no more than anyone else, wanted to seem to be one of the "parrots" that Mr. Churchill said sometimes swarm down on the eagles. Then Mr. Greenwood was through, interrupted notably only by Mr. Churchill's magnificent blowing of his nose in answer to a rhetorical question, the Prime Minister rose and moved out, and soon after, so did all else, out into the wintry afternoon on Whitehall, where the great red buses, like Spanish galleons, sailed steadily in convoys along the old avenue.

2. THE DRAGON'S TEETH

To: OC Main Can Press Camp
From: Cdn ADPR, 21 Army Gp
OC Adv Cdn Press Camp
Jan. 27, 1945

Facility Visit—Mr Olsen [*sic* throughout]
Correspondent for *Time* & *Life*

1. The m/n correspondent is assigned for a four or five day facility visit on the Cdn sector.[87] He is presently touring the Second British Army front.

2. Capt Cassils will detail a conducting offr from the Adv Camp to report to the British Press Camp, Eindhoven, for lunch on Monday, 29 Jan 45. After lunch he will take Mr Olsen back to the Adv Camp for the night.

3. Mr Olsen is particularly anxious to secure infm and background regarding flooded areas, winter patrol activities and so forth. If possible, a visit should be arrange [*sic*] the following day to an Inf Btn or Bde HQ.

4. It is suggested that Mr Olsen might like to meet Gen Simonds if this could be arranged through the Gen's ADC. It is also suggested that on his way to the Main Camp at Tilburg he should drop in and see Gen Volkes at 4th Div HQ and also the CRE at that HQ for infm on Engineering problems. If the conducting offr should get through on the telephone to Gen Volkes or his ADC, and, using my name, suggest that Mr Olsen would like to meet Gen Volkes, it is altogether likely the Gen would invite him in for lunch, tea or a drink.

5. On arrival at the Main Press Camp, either Tuesday night or Wednesday, it should be arranged for Mr. OLSEN to get an OPs briefing from Col Ducette. If Mr Olsen desires, it is also likely that Gen Crerar would grant him a few minutes interview. Should this be the case, Maj Austin should be asked to arrange it.

6. En route back to Brussels Mr Olsen indicates that he would like to have a look at the Beveland-Walcheren area, background to the Antwerp

story. It might also be arranged for him to visit the Fort Comds' office at Antwerp where he could secure a brief outline of the ports development. If necessary being billeted over-night in Antwerp by the Town Major. The conducting offr should then bring him back here to Brussels.

7. Mr Olsen's light-weight American uniform is not considered suitable for his activities on this front and he has had no opportunity of picking up warmer clothes. Please instruct the QM at the Main Press Camp to issue him, if possible, with a Cdn battle-dress and an issue sweater.

8. All informed.

Lt. Col R.S. Malone [handwritten]

Copies to:
War Correspondent Mr. Olsen
DADPR, Main HQ First Con Army

SUNDAY, JAN. 28, 1945
Sittard, Holland [Field Notes]

Someone said: "Do you know? It's Sunday!"

This was quite a shock, Sunday always looks different from other days; the sunlight has a special quality; the day feels different.

But out the broad glass windows of the press camp you could see the Dutch people going to church. A youngish mother, about 35, a black felt hat set carefully on her head, led her young son, about 9 or 10, off toward church, his yellow hair neatly parted and plastered down. Others passed, walking slowly, their meager breakfasts still warm in their stomachs. A little girl, about seven or eight years old, came along, rolling with great difficulty a woman's bike, through the snow, and across the iced streets. She wore pigtails, a maroon coat, and long white stockings. Like the others, she looked perfectly American, a cute little thing, with rosy cheeks in the chill day. There had been a light fall of snow during the night, lying lightly and thinly on top the heavy older ice.

This is only a few miles behind the front lines. The people refuse to pay overmuch attention to the war. At the schools yesterday, at recesses, they were sliding down the ice-slides exactly as American children do; or sleighing on even the slightest slopes. There were differences; the schools were damned cold, and not much lighted; I suppose they wore their over-coats indoors, as so many people must in Europe now.

This is a most Catholic area. Roadside shrines everywhere, even in the busy city streets; and in the houses, crucifixes of all sizes, over the doors and on the tables, usually with a bleeding Christ hanging from them. And everywhere wheeling through the snow on the omnipresent bicycles, priests with their robes blowing in the wind, their little black sombreros pulled down hard on their heads.

Things to remember about Brussels, Louvain.

At Louvain the Hotel de Ville, and the great Library re-built by the Americans. The awful bomb damage, and V-bomb damage, much of it fresh. The British soldiers queueing for tea. $2 equals 10 shillings equals 100 French francs equals 88 Belgian francs equals 0 guilders Dutch.

The neatly pruned, oh, expertly pruned orchards of Belgium and Holland. What a comparison with Britain, where the manpower situation has been so tight so long. Things like this really reveal the extent of a war's impact on a country.

The canals. Another Bridge Built by Company A....

Slang: bit of a bind, that. What's the form? The form is. ... The golf course: you'll have to play the last nine first, but after lunch I'll have the 5th and 7th holes cleared of Germans . . . if you don't mind. The pheasant-shoot: pheasants flew north into the woods. But those woods are full of Germans. Oh no, old boy; I ordered a small attack this morning; the only thing is that we'll have to have the beaters work back toward us.

In Brussels, the hotel at breakfast. The lanterns placed on chairs set up on the tablecloths; the lights, off at 7 a.m. The deadly chill. The breakfast: bacon and sausage, porridge; the butter, sugar and cream that any Briton would give an eye for; good tea or coffee. Cigars. Cognac, champagne, *bière*.

The department stores; toys; food, Churchill cigars of confection, but mostly the cakes known as Madeleines; the gloves; 500 499 [*sic*] Belgian francs. The window display of rations; see red notebook—1650 gr, for 2450 gr. of food....

The nightclubs: *Sa Majeste*, Variety club. The one in the cellar. The bands. The dancing. The women. The drinks. The prices.

The very narrow streets. Wooden shoes. Describe the varieties of shoes and boots seen.

Takeout of Paris stores. *Le Soleil!*

Never have a house by a crossroads, by a canal, by a rr station, along a river or a main street.

Talk to couriers about how they keep warm; their clothes.

Description of a hellhole in a brick wall. An exact description, like CSF. Bullets in the walls. Rolls of barbed wire across the fields full of frozen Brussels sprouts.

This country was nobody's cup of tea for quite a bit.

The upended riddled cars; only exact description of these would be good. Very close descrip all the way. Hongen. The shattered trees.

The use of the word liberated. Hongen was totally liberated. Liberated horses and cows; villagers cut off steaks at night.[88]

Cans on the barbed wire; they can tell whether the rattle is from the wind or by men; and they fire anyway.

The evacuees camp; new Germans and Belgians.

Fortresses, I expect, as the mighty rumble rolls across the sky, unseen, steady.[89] The quarters in the barn and house around the little court.

The line of tanks going by, and skidding into the ditch at the same point. The top hats; umbrellas; the easy chairs; the liberated piano; the tea kettles; the faces of the Germans in trucks; *the b - - - - - - f - - - - - -*, said the soldiers; or *You started it*. The mutters. The children and the old and the women; the goat and cattle liberated; off to be milked.

BLA—Burma Looms Ahead.

Heinsberg; lib. 9 one half miles SE of Roermond, 6 one half miles north of Geilenkirchen. The damage, the damage, the damage. Lib, from the house of Hermann Pape and Joh. Peters, the tray. The recipe book; the exquisitely clear handwriting, so careful and even, of Frau Pape or Peters; so careful to inscribe these recipes so that she would have them always. Is she dead? Liberated, unquote? Back farther in Germany? Forward in evac. camp? Now the winds blow through the house she tried so hard to keep up. As to so many Greeks, Yugoslavs, French, Belgians, Danes, Norwegians, Russians, Japs, Filipinos, Africans and on and on their household gods and goods scattered and shattered or looked on by the curious, or felt delicately to see if mines. The phone book fluttering on the windowsill. The little graveyards—mined? The next sexton—who will he be?—will find out when he digs new graves; and there will be lots of new ones when these people come back, all over the world; as they probably will, mostly.

Silver birch along the road.

The street names and numbers that are meaningless now; no one is going to call up; no one is there. Only military signs, and men in cellars warming tea, and discussing loot.

The little church with the roll of honor, at Schinfeld, near Straeten and Putt. Silk on jeeps, and the spine.

The real cold. Exact. The dead purple hands, too numb to more than flutter. Horses loose in the fields. The bawling cows in the barn. Udders aching. Cold. Oh, they'll step on a mine soon.

The tin threads of colored wires along the roads, on hedges, trees. The verges cleared signs. The mined areas markings. The waits for tanks and trucks. The talks with the men. The sgt. with the doll for the major. Saeffelen. "Sunshine roof."

B traps—Keep Out.[90] Camouflage fluttering on the helmets. Snow white tarps on tanks. The tapes along minefields. Tanks printing their treads stead [sic] along the snow. The thump and crack of shellfire in the distance. My first hearing of shells.

Leather overstuffed chairs; the awful chandelier.

Harsh grind of the cold. British leather jerkins, like so many bereted Robin Hoods. The gauntlets. The battledress.

Sidney Olson Cable Unnumbered
From Holland to David Hulburd
Sent February 4, 1945; Rec'd February 4, 1945

Attention Calhoun and Battlefronts

I have just learned that Busch's Wilhelmina profile was actually the Holland diary so understand why no sale,[91] but just to make you wish you were here now follows a catalog of items which I will herewith throw away:

An interview with General Crerar and tour through his special caravan wagon seized from a Belgian collaborator who was building it for a German general.[92] It is a seraglio on wheels with built-in imitation marble fireplace, multiple liquor closets, superb baroque bed, lounges, easy chairs, refrigerator, galley, closets. Crerar now uses it for big-shot visiting firemen such as Eisenhower.

Lunch with Major General Chris Vokes, the red-mustached Canadian fire-eater who told men on leave to go home and breed and who has heard from his wife about this—all this off-record unless you want—and who drinks straight gins like Duke Ellington.[93] Check Tom Griffith on this.

Watching V-bombs corkscrew up from the northern tip of the corner until they shoot up into the strato.

Life in Antwerp today interview with the American port commander who refuses to regard the Belgian strikers as anything but the most patriotic, hardworking, underfed brave men he has ever seen.

Evening in a Dutch home discussing modem art and some dope on the newest continental school of modern painting since surrealism, an absolutely photographic but superbly imaginative style whose Dutch masters are Jan Sluyters, Piet Wieman, Raoul Hynckes and Jan Voerman.

Watching British tanks come out of the German clean-up battle, each tanker wearing a German top hat with liberated easy chairs tied on to tanks and trucks full of liberated pianos followed by Tommies driving liberated goats, cows and horses.[94] I liberated a silver tray.

Life in the tip of the British Canadian corner of the front where Canadian woodsmen have dug into forests so expertly that they all have bed-lamps, automatic doors and laid stone floors in the midst of snow-filled pinewoods wilds.

Night life in Ghent. Wow! Night life in Brussels. Four wows! Night life in Paris. Bah!

Trip through smashed Holland north of Ghent to Breskens to find how the Dutch are moving actually back into hopelessly Aachen-ated places and bravely lifting the unexploded shells out of their kitchens.

How you get steak and champagne at the front with lots of hot baths, and Spam and beans and post-liberation cognac which tastes like used mouthwash back in the rear bases such as Paris, plus no baths unless you like ice water.

How a British patrol feels at night with Germans infiltrating around them.

I sent Canadian battle stuff on to Battlefronts if the censor will let it through.

Sidney Olson Cable Unnumbered[95]
Sans origine to David Hulburd
Sent February 5, 1945; Rec'd February 5, 1945

Shorty for Battlefronts:

When Rundstedt struck towards Namur last Christmas in the now vanished bulge, he posed a heavy secondary threat along the lower Meuse above 's-Hertogenbosch, massing divisions and armor there second only to that committed to the bulge.[96] If the stab farthest east succeeded the second pincer would be thrown across the lower Maas in a giant clutch at Antwerp.[97] Farthest east on the flooded coastal islands he also made ready a third thrust, a subsidiary to a subsidiary, whose mission was to be the retaking of Walcheren, Zuid Beveland and Flushing (Vlissengen). In preparation for the middle thrust, German paratroopers took the island of Kappelsche Sveer on Christmas Eve last.[98] This gave him a toehold for a crossing in force farther down the river if the battle of the bulge went well.

This little place looks like the side profile of a heaping teaspoon sugar. It only shows on the largest scale maps, on the Maas a few miles north-west of 's-Hertogenbosch. It is easily on oof the most worthless pieces of land anywhere. Even the land-thrifty Dutch had only two houses on it, one at the end of the spoon-handle, which the Canadians still held, and one at a point where the handle joins the spoon. The handle was several miles of grassy dike about forty feet high and about as wide as a football field; the spoon part was about a mile wide and absolutely flat. With their usual superb industry the Germans dug sideways holes through the dike out of which they could pop to harass the Canadians across the river and into which they could pop for complete safety against any attack.

The high command wanted this island back badly. First they sent Poles against the flat part of the spoon in a night attack. When daylight came the Poles still hadn't cleaned the flat of Germans and they were driven bloodily off the flat. The command tried a new strategy. Commandos in snow suits in white-painted boats were sent by night down the river at the intersection of the spoon and handle behind the Germans. But unexpectedly the moon came out and the commando boats were spotted easily. Scores of smoke pots had been made ready for this but a shifting wind drove the smoke back on the Canadian side of the river, exposing the commandos who were bloodily repulsed and made their way back as best they could in daylight. With two defeats the command turned the problem over to the Royal Canadian Engineers, who all seem to be six-feet tall, blonde and blue-eyed. The decision was that the only way to root out the Germans was to get tanks on the island. The obvious place to build a bridge was at the handle which the Canadians still held, and then run the tanks along the grassy terraced sides of the dike firing into one German foxhole after another. The problem was how to build the bridge. Twice attempts failed when the Germans heard Canadian trucks trundling Bailey Bridge materials up the road. A Canadian engineer major finally had the idea: He commandeered a Dutch farmer's rubber-tired farm wagon and one night beginning at twilight his men wearily dragged this cart back and forth until the bridge was up.

The bridge is a fantasy of makeshift with one Bailey section bolted in among nailed wooden sections that soop [*sic*] up and down like a Coney Island giant racer. The men got it in place complete with a painted sign naming it the mad whore's dream and the tanks began crawling delicately over it at midnight while a heavy artillery barrage on the opposite shore was laid down to foul up German attempts to find out what was up. The Canadians, their faces stung red in the dark by a stinging sleet storm, worked along the dike methodically firing in short bursts and tossing grenades. Whenever they got a heavy answer, a trundling tank would pour in supporting fire. It was a nasty night. The heavy sleeting rain soon melted the snow that had iced the dikes and the troops tore off their snow suits which began to make them targets against the grass.

By dawn they had cleared the whole handle and a secondary attack on the flat had driven the remaining Germans into a knot at the intersection of the spoon and spoon handle. By nine o'clock all the Germans were dead except for forty prisoners. These were no old men with glass eyes and wooden legs, but tall, tough, arrogant paratroopers, young and surly. Under interrogation they were cold and hostile, with only the occasional nerve-twitch of a cheek-muscle to betray weariness, not weakness. Of the house that once stood at the joint, nothing remains but a brick cellar big enough to hold only two men and maps and a candle at one time. Below it is the airless horror of the dugout where Germans slept. Half a German officer lay on the top of the dugout with his face smiling into the mud. Below him all along the spoon and handle were strung the battle-green uniforms of his men, seeming arrogant even in death. Here and there lay a Canadian—and this may be only a trick of the imagination—but they all seemed relaxed and peaceful. This tiny action was finished January 31st. It has two meanings. First, to show the extraordinary difficulty of fighting in this sector where the only possible progress is along narrow pothole roads between vast vistas of ice-choked, flooded grey waters unrelieved even by trees—a landscape incredibly grey and miserable—and second, to point out the obvious fact that whereas once the Germans had a foothold to cross the lower Maas we now have that foothold. In communiques, incidentally, this action seems only to appear as "vigorous patrolling."[99]

From: Sidney Olson, W/Corr.
P.R.D. SHAEF
A.P.O. 757

To: Mrs. Sidney Olson
c/o A.E. Holmgren
Bear River City, Utah U.S.A.

FEBRUARY 5, 1945
Darling Supreme B.G.—
    This short note will reach you sooner than much longer letter I'm also writing tonight. In case you're blaming the mails, I haven't written since mid-January. I've been traveling ever since and generally in places where I couldn't get off a letter. Mostly I've been too busy learning and seeing. But I blame the mails plenty. I still haven't heard a single line from anybody back home since I left you at the Larchmont train station that night. Nothing had come through when I left London Jan. 21. But I love you all dearly and I'm sure you're writing me. Even a letter from John would be terrific. Hope you're getting occasional packages I send. Got you something cute in Brussels Saturday morn (this is Monday). Am putting love in other letter; this is only news. Spent two and a half days in Paris, oh wonderful beautiful Paris, even though three feet deep in snow and ice and no hot baths. Then flew to Brussels in an hour and waited three hours at airport for British to pick me up. Spent all next day driving toward front. Sunday the 27th I spent in Germany, in a heap of bricks that used to be the town of Heinsberg. There I "liberated" a nice little silver tray. We are wrecking Germany inch by inch. But somehow I can't hate the German evacuees I have seen, mostly old men, mothers, and children. One little blonde girl, age 7, hair in pigtails, was almost a ringer for Whitney, even to her way of skittering about. They squirted her with delousing powder but she didn't cry. I am more used to the *boomp boomp* of guns now. Then went up to Eindhoven and on to the little northern corner of the front at Dutch town of Nijmegen: look on your maps. Spent some time there with Canadians and then followed operation to clean up Germans on little island of Kappelsch s'Veer on which I sent story to

Time for next week. Canadian four feet on my right was killed by snipers bullet, but I was on bottom of dugout with my puss in the cold mud. Otherwise I have stayed well out of danger and will continue this policy until I get back to you, when you are going to be in plenty of danger. You'll think you have five husbands, all of them commandos, when I get my clutches on you. I miss you terribly and Whitney and John something awful. Be sure to give my folks the dope. Hope everything is all right, but with the mail the way it is, I don't know a thing. If anything happens, have Hulburd cable me. He can always reach me in a few hours. Men all around me are getting letters dated Jan. 26. In one hour and 45 minutes recently I was in three countries: Germany, Holland, Belgium. I can fumble along in French well enough to get by in France and Belgium, but the only Dutch I know is Cleanser. All of these people are wonderful though, and I'm collecting all the dope for our own peacetime world tour. I played poker last night here (am with Ninth Army, Americans, look at your newspaper map) and won 300 guilders Dutch and 1000 francs French. I knew the francs were worth $20 but I had thought the guilders were so many pennies. Actually the 300 gs. are worth $100! I almost fainted and have given up poker. Will stay at this front 3 wks.

Love, Sid

SIDNEY OLSON CABLE UNNUMBERED[100]
FROM HOLLAND TO DAVID HULBURD
SENT FEBRUARY 7, 1945; REC'D FEBRUARY 7, 1945

Attention Eleanor Welch and Mr. Matthews:
Simpson:

William Hold [Hood] Simpson, 56, is six feet one tall, slim and spare, built very much like a tailor's dream. His beautifully cut battle jacket and trousers sit on him with an exact perfection of drape that is the despair of his rumpled juniors. His stomach is absolutely flat, his waist lean and there isn't a trace of jowl on him anywhere.

On this trim body is set an extraordinary head, a lean, bony, Cyrancsed [sic] egg-bald skull. His mouth is wide and thin, his projecting ears the shape and size of demitasse saucers and his lantern-jaw thrusts out and down like a locomotive's cow-catcher. Above the ears and about the projecting bony back of his skull is the faintest brown-grey shadow of very closely cropped hair. On each side of his long, great-grandfather's nose is set a tiny, keen, shrewd, sparkling brown eye. They are remarkable eyes and seem at first glance much like the lumps of coal children sometimes put in a snowman's head.

Those small, warm brown eyes dominate the whole face. You forget the face and talk direct to those eyes without noticing whether the long, bony face is smiling or expressionless. Simpson's voice is low and tangy; most of the time he deliberately keeps it flat and without inflection. From the first he gives you the impression of extraordinary force kept in tightest harness, of a keenness carefully schooled for many years in the rigidity of discipline. He is like a poet who has mastered the sonnet in the sense that he has learned how to keep strategically and tactically flexible within the limits of army discipline and the long array of army manuals that tell you how to do everything and what to think when anything happens. His first precept is "go by the book" and he believes implicitly and almost religiously in those scores of army manuals and is merciless to any feckless subordinate who indicates that he might prefer a sudden inspiration to the grooved perfection of action that results from the perspiration of knowledge as absolute as it can be made.

His hands are long and lean, with the kind of forefinger you'd hate to have pointed at you. His only ornaments were a West Point class ring, 1919, the three stars of his rank with the green band below the middle star that denotes he is a commander, and three-and-one-half rows of ribbons. He works before three windows on the second floor of a building in a Dutch town, with ceiling-height maps on the wall facing him and to his right. Long brown curtains on wires are carefully drawn over the maps when visitors are present. He is a bare-desk man, as you might guess. But it is hard to get away from those compelling little brown eyes in order to look around.

He loved polo above all things, but his wife grounded him in 1925 after he had injured his back riding off another player. He took up golf and would give anything to play again but hasn't played since two rounds early in 1941. For diversion he goes to the G.I. movies and walks. As your Bio will show, he made all his staff take a 15-mile hike weekly with full pack through the sand of Louisiana until two years ago. Now he still manages to get in a brisk, one-hour walk three times a week. And by brisk he means brisk all the way for the full hour.

The one book he quoted from is called *As to Polo*, by Cameron Forbes, and he still remembers the opening sentence: "Matchplay is the best school for polo." This seems to him high military wisdom in that he regards battle as the best school for soldiers. Although he is one of the greatest of all American trainers of soldiers, having processed hundreds of thousands of them when he was Lesley McNair's prize jewel, he says that there is no substitute for battle experience. He acclimates his divisions slowly and carefully, putting them into the line in quiet defensive sectors and grooming them through patrol actions until the troops are familiar with all the sights and sounds of war.

In evaluating Simpson, I would suggest that while it is early to guess whether or not he will turn out to be one of the great American generals, it is fully safe to say at the minimum that he is keen, sensitive, quick, intelligent and flexible of mind; that he is one of the most exactingly thorough of all our generals, if not the most; that he believes in taking the extremest military precautions to save American lives and as such is a great believer in machinery, artillery and ammunition. When he talks to you about the need of ammunition, without raising his voice or stressing the words but only by letting his brown eyes glow like hot coals, you are not likely to forget it. It is also safe to say that if and when Simpson gives the Germans a crack it will be one they will never forget, either. He is attack-minded utterly and one of the main reasons is that he believes attacking is the most economical way to fight a war. He says if the Germans want to fight all the way back to Berlin, as they did for Aachen, he will be only too happy to wreck the country inch by inch as the Americans wrecked Aachen.

I personally believe we should add the word "Aachenate" to the language as the destruction of that great and beautiful city is something incredible and sad, a monument to man's savagery to man.

Sidney Olson Cable Unnumbered
From Holland to David Hulburd
Sent February 28, 1945; Rec'd February 28, 1945

Attention Eleanor Welch:

Dateline: Written February 8th—held by censors.[101]

Not too far from Germany in a small Dutch town, there is a cloister of Ursuline nuns. The nuns are mostly youngish, rosy cheeked and gay of temperament. When the snow and ice was thick on the ground they brought out two small sleds in the flat little convent garden. They took turns, forming a giggling queue. The procedure was the same each time. One nun would board the sled, tucking up her habit and the other would drag her down the grape arbor path, trying to get up enough speed to throw the sledder off when they reached the turn. Usually the lurch was successful and the sledding nun would roll off into the snow with a great flurry of black skirts while all the nuns in the queue would gasp with laughter.

Also laughing were several hundred American officers and men of the Headquarters of the 13th Corps of the 9th Army, who cheered the spectacle from the windows of the big, weathered red-brick building, which they have commandeered. The nuns serenely ignored the cheers and proffered advice: they go their way with a kind of timeless calm stubbornness of indifference to the war around them. They have seen much with the sharp, clear eyes behind their gold-rimmed spectacles. For one thing, half of their convent itself has been taken over by the Army and some hapless GI is always being caught buttoning his pants by a pair of quickstepping nuns swirling around a corner, and his feelings are not salved by the demure twinkle in the calm eyes that ignore him. Many of the nuns speak excellent English and they are not the least awed by gold braid or bashful about asking for their rights.

One night this week one of them marched firmly past the M.P.s at the Headquarters entrance, climbed the stairs, walked down the hall and on into the room where sat Major General Alvan C. Gillem of the 13th Corps, hard at work. As the General stared up from his desk she coolly explained to the flustered aides trying to intercept her that she wanted some of her books which were in the tall green bookcases. The aide pointed out that to get them he would have to move the whole ceiling height wall maps. The nun was firm; the aides but mere men, and the General smiled. She got the books.

The next day a khaki-green sedan with four stars on it drove up to the Headquarters and out stepped Generals Eisenhower and Bradley making one of the key visits of their carefully timed tour of the fronts that week. They walked through the door and on up to General Gillem's office, to which order had been restored again. A few minutes later the three together with a number of divisional generals had gathered in another room which is now the war room, where all the secret exact dispositions of U.S. troops and all the known dispositions of enemy troops are carefully marked hour by hour, day and night. A bank of 32 wooden chairs had been set up before the maps with empty C ration cans tied on to the backs of the chairs for use as ashtrays. But the generals stood in a circle around the maps and tossed ashes on the floor during a fast half-hour conference that moved with the easy speed of technicians discussing a subject on which they are all completely expert. The conference served to brief Eisenhower on the immediate situation rather than vice versa. He asked a dozen sharp questions, inquired about some old friends and then the conference adjourned by car to a little tile-fronted restaurant on another street.

Here great preparations had been made to receive the biggest man in Europe outside of Hitler and Stalin. The GIs had made preparations to the limit of their ability. Dutch oysters had been flown in fresh from the sea at a cost of two guilders per oyster (roughly 75 cents per oyster). Steaks had been wangled from somewhere no questions asked and a chocolate cake had been baked. The staff was Technical Sergeant Albert Woodward of Hartford, Connecticut; Sergeant Edward Kroll of New Jersey, Sergeant James Fisher of Oklahoma, Pfc. J. L. Cruise of Tennessee, Pfc. Shelley Johnson, Jr., of Kentucky, Stephen Dowd of Tennessee and Pfc. Vincent Yaklin of Michigan. The blue-and-white oilcloth on the three little tables set in a capital T shape had been scrubbed into a high shine, little pots of white hyacinths had been scrounged from some Dutch *vrouw*'s winter window display and a hand-lettered sign set under the old carved wall-clock. The sign printed in big red pencil capitals simply said: "Guests today 12:30 The Boss."

Eisenhower sat down in the middle of the top bar of the capital T and said a short censorable oath of utter happiness when he saw the oysters. Several moments later he doubled the same oath when he was served a tall vase-shaped glass of beer—which he immediately recognized as German beer (I had a glass of this same beer a little later and you can tell Fuerbringer, Purtell and Alexander that I now finally understand the meaning of beer). In short it was wonderful. The GIs happily noted that Eisenhower eats like a soldier, which means very heartily and at breath-taking speed and I mean speed. In the Army apparently anyone who takes a full fifteen minutes to finish three very hearty courses and two cups of coffee is considered a finicking sissy or something of a Lucius Beebe. Ike made the full course in the approved time.

One most significant point that you will be glad later that you stressed now is that on the dinner table directly in front of Eisenhower in this General's mess sat a little tin can with a slit hole in it with a sign wrapped around it saying: "One guilder fine for every mention of ammunition." In case you don't get this I will lean on it hard: ammunition is such a sore spot with American generals that they are sick of hearing each other bitch about it. (Bitch is army slang for gripe.) Anyway no one mentioned ammunition at the luncheon but you may hear more about it later.

Eisenhower and Bradley sped off on their tour of the front. The significance of this tour, impossible for me to point out when this was written, was that these were the final conferences before the February 10th jump-off date, later postponed.

SIDNEY OLSON CABLE[102]
FROM HOLLAND TO DAVID HULBURD
SENT FEBRUARY 10, 1945; REC'D FEBRUARY 10, 1945

For Battlefronts:

(This will be an attempt to give the cover story writer the look and feel of the terrain along the Ninth Army front, although I will necessarily avoid using place names that might be censorable. But you can pretty generally figure out about what points I am describing.)

The Ninth Army's terrain begins in the United States, a nation which does not produce enough ammunition to satisfy me. Like all other American armies, it has certain basic advantages and certain disadvantages militarily. Its artillery is the best in the world, perhaps one and one-half times as good as the Russians; its infantry is the most intelligent, the keenest command is now extraordinarily battlewise; its motor transport is fantastically superior to any ever dreamed of; and its food and standard of living are the best and highest. It has no tank better than the Germans' or Russians' best tanks; many hundreds of thousands of its finest physical specimens are ground crew men in the airforces fiddling with spark plugs or filling gasoline tanks, while married men recently drafted and not Tarzans by any view go into the front line as infantry replacements; its heaviest winter-weight wool clothing seems shoddy to me beside the superb woolen khakis of the British and Canadians; boot for boot and shoe for shoe, from the airfare to the infantry the British and Canadians are much better shod; heavy, clumsy canvas things over their heavy boots, which builds character but makes for slow footwork, while the Canadians, especially, have a light, most excellent all-rubber boot in which you wear one light pair of socks and two heavy woolen socks and which keep your feet perfectly warm and dry and are not much heavier than sneakers. (I can testify to this as I scrounged a pair of them after having ice-cold, wet feet for days in American boots.) The German adaptation of the prize American bazooka is also generally considered superior to our model.

But, advantages and disadvantages are so much argument and perhaps Washington is all-wise. What is not arguable is that General

Simpson has under his command one of the best American armies ever put together, if not the best, and I mean in all respects—even including for comparison purposes any of the American armies which landed in France last summer and fought their way all through France. The cover writer can go all-out on the limb in this respect as no one later will ever deny that the Ninth Army is about as near perfect as Americans can make an army.

On the basis of these points consider carefully the terrain on which this army is based and that along its front. As you go forward toward the Roer River keep these points in mind. Almost all Dutch roads are superb and are even excellent after their long, incessant pounding by trucks, tanks, half-trucks, jeeps, tank carriers and mobile guns and scores and scores of types of fantastic mobile machinery, awe-inspiring in its diversity and numbers. (The British call all these screwy-looking things going down the roads "the funnies.")

The Dutch countryside is a long series of gentle rolling fields in easy dips that are called valleys, and easy slopes that are called hills although seldom more than a hundred feet high. In the February thaw with all the snow rained away, the short-grass fields that roll endlessly to the horizon are all bright-green with grass and Brussel sprouts, although here and there a duller green where the withered tops of sugar beets droop. Up and down this rich green panorama march the strings of fences that proclaim how carefully and thoroughly all the land is farmed. Spaced thickly in ordered groves all through the green lawns are the carefully pruned, expertly tended orchards of the Dutch, predominantly apple trees of numerous varieties but occasionally pears. It is safe to call them young orchards as the Dutch regularly put in young trees and I have seldom seen apple trees as much as thirty years old. . . .

In the dips and on the slopes of the stretching green meadows are set the little old Dutch farmhouses in the palest, gayest pastel colors, the most surprising turquoise blues, fresh salmon pinks and lilacs, and forsythia yellows. . . .

As you go down nearer the front the pastel-colored houses begin to gape with shell holes through the side walls, the tiled roofs are shaken loose and the orchards include broken trees until you reach the roads where the Germans blasted every other one of the great poplars care-fully across the roads blocks and then mined and wired the fallen trunks while retreating to points that could sweep the roads and hold the mined, green farm fields, deadly empty by daylight. The German road-side sign for minefields is much simpler and more graphic than ours or the British: They just hung a black plate of tin on the wire fences, with a grinning white skull-and-crossbones on it. Our more prosaic signs say simply: "Mines." You don't have to be able to read the German signs. It is odd to look at these empty fields, so like the other farm fields, and imag-ine that the grass is a more poisonous green just because you know there is quick, shattering death sown as carefully as a crop there.

The Dutch on bicycles and in wagons still pour up and down the roads, old men and women dragging their goods on heavy carts, ker-chiefed, fresh-faced Dutch girls, usually wearing knee-length leather or rubber boots bicycling gaily past and the omnipresent clouds of Rubens-plump children chattering as they hang admiringly around the American troops and say the American words they know: "Hello, gum?" (Europe has been ruined by chewing gum—even in Brussels nightclubs it is considered a mark of sophistication for the girls to chew gum as it shows they know Americans and are thus cosmopolitan.)

Then suddenly you enter destruction where house by house each brick is smashed and the household goods and gods lie exposed and moldering in the rain, where the streets are lined with signs in American: "Danger—Falling Walls" because the topless ruins totter and crash in the least wind, where the streets still stink with the memory of burning ruins and where the only civilians who still live in the absolute desolation seem quiet and hopeless as zombies. Then you know you are in Germany, even before you see the hooked black script of the signs on the bullet-pocked walls or the slag piles that are the only mountains in this flattened country of the Ruhr or the grey-green dragons' teeth of the Siegfried Line, looking much like a curious kind of military cemetery composed of modernistic concrete tombs placed regularly in great ditches that curve along the sides of the valleys.

If this is what is going to happen to all of Germany—incidentally the old Germany can never be again, no matter how its traditions are cherished by any new *Fuehrer* of the future, for any culture needs some kind of nucleus of monuments and shrines on which to build, and I cannot stress too solemnly how thoroughly that old Germany is being smashed, house by house, stone by stone, shrine by shrine, a destruction that here and there actually reaches the point of annihilation of everything that was once there. London was hurt terribly but London is still there; many German places are just no longer there. The very soil is rancid with the stink of what has happened on it.

But on the Ninth Army front we are deepest into Germany and well past the Siegfried Line. As you go on toward the winding little Roer, which is now rain-swelled, some seven or more feet deep and sometimes reaches one hundred fifty feet wide (most Americans would regard it as a good-sized creek but not a river), you come into down-sloping, flat, open country which can be observed for miles from one ridge that the Germans hold over the river. The American front ends here at the Roer in little farm towns horribly smashed by the artillery of both sides, where American troops live in the concrete, white-washed cellars of empty, wrecked, windowless, roofless, shell-smashed German homes or are dug in along little folds in the green meadows that slope in long, flat sweeps to the river.

Ending this description in generalities of the terrain, please bear in mind that it is in this country described, from the rear echelons in rolling Dutch farmland on through the Siegfried Line into Germany, that Simpson has concentrated his marvelous army and it is out of this terrain that he will mobilize and strike whenever the High Command gives the word of attack.

FEBRUARY 10, 1945 [LETTER TO ZEMBRA]

Dearest darling I.B.G.

    I'm writing this in the Ninth Army press camp and you'll just have to guess where that is because of censorship but a look at a newspaper map will give you a guess. It's in Holland: I can say that much, not far from the German border; and I drive through the Siegfried Line in a jeep about twice a day from here into Germany toward the front, which I visit at some point every day.[103] I haven't written you since the V-mail letter three days ago because I have been very very very busy day and night since working on the cover story for *Time* on General Simpson for next week.[104] Before that letter I hadn't written you since before I left London, for one good reason: I was on the move all that time, traveling all day, sleeping a few hours in a different bed every night and then getting up in the black dawn to travel some more and see things. Here I have settled down for almost a month, which should give me about three weeks more here.

    Since I last wrote you in full many things have happened of course. In London I got my combat boots, more shots, my bedroll (canvas with three blankets, and oh how lovely warm they have been) my canteen and some GI clothes for roughing it in. I traveled to RAF bases and Eighth Air Force bases and toured some of the English countryside; lunched alone with Lord Beaverbrook in his town house; met Brendan Bracken;[105] had lunch in the House of Lords chessroom with some Members of Parliament; had dinner with Aneurin Bevan, leader of the opposition to Churchill, and his wife labor writer Jennie Lee and Donald Tyreman editor of the London *Times*, the famous *Times*; and spent with Ragsdale and Noel Busch a weekend in Dorset, in the very heart of the Thomas Hardy country, traveling and cycling and walking over the very places Hardy described in the books we know so well—this weekend at the home of Alice Astor Something Von Hofmannsthal Harding,[106] the sister of Vincent Astor, and only daughter of the John Jacob who went down with the Titanic—in a lovely 17th century pre-Georgian and Georgian country house that cost her $28,000 a year and on which the annual taxes are $100 . . . hmmm. Next day Noel and

I caught the boat-train from London to Paris, reaching there 17 hours later, at 6:30 a.m. There I stayed at the Hotel Scribe, one of the three hotels in Paris which have electric light and heat, due to the desperate fuel shortage; saw Hemingway, who looks 8,000,000 years old, drinking cognac with *Time*'s Mary Welsh, a young English dull-looking blonde with whom he is living at the Ritz and for whom he is divorcing Martha Gellhorn;[107] drank champagne with the Wertenbakers three or four times a day; and walked and walked and walked and walked in the world's most beautiful too beautiful city with those wonderful French people bubbling around all the time, and stamping their feet in their unlit unheated offices and homes but screaming in the streets *"Le Soleil!"* for sheer delight when the sun broke through. Ah Paris. . . . Ah Europe, where every woman from the age of Whitney to the age of 90 wears high leather or rubber boots at least to the knee and often with high heels, in all countries, all winter. It hasn't done me any good because I've mostly been traveling fast through the streets to an objective. They're attractive, but somehow when a truck driven by two ordinary freckle faced American Red Cross girls goes by you want to marry both of them just because they look so damn American. You are not only the most beautiful woman in the U.S., I am now certain, but of Europe, too. Just get over here and get some boots, toots. You'd never believe some of those I've seen: just imagine the boots of your top dreams—they've got 'em.

But I only stayed in Paris two and one half days learning gin rummy from Wertenbaker (playing for free). He owes Photog Capa 2,000 pounds ($8,000) in games they have every night while Lael sits quietly by supervising and reading a book.[108] Wert doesn't stray off the path for a second—he can't. Then flew to Brussels in an hour and spent a night and a morning there—ah, Brussels, where every building is a night-club, and where the best new act is a man and a woman dancing with live pythons twelve feet long curling around them with their tongues flicking at the ringsiders. But I haven't led a gay life: actually I've been in some 43 churches or cathedrals thus far in England and here. I might make a career of it. The Eglise de Saint-Bavon in Ghent has little iron stoves along the aisles with stovepipes that go 200 feet high into the dim top of the vaulted roof above like crooked pillars. The Church of St.

Servatius in Maastricht Holland has tombs from the year 700 A.D. and Charlemagne was often there, although his seat of empire was at Aachen, now destroyed stone by stone in the battle we fought and won there; and all the priceless things are smashed into junk-heap city dump refuse. You can't imagine the destruction. Think of our house as smashed into a pile of broken bricks with maybe one crumbling piece of wall standing, stinking with undug bodies and broken sewer pipes, part of the wreckage burned over; with pools of muddy rainwater all through it in which floated broken pieces of your china and my books, with muddy boots long since tearing up the carpets and the drapes used as blackout curtains for the cellar, in which German or American troops live, with a little iron stove down there for heat, with the stovepipe sticking out of one of the front basement windows; the lawn all churned up with huge shell holes filled with rain and the trees shattered by shellfire—multiply that by a city three times as big as Salt Lake and 1,000,000 times as historic, and you've got Aachen. But even then you couldn't imagine it. It has to be seen. For instance I looked for about 15 minutes at one curious shape of brick and stone ruins and then gradually made out that it had once been a church, by the shape of the fallen window frames and a piece of a statue of Jesus. Later I found it had been one of the worlds most famous cathedrals. Well, they started it, and we're finishing it, but that won't bring back the London that was destroyed, or these towns either.

But to get back: from Brussels I drove into Holland with the British and up to Nijmegen at the tip of the front, where I got myself a pair of Canadian rubber galoshes, light as a feather and very warm, in which you wear only three pair of wool sox, no shoes. My feet had been cold and wet for four days in the US combat boots which are no good in cold or wet weather. I also scrounged a suit of British battledress, much warmer than ours. I lived near the front where they start the V-bombs off on their way, the b - - - - - - -! Heard them pooping along overhead, a most eerie experience, and I was glad it was only eerie and not personal. Went along on a small battle in very tough country with the Canadians, to get my baptism of fire, and was very careful not to be in danger, although Chickering's death shows that no place is really safe.[109] Then south to Antwerp, where I never want to return, and south to Ghent and up to the tip of

Holland at Breskens, across from Flushing, to look at the way the dutch are coming back in their ruined homes and then to Brussels for another night in the nightclubs and off next day for here. When I got to Brussels I had been about ten days without a bath, washing and shaving in absolute ice water, and sleeping in unheated dutch homes. One of them was very nice, at Witchen, where I had coffee AND tea each evening for two evenings with a Dutch artist and his wife who spoke a little english and who gave me a dutch lesson. I have Dutch Belgian American French and English money in my pockets right now and still don't know really how much is how much and which is which. The french money is the prettiest although the english is fine too. Here I have met Gen'l Simpson in a 90-minute interview, and ever since have been touring right along the front, looking at the Germans through binoculars from observation posts in the third stories of wrecked houses and churches. This keeps me spry and teaches me to tuck my fanny in as I see what happens to Germans who don't. I have seen a lot of dead Germans and seems to me British and Canadians but no dead Americans yet thank heavens because this has been a quiet front.

The German people who live so sadly and like dead people in these little German towns are very interesting although I have only seen them on the streets and passing through interrogation centers. They are only the Germans who wouldn't leave when Hitler ordered them to evacuate and lived in cellars until the Americans won the battle over their heads. They are mostly old men and women and children.

I am sleeping two in a room with Max Lerner of *PM* here, which is plenty strange bedfellows for me.[110] There is much hot water here—the Americans manage well always—and I bathe every night in one of the two bathtubs that 65 of us use here. It's on the next floor down from me. I am working very hard and sleep like a rock, am in the open air all day every day, eat like three horses, including all of my candy ration of five bars a week—the food is excellent and solid—and honestly and truly feel fine in every way except that I miss you so terribly and the others so very much. John saying whole sentences absolutely breaks my heart.[111] But I am having such wonderful luck all the way darling—knock on wood—absolutely unbelievable luck—that it seems that this trip is the right thing for me to do. For instance Churchill speaks fairly rarely—but I heard him in the House of Commons. De Gaulle hadn't had a press conference in three and one-half months. I am in Paris two days and get to see him from the front row of a press conference! Night before I had dinner with the editor of the Paris *Figaro* and Mlle. "Miribel" the brains of De Gaulle, a thick-voiced moosy gal who is very smart.[112] Etc etc etc. I could cite you a million examples of sheer luck such as that. I don't expect any more good luck all the way, as a result of so much so far, but I won't mind a bit, because things have gone so well up to now.

[The bottom of the page was cut off, and there is a note handwritten in pencil on the back side:]

B.G.—P.S. I just got all of your letters through No. 3 of Jan. 20. Hadn't heard anything before, at all, from anyone. Also got folks' mail. Get ready for when I come back! —S, the S.

SIDNEY OLSON CABLE 20[113]
FROM HOLLAND TO DAVID HULBURD
SENT FEBRUARY 12, 1945; REC'D FEBRUARY 12, 1945

I will call this number 20 as I have not been numbering my file. In my unnumbered of February 5 I was indicating the present Canadian offensive as the Kappelsch Sveer action cleared a dangerous flank.[114] The towns of Cleve and Goch are gateposts to the Siegfried line. I personally regard the capture of Goch, when it comes, as the most important since it is a crossroads town.

I am desolate at my inability to flesh out the Simpson cover with the kind of detail you are looking for.[115] In studying the Ninth Army terrain I went to nearly every forward observation post so you can query me about any point thereon at any time henceforth. I have now called down an even more extensive curse on the combo of February thaw and the German blasting of the Schwammenauel dam gate. The Roer river, which I could almost spit across, is now 1100 feet wide in some places. The German side of the Roer is actually much more flooded than our side and the fact is that the Roer river may remain at its present width and depth indefinitely since the dams no longer impound the normal flow of water and the Roer has resumed its ancient broad reaches. All this is approximate generalization but basically accurate.

In the long piece I sent you on the Ninth's terrain I deliberately presented it as so much geography. I had hoped before closing to be able to brush in on that landscape a great picture of an army. Now the best I can do is fill in some of the picture along the following lines.

Along the roads over that landscape endlessly pound trucks forward and back. Interspersed in the traffic moving both ways are innumerable jeeps, most of them with tops down. (Have you ever ridden eight hours in sleeting rain at fifty miles per hour over potholed roads? It builds character.) This great stream constantly flowing up and down in all American armies is hereabouts peppered with audacious Dutch cyclists and scores of creaking wagons usually loaded with sugar beets.

Under each apple tree in the sloping hillside orchards troops warm themselves over little daytime campfires on the green lawns close to the brown clay gashes in the grass that are their foxholes in case of air attack. It is not unusual to see some Dutch *vrouw*'s weekly washing hung between the trees, flapping in the wind, with occasional fresh-washed khaki shirts along the lines, denoting that reverse lend-lease is operating well. Roosters chase attractive hens as of time immemorial and American troops make passes at comely Hollanders and vice versa. But the great love affair here is between the troops and the Dutch children who flock for miles around, running nimbly in wooden shoes to put their warm little hands in the troopers' big brown paws and say their entire vocabulary of "Hello chum, gum?"

Nearer the front, as you pass into the dark, blasted land of Germany where the flagpoles of the Ruhr landmark the sky like the regular, even black triangles that children draw for mountains, a pall seems to fall over the blighted land. The minute you pass the border there are no civilians, except the German miners, allowed out twice a day to and from work, and one hour daily the German women are permitted time to shop and visit and buy a copy of the singe-sheet German language newspaper published in Aachen, the only news they get here. The countryside is more and more marked with mounds out of which project sky-pointing barrels of anti-aircraft guns, usually placed in the open for a clearest view of the horizon. Only with a careful guide can you find the heavily camouflaged great guns which occasionally register fire on German positions in great booms that gives the sky concussion. Out of each cellar sticks a little puffing stovepipe to show that Americans are living in warm squalor in German basements. Beyond these generalities I cannot go brushing in the picture of an army along the front, whose geography you have, but I hope some of these details will be helpful in visualizing where Simpson's army lives and works. I still refuse to apologize, although I appreciate your difficulties in going to press. All regards to the hapless cover writer, whoever he is.

SIDNEY OLSON CABLE 21[116]
FROM BELGIUM TO DAVID HULBURD
SENT FEBRUARY 17, 1945; REC'D FEBRUARY 17, 1945

For Eleanor Welch:

I have been with the First Army for a few days to survey the terrain here and better inspect the Roer River dams from the air. Earlier in the week I flew in a Piper Cub along the (Omission?) Army front from south of Julich to north of Linnich, not far from Heinsberg. Yesterday I flew (?) Army front in a Stinson L-5 from Duren to Schleiden, following the river curves all the way.

For Battlefronts, for overall Western front action story:

The Roer River dam area juts into our front line like a clumsy nine-fingered mitten that the Nazis have laid on the map. The Roer from Gemünd to Heimbach is a fantastic series of looping curves through the low, heavily wooded hills of the Kermeter Forest. It looks from the air like the hairpin curves of a Colorado mountain road as the river doubles back on itself at least eight times. The Germans long ago built dams at various places along the river, but most importantly along each side of the wrist of the multi-fingered mitten, impounding water in a series of reservoirs that fill the loops at the fingertips. But then, to control the flow of water with easiest efficiency, they then cut a conduit directly across the wrist so that the flow from the uppermost dams could be fed directly to the lowermost dams without having to go through all the loops of the river in between. The Germans and the First American Army have long been fighting for control of this most important area, off and on since last October, I believe. Angry at the first defeats, the First Army has fought with greatest bitterness in the present campaign now simmering down to artillery action as we hold areas at the east of the wrist and are along the Roer curves through all the twists. But the Germans still thrive on the fingers and palm of the mitten, which are superb vantage points whence they can from most excellent observation points fire at us in all directions. The RAF long ago realized the importance of the dams, but in a series of bombings failed to do more than create small breaches and leaks in some of them, although you can see vast water-filled bomb craters all about the dam areas still. At that time the high command wanted to create a flood behind the Germans and then win(?) [pin, probably] them up against that flood. Later when the Germans held but a thin strip of bridgehead along the Roer the high command wanted to keep the Roer at the low state of creek-size trickle below the dams to make a crossing easy, and therefore struggled hard to gain control of the dams before the Germans flooded the Roer to create another tough water crossing for us. At first the belief was that the Germans had all the dams mined to be blown almost in concert, creating a great high-crested flood which would crash down the Roer River valley, wiping out any river bank installations we had. But as often happens, the Germans outsmarted us again. When American engineers finally captured the lowermost dams known as Schwammenauel where ends the conduit across the wrist, they found that the Germans had merely destroyed the Penstock and floodgates at the conduit's end. This removed the fear that the floodcrest would wash down the valley with considerable havoc all the way to sea. But the result was even more satisfactory from the scientific, war-making view of the Germans, as it let the series of dams' entire stock of impounded water leak out at a steady rate of flow which they could calculate pretty exactly, thus knowing just how long the Roer River valley will be in a flood state. I based my calculations in Cable 20 on a personal estimate of German war-making skill.

More coming.

Sidney Olson Cable 22[117]
From Belgium to David Hulburd
Sent February 17, 1945—February 18, 1945

For Battlefronts—continuing Roer dam analysis and front situation:

The penstock and other dam workings at Schwammenauel are so blasted, according to American engineers, that they cannot be repaired by swift improvisation. There was nothing to do but to let nature take its course as planned by the Germans. The result was that the Roer rose to its present width and speed of current swiftly and that the river became roughly five times as wide along much of its course and even wider at some points. At some points along the river before the flood it was actually only about seventy-five feet wide and knee-deep and with a hard-pan bottom ideal for tank crossing. The current was lazy and steady. Now the river is more than a thousand feet wide in many places, at least three times deeper, and the current is rapid and erratic. From an artillery observation plane you can see that most of the flooding has spread on the German side of the river as I reported before but whereas before the river had regular established banks in an old channel, now the swirling brown waters spread over forested flatlands for miles lengthwise so that any crossing would involve long boat trips through all kinds of obstacles, would make bridge building correspondingly more difficult, and you can visualize the difficulties of ferrying tanks over.

A point to remember once again is that the Nazis are playing for time as always. In case you ask what for, here are the best answers I can personally give, entirely without reflecting official views. The class of 1928, Hitler's last reservoir of fanatical young Nazi manpower, will graduate in the spring as pretty sophisticated young soldiers averaging seventeen years old. The best guesses made in London last fall and winter were that Hitler's newest secret weapons would graduate about April. The censors permitting, I believe it is safe to tell Time Inc. that German jet planes have been seen flying in formation recently, which I believe may be an indication that they are finally learning to tame the monstrous speed of this latest military fantasy.[118]

For all these reasons and others unmentionable, it is safe to guess that April is a most important month for Hitler. He will have a number of new divisions of hot young Nazis—*Time* may speculate on how many —new weapons and more precious time in which to dig in.

The problem before the American and British strategists is how long to give him while mounting their own offensives into perfection suitable even to Montgomery, who will never move until the last stock of chewing gum is on hand.

Back to the river again: from Linnich south past Duren it seems wide and placid from the air as it flows through the west end of the great Cologne plain, with only small knots of woods and small clumps of houses along the banks. On the Nazi side of the river in this area, ending at Duren, there is a low but important ridge from which the Nazis have observation of American movements for miles on our side of the river. I have been down to almost all the forward observation posts at Linnich, Roerdorf, Flossdorf, Bourheim, Kirchberg, etc., some of which are now under water, and I always went with that naked feeling you have when you know Nazi artillery eyes are watching you ready to lay a mortar on your jeep. Along these roads no jeep stops except on the lee side of a crumbled red brick farm building, and then only long enough for you to jump out and duck into a cellar. The Nazis have all roads long since zeroed in and can wipe out a jeep if it only stops in the road long enough to turn around. At night they pour artillery into these little towns, especially if they believe we are hauling in stuff which will be well concealed by daylight. You might note that the Nazis used buzz bombs against an infinitesimal town recently. I hope they wiped out the building where I watched them through glasses as I fell halfway through the rickety ceiling of the place. Yesterday a corps pilot in a Stinson took me over Duren by mistake; he thought the Americans had taken it.[119] Buildings were burning and shells dropping steadily all through the little city, the middle of which is not just rubble but has been powdered into brick dust, and my pilot was angry because he thought these were German shells falling on American troops, so he swung down low to get a better look. I finally convinced him we were on the wrong side of the river and violating the usual military etiquette, which is that the Germans will let you make one pass over their lines without firing at you but will blast you quick if you make two passes or if you want to hang around. The pilot thought I was wrong and looped down until we could see figures scurrying around the blazing houses. But suddenly shots began to crackle around us and then a blast of ack-ack and he ducked out of town at full Stinson speed, maneuvering like a man dancing on a bed of hot coals. The reason I could tell sooner than he could is that I have a very sensitive fanny. Also as we flew through this brilliant sunshine I had watched pools of water along the roads and in shell holes and bomb holes wink at us as they flickered in the sunshine; but when I saw alot of things winking steadily at us from one position I knew they were not puddles.

Aside: Cut out all this personal stuff, this is just for office edification.

Below Duren the river swings in those crazy curves through rounded low hills running endlessly to the horizon of the Ardennes, one vast carpet of green pines making for a nasty kind of fighting like the Hürtgen Forest. Occasionally the evergreen carpet is broken with small clumps of silver birch or linden bare of leaves now, but pines is a safe generalization. The dams are not much to see, they are just long low dams, mostly an earthen core with concrete shell, weathered yellow. Dam water level has naturally dropped steadily under continuing leakage while the speed of the down-river current and the depth of the Roer has been dropping perceptibly, although far from enough.

In analyzing the lull on the Western front, please note we have had three straight days of the most brilliant blue-sky weather in April-like foreshadowing of spring, although today was gray but not rainy. Already hard-surface roads throw up dust and vast road gangs have had a most welcome chance to dump tons of red bricks from bombed buildings into great potholes in secondary roads and I do mean secondary. The highways are crowded with trucks labeled "Priority—Road Materials."

Spring signs in this area: GIs playing catch with baseballs in narrow little Belgian and Dutch streets, throwing their arms out on the first day as they always did in America; the miles of evenly planted little apple orchards show neat piles of pruned branches below the trees and workers swing cleavers along the hawthorn hedges at roadsides, while for miles around on all sides you can watch white vapor trails of Fortresses converging in the blue bowl of the sky in great, rising circular corkscrews as they rendezvous before packing into tight formations out of sight in the blue on their way to Germany. There cannot be many greater spectator thrills than to see flight after flight of those silver specks sailing steadily on toward Germany minute after long minute, a Stars-and-Stripes thrill for the bombers' friends but a deadly spectacle to the enemy. If there is one thing I would wish everyone in America could see it would be this testament of war power combined with beauty.

This present West front lull is becoming almost spectacularly long. In some areas not even one German prisoner has been taken and that is one of the most significant signs, as it means absence of the "vigorous patrolling" which is war. It also means absence of the enemy from near ground, it shows the difficulty of crossing the Roer in lone boats even at night. I have not yet seen the Simpson cover so I cannot tell what your estimate of the situation is, of course, but I still stand by the material sent in at that time. During the present lull the Nazis, eager beavers all, feverishly dig and dig. Our troops don't like the lull; many of them are all "browned off" (slang for disgusted), not because they are anxious to fight and die but because they know that the sooner they get going the sooner the war is over. Also they well know how much deeper a Nazi can dig in during even twenty-four hours.

If you need exactest dam details, heights, etc., I can forward them but I have kept the picture general for easy comprehension.

SIDNEY OLSON CABLE 24
FROM HOLLAND TO DAVID HULBURD
SENT FEBRUARY 24, 1945; REC'D FEBRUARY 24, 1945

For Battlefronts:

General Simpson's Ninth Army struck across the Roer river this morning in great force. Tonight the army holds a slender bridgehead across the Roer all along its front. The worst is probably over. The extremely delicate and dirty business of getting an army on its way across a river has passed the trickiest stage. Tonight more troops are going across the swaying treadway bridges at many points despite the flat crack of heavy mortar fire. Before them, the spearhead, lies the great Cologne plain, with the Rhine river only some eighteen miles away. Behind them General Simpson has packed in an extraordinary concentration of military power.

Battle-wise units of those superb, slouchy, casual American infantrymen are piled in along this front in the midst of masses of artillery and machines. The Ninth Army front points at the Germans like a piece of pie after you have forked off the first bites. From the wide spread at the rear in the rolling Dutch orchard country on down past the slag piles of the German border coal mines into the open flat lands of the Roer river plain, this sector has gradually become a great steel weapon, built up gun by gun, truck by truck steadily throughout the long weeks of waiting and inaction.

Day after day the trucks and guns and unnameable steel monsters roared and clanked forward over the wide tree-lined Dutch roads, throbbing through the little Dutch towns in an endless parade, watched with tireless enthusiasm by Dutch women from second story windows, their arms never too weary to wave the hundredth time at grinning Americans jouncing past in trucks, jeeps and half-tracks. Under the trees, beside barns and houses and haystacks they snuggled in for shelter from the darting German Jet planes on reconnaissance, choking in together in alleys, the barn courtyards and farm lanes for miles and miles down into the masses of smashed bricks that are German towns. Into these the movement was more carefully controlled as the front neared. Into the little Roer plain towns the forces moved at night with lights dimmed, vehicles traveling sixty yards apart, the men not smoking or using flashlights as the trucks and machines sank and pounded through the deep-rutted, pot-holed German secondary roads.

The offensive had been postponed when the Germans, fighting with desperation and scientific skill, slowed the American First Army attack on the Roer river dams down until they had blasted the penstock gates, changing the sleepy, winding, little creek-sized Roer into a wide swift-swirling obstacle. The big offensive, set for 0530 hours Saturday morning February 10th, had to be postponed until new engineering plans and materials could be brought together.

For weeks Nazi commentators have been predicting a supreme offensive by the American Ninth Army, venturing even to suggest that this would be the most powerful blow struck by the Allies on the western front this year.

Yesterday was a perfect golden day, a little chill but not enough to keep the doughfeet from playing catch in their shirtsleeves.[120] The sky was a brilliant blue most of the day, and early in the afternoon you could see the big nickel-colored moon. All day great formations of bombers ground away overhead, with Thunderbolt P-47s skitting past below them on their own destructive business.[121]

Almost all movement was forward. The front was quiet, eerily quiet until late afternoon when just before sunset the Germans sent reccy planes over in the evening haze.[122] Ack-ack began to tear the sky, the black puffs of the heavy flak marching up through the clouds toward the fleeing little black planes.[123] A Thunderbolt caught one and got on his tail in a swift flurry of maneuver and soon the German started to smoke and was suddenly sucked down to the horizon. Watching doughfeet who had been lining up for chow with mess tins in hand had broken lines to run around cheering and shouting and clanging their mess kits happily. As always, they roared up at the Thunderbolts as they swept overhead: "Oh you sweet bastards, oh you sweet pretty bastards!"

Then suddenly it was evening, and the evening sank into night. But the moon, a great gibbous moon like a green gold coin pasted on the rich, pale blue night sky, shone clear and serene in the deadly, nervous, tense quiet. Long strips of cirrus clouds appeared and floated under the noon to give it the halo that is supposed to mean a wet morrow. Down near the river banks the great artificial moonlight searchlights shone steadily to the rear adding millions of candle-power to the moon's searching clarity. (The Germans never seem to shoot out these searchlights—perhaps they are one of those mutual conveniences that enemy armies seem sometimes to permit.)

Then the Germans, evidently nervous at the quiet of our artillery, shot over more reccy planes, cutting fast through the swift-floating cirrus where the uneven beat of the German motors, not so exactly synchronized as American engines, could be heard, but the planes could not be seen by uninstrumental eyes. At once began the sight so beautiful to men on the ground, so dreadful to men in the air, of ack-ack tracers sailing into the sky, a kind of state fair fireworks, as the tracer bullets, looking exactly like short, red-hot pokers, streamed up in graceful arcs from several points at once, converging as several flak batteries got together on a plane's location, and then crisscrossing in red streams across the washed blue moonlight sky as they chased the Germans back and forth.

More coming Saturday.

SIDNEY OLSON CABLE 25
FROM HOLLAND TO DAVID HULBURD
SENT FEBRUARY 25, 1945; REC'D FEBRUARY 26, 1945

For Battlefronts:

In writing these dispatches I am mainly endeavoring to picture the scene for you so that you and your writers will get some visualization of the battlefield as far as one inexpert war reporter bumping around can give it to you. I have traveled the whole terrain on which the attack was based in both armies; I have flown most of the front repeatedly in Piper Cubs and gone on a Thunderbolt mission deep into objective territory to get a good view of the terrain ahead. I have stuck my neck out as far as I can and so far have only had my helmet blown off once. The point of this is that I am prepared to answer all possible questions to the limit of my ability as far as you shoot them from here on in. Do not be afraid to put me to work; I'll be happy to do whatever I can to help *Time* get the best possible coverage of this attack. Suggestion: I have just seen the Simpson cover story, which I thought swell save of the snafu when postponement of the offensive came due to the Roer flood. My only regret is the occasional note of slight caution in the story, which of course is natural. But whatever *Time* says this week don't put it on the side of underestimation. The censors must naturally cut out any copy by me which indicates the actual extent or lack of power of this drive so you will have to roll your own.

Continued coverage of the Roer crossing from Wireless 24:

The Germans sent jet planes over several times in the early evening, peeking and poking about. This gave the lonesome ack-ack crews something to do. But that will be the day, that will really be the day, when ack-ack brings down one of those streaking jets. They seem to go past a Thunderbolt as a Thunderbolt passes a Piper Cub.

But very soon the deadly quiet settled on the evening all along the front. Usually these little smashed towns at the front shake from time to time as the great guns boom from below the green camouflage nets set over the gunpits dug into the brown clay of the German cabbage fields.

All night the guns would fire sporadically, and the loose bricks and plaster and smashed furniture would clatter down from the second stories of the rows of little red brick houses facing flush on the rubble-filled streets. Occasionally too the Germans would smash away all night at some little town, pouring in rockets and 88's for hours,[124] while the sleepy doughfeet, cursing, would hug themselves close to the basement walls in their bedrolls in the deepest cellars they knew, grumbling "Oh stop that - - - -!"

But on this night the quiet kept on minute after long minute, the time creeping as slowly as the moon rising high in the rich blue sky. At long intervals there would come the thump and boom of some big gun registering fire on a German target but this only accentuated the stillness. This quiet was a thick, deep thing, one of the elements, almost. But it was only seeming; as the Americans knew only too well and as the Germans seemed to know.

The doughfeet had slept most of the afternoon and then had eaten early chow. Then they had horsed around in the early evening, playing catch, playing volley ball on clear spaces of lawn such as around smashed German churches, writing V-mail letters telling their wives and folks not to worry, I am eating fine and get lots of sleep and how is Uncle Ed's rheumatism?

But as the quiet evening went on they dressed carefully, filling canteens, checking their pockets, but mainly idling and polishing up their old Betsys.[125] Farther down the front, the empty flatlands by the river began to fill up with the strange agglomeration of material needed in a river crossing. The roads, wide and tree-lined, converging at such one-time bridge sites as Julich, became one long vista of vehicles parked on each side. Only a few yards apart for several miles stretched the lines of vehicles on each side of the roads, spaced with some tanks, tank destroyers and trucks of fantastic variety, from the monsters that are movable cranes to bulldozers large and small to the mammoths that carry the huge rubber bridge pontoons. All of them down to the last candy bar in the last man's pocket as he sat quietly reminiscing of Rantoul, Illinois with his fellow tankers or engineers, were in planned positions ready to surge forward when their turn came.

Jeeps swept past the double lines on down the lonesome road, carrying officers and correspondents to their positions. The last group of houses five hundred yards from the river at Julich was an assembly area for assault boats which had been trucked up in stacks like a housewife stacks the mush bowls in the cupboard. These are like big, heavy rowboats lightly plated against bullets, with handgrips so that twelve men can carry one of them to the river edge. At the sign nailed to a tree saying that lonesome word "Front" all movement by vehicle ceased, as Jerries could and often did sweep the road straight up with machine-gun fire and had a bad habit of shooting 88's point-blank up it from their side of the river.

All along the front this scene was repeated scores on scores of times; the tree-lined roads stocked with vehicles chockablock down to the last possible point. Beyond that point the infantry and the engineers left the road and the bright moonlight and ducked down into the muddy fields, following carefully and exactly the very footsteps of the man ahead as he walked along the white tapes set in late that afternoon by engineers. This was much like any hike through woods in the dark, slipping and stumbling through the mud, with bushes whipping unexpectedly back into the faces of the men. But they kept their curses to themselves and no man dared cough or even clear his throat. A sneeze can be heard some distance and the jump-off point for the attack across the river at Julich was exactly on the river bank, which at that point was channeled only thirty yards wide.

The HQ for the Julich attack (which I selected because I could get closest with the least danger) was in the ancient catacombs, those massive brick moat fortifications built in the 16th Century across the river from Julich and long since heavily overgrown with bushes and trees. This would stand direct hits from everything but the biggest bombs, it was believed, except of course around the tree holes on which it opens onto the river. Down in the days [*sic*, depths] of the catacombs the night was still quiet. Unless you were foolish you didn't look out much over the river at Julich; you looked out the other way over the moat toward the American rear. The deep moat, flooded into a great pond, was thick with torn up trees. Up and down these logs ran great rats disappearing down by the water or nosing up past you to dash into the bays of the catacombs.

In those bays slept engineers and infantry rolled in their blankets on the dirt piles in the dark, muttering as couriers stumbled over their feet on their way to the inmost catacombs where the command post was set up for the 175th Regiment of the 29th Division. Some didn't sleep; if you stood near them you could feel them trembling. The command post was a telephone switchboard, a kitchen table and a lot of liaison officers—tanks, tank destroyers, air force, engineers, artillery.

The cave-like bays of the catacombs were lit only by occasional guttering candles which the doughfeet produced. The command post had the supreme luxury of a pair of kerosene lamps, one by the telephone switchboard and the other by the map table. In general, then, the broad picture of the early evening was of equipment moving by all roads slowly and carefully down to the edge of the Roer river along nearly all of the Ninth Army front until the curving muddy river bank for a half mile deep was one long welter of troops and boats and bridging equipment. Behind them, parked silently on all the roads, waited the armor and supply trucks that were to pour in once the bridgehead was won and consolidated. Before midnight practically every item and man was in place in a long grand welter of what seemed like absolute snafu confusion to laymen and often even to junior officers cursing a missing man or a needed roll of wire. Actually the operation was in perfect shape but on such a scale that only back at division and corps HQ could its smoothness be properly assessed. But one point will suffice: not one man of the 29th Division which took Julich was lost in the movement down to within short pistol-shot of the enemy. Then the waiting began again. Once in the little scarred woods opposite Julich an American tank turned its engine over as the driver nervously checked the ignition. The sound seemed to raise hell in the quiet and startled German machine-gunners sent tracers ripping gaily through the woods at the sound. The tanker cut his engine and all was silent again.

This silence until a few seconds before 0245 hours. Then some artillery officer decided to fire the first shot and the greatest barrage in all artillery history, according to authorities here, was laid down on the Germans from the river bank on back for many miles.

The moon seemed shrunken and the light dimmer. For the sky was literally a sheet of pale yellow fire for miles on all sides, the light flickering like summer "heat lightning." Perhaps the best description would be the colloquial "all hell broke loose." The noise was beyond all absorption by the ears: it was like having a doctor pound your eardrum with a chisel and a mallet. This went on for forty-five full minutes. Then came H-hour at 3:30.

At 0300 hours combat infantrymen dressed in Mae Wests[126] had shoved directly across the river in assault boats to clean up the riverfront houses on the opposite bank to hold the bridge sites. At 0330 hours the combat engineers began work.

Bulldozers armored like tanks shoved their big blades through the ground preparing approaches while bullets bounced off their hides. The trucks loaded with pontoons crept closer to the water's edge. Down on the water itself the engineers, ducking and sweating, cool yet trembling under the flat vicious splat of heavy mortar fire, were fastening the planking and steel connections together with cold fast-fumbling fingers while covering fire was laid on against occasional machine-gun interruption from the other bank.

All during the barrage the dogfaces had listened with great shudders of satisfaction, saying over and over again at little intervals, "That's outgoing." But after the barrage had lifted and the Jerries began to react with mortar and 88 gunfire the doughs began to squirm and shrink down beside walls for protection, saying over and over again, "Boy, that's incoming." Someone would always argue, "Nuts that's outgoing, you didn't hear any whistle, didya?" But the answer would always come back, "Ya screwy, that's incoming mail." Sometimes they would say, "That's incoming mail with the right address" or "aimed right for the basket." Actually the river crossing, seen in the light of later events, was fairly simple. In what the experts call the Big Picture the casualties were astonishingly light and the opposition light to moderate. The Americans had carefully prepared an elephant in order to step on a fly. This was nothing to be ashamed of; this should be an occasion for extremest satisfaction because it is thus that lives are saved to fight again another day. In the whole operation there was actually little gamble and only a few critical hours, these latter mainly coming around the 29th Division when they had been unable to get treadway bridges across before daylight came. Actually when the broad, beautiful, blue-sky day dawned on the red-eyed troops the situation was fairly ticklish in that only two companies had crossed over the three little foot bridges in operation while the treadway bridge for tanks and vehicles was completely fouled up by German machine-gun opposition and by the fact that three successive vehicles, an alligator, a bulldozer and a crane on wheels had been smashed by mines at one bridge site. The combat engineers finally had to dynamite them off the road seriatim[127] before they could begin work again. Building a bridge in that naked daylight of a beautiful cool spring morning under direct enemy observation is no career. But on the other side the doughs kept jumping from house to house burping their guns down cellar windows or unpinning grenades from their shoulder straps to lob down into the holes. There would come a short muffled boom and then quiet, after which the dogfaces (put?) a gun down the hole and burp it about the room a bit before passing on, while clean-up squads cautiously poked down into the basements as the house-to-house crews went on. But suddenly things began to speed up and by noon two whole battalions of infantry were over the river and house-to-housing the town while the engineers still struggle against mortar fire from behind the town to get the tank treadway bridges over so that supplies of food and ammo could flow over in quantity. That was the way it went all along the river on the Ninth Army front. During the night some companies had rushed around the towns knocking out pillboxes and bunkers and slit trench emplacements to reach the high ground of the ridge that dominates the far side of the river from below Julich up to Linnich. They took this with comparative ease and by noon were all along the ridge looking down into the plain at the other end of which lies the Rhine river.

Attention John Walker again: I assume you have ample coverage of the taking of the citadel in Julich, which I witnessed yesterday. I am not sending it as it was the grossest example of elephant versus gnat yet, although I most heartily sympathize with that policy. But I am standing by to send any amount you may need as it was a very pretty show of flamethrowers squirting directly into the enormous fortress. One detail which I believe other corespondents *[sic]* may have missed: carved on the stone of the ancient fortress above the great stone clock is a Latin motto which must have given the citadel defenders ironic smiles as their numbers diminished. The inscription: *Vita cum horas fugit.*[128] That will be pie for Matthews as even I could decipher it.

SIDNEY OLSON CABLE 26
FROM HOLLAND TO DAVID HULBURD
SENT FEBRUARY 26, 1945; REC'D FEBRUARY 26, 1945

For Battlefronts:

Erkelenz is falling and when Erkelenz falls all hell and heavy mortars cannot stop General Simpson's divisions in that area. I personally expect a breakthrough tomorrow and that the Ninth Army will reach the Rhine on a broad front by Sunday despite the flow of German reinforcements and possibly stiffer resistance. Yesterday Simpson visited several divisions at the front and pinned decorations liberally on battlefield heroes. He is a great believer in recognizing merit swiftly. One of the worst moments of his life, he has told friends, was when about 1940 he had to decorate two sergeants with medals they had won in 1918. This is just a last-minute plug once more not to under-estimate the power of this drive. Developments by the time this issue is on the news stands will make clear how Simpson will benefit by getting elbow room. So far this battle is generally characterized by slow digging out of Germans from slit trenches, bunkers, small wooded clumps and minuscule towns which are little clumps of houses around a road crossing. One more point to make: this action is said by experts to be unique in the utter confidence and precision with which it is being fought. Everything is in place at the right time and going beautifully. I give all credit for this to Simpson, who is sure, steady, confident and tough. They told me before he visited the divisions yesterday that the boys would spurt today and certainly enough they did, generally clocking off three miles per division. They always spurt after the old man gets up there.

Reverting to the general character of the battle: observers in Piper Cub planes and in most forward farmhouses point out low brown clay mounds of German bunkers and zigzag of trenches to the artillery, which pounds it a few times, and then doughboys file through the fields, crouching and stepping carefully in the footsteps of men ahead, spreading out carefully as they near the objective where the Germans have to keep their heads down and under against our artillery fire. Suddenly the artillery fire lifts in perfect timing, and the smoothly working, battle-wise doughfeet rush the bunker under cover of chattering small arms to lob grenades into the dugouts and trenches. All this goes on hour after hour, steadily on and on. The problem for correspondents now is to find the front as the landmarks of the weeks of waiting vanish into the background. When you do you are as likely as not to overshoot it. The doughs are now going so fast that all the roads are still packaged with dynamited sticks wired into the near side of all trees along both sides of the tree-lined roads. This is the German night-time tank buster so that when tanks are bumping along black country roads at night they might nudge a tree and be blown up. This also keeps tanks in the center of the road so that the Germans need only mine the centers. But thus far, despite long weeks of waiting, this battle is characterized by an unusual lack of mines which you may be able to explain.

Sidney Olson Cable 27[129]
From Holland to Time Inc.—3/1/45

For *Life* Newsfront: Suggested Title: "One More River to Cross"[130]

With the Ninth Army, Wednesday night, February 28—soon, with luck, spearheads of the Ninth Army will reach the Rhine river. Without luck, the operation may take longer. But certainly sooner or later the whole army will be camped along the banks of the ancient and beautiful stream, the last great natural barrier before Berlin.

The beauty of the Rhine will be largely lost on the American troops. They have two red hot ambitions: to commit a nuisance in the Rhine, and to cross over and thus end the war.

But of all the American eyes focused on the river, perhaps the least susceptible aesthetically will be the small, hot, dark brown eyes of the Ninth's commander, General William Simpson, and the large, cold, grey eyes of his chief engineer, Colonel Richard U. Nicholas. For they are the authors of the crossing of the Roer River. Only five days ago they made an almost perfect success of the infinitely delicate and dangerously tricky business of getting one of the world's most powerful armies over the little Roer. Yet that was only a dress rehearsal for the crossing of the Big Ditch.

General Simpson knows exactly how difficult the Rhine Crossing will be. For months he and his chief of staff, Brig. General James Moore, and Colonel Nicholas, have been studying maps and data on the Rhine River, and more important, have spent many happy working hours over an 18 foot long scale model of the Rhine area, prepared for them by British map artists. As yet only General Simpson knows exactly where and how he will pass his troops over the historic river. Only he and Generals Hodges, Bradley and Eisenhower and Field Marshal Montgomery know exactly when.

But whenever he orders the crossing, the citizenry back home should know two things: all the decisions will be his own; and he will be supremely confident. In such operations as the Roer crossing or the Rhine crossing, army generals work under a kind of carte blanche permission. The supreme commander, Eisenhower, and the army group commanders, such as Bradley and Montgomery merely tell the army chiefs such as Simpson and Hodges and Crerar of the Canadians to "attack when ready." In short Eisenhower's job is to defeat the enemy; Montgomery and Bradley's jobs are to coordinate attacks, and Simpson and Hodges and Crerar have the job of attacking.

General Simpson's confidence is one of his stock of man merits, all of them plain and familiar as old shoes. For the general is like a platitude come to life, like a set of old maxims clothed in flesh. He is a simple, clear-cut, strong-willed, clean minded old soldier, steady, dependable, solid and sure. His confidence, as for instance about the Roer crossing, has nothing in it of the gaudy cocksureness or even arrogant showmanship of some American commanders. But somehow he can make the most Rotarian-sounding remarks carry such absolute conviction that men go out to fight, perhaps to die, uplifted by his transparent sincerity.

There is something Biblical about the man. He is tall and lean as a whip, always dressed with such creased and shining perfection that a mere fleck of lint would show on him as the fleck of red that the English painter Turner often put near the center of his canvases as an eye catcher. Atop this trim body so much younger than his fifty-six years is an almost unique head. At first glance it seems so bony, so cadaverously lean that you think of it as a kind of friendly skull. He has a wide, reassuring smile, friendly and honest. But his eyes dominate his face: they are almost hypnotically compelling. People find themselves talking to his eyes. When he is deeply interested or angry they glow like hot coals. As a matter of fact he is probably one of the few men who can actually give a burning look. When he dresses down some one for incompetence or stupidity the operation is simple: he merely sears the hapless offender.

One of his greatest merits as a commander is one that is not easily appreciated by the masses who have never had the occasion or opportunity to manage groups of people. This is simply his experience as a commander. Unlike many American generals, who skipped a grade or two in their careers, General Simpson rose steadily and exactly through every command rank in the army. As a result he can appreciate to a technical nicety the needs and problems of, say, an assistant division commander. Command has become a habit with him, as integral a part of his makeup as the sense of being nobly born was an almost unconscious factor in the conduct of aristocrats in other days. Thus he does not need to exaggerate his orders in order to get them obeyed. He merely says what he wants done in the obviously clear expectancy his decisions will be carried out. It is always easy to work for a boss who knows his business. Simpson is such a boss.

Field Marshal Montgomery, General Simpson, General Bradley, and General Hodges were conferring in General Simpson's office on the second floor of a Dutch building. This was Wednesday afternoon, February 21. They had been discussing once again the topic that has become an obsession with them since the day last October when the First and Ninth Armies reached close to the Roer: the depth and width of that tricky stream. The engineer, Colonel Nicholas, had finally risked a last guess on when the Roer would be bridgeable. They were all agreed they could set the hour at 3:30 a.m. on Friday morning, February 23, to be preceded by a 45-minute artillery barrage beginning at 2:45 a.m.

General Simpson stood up and whipped out his wallet. From it he tenderly extracted a four leaf clover sent him long ago by an admirer. Solemnly but delicately the Field Marshal and the three generals rubbed the little good luck symbol. Then General Simpson tucked it back in his wallet; they all shook hands. Thus simply was set in final motion one of the most powerful combinations ever sent against an enemy army. The same offensive had once been scheduled for 5:30 a.m. on the morning of February 10. All had been in readiness, everything had been made ready. That afternoon correspondents took their bed rolls out to the divisions that they had chosen to follow into battle and found the troops oiling their rifles, the battalion commanders calm and confident, the engineers ready to the last assault boat. About five o'clock word flashed over the area: the offensive had been postponed for 24 hours. Early the next afternoon came the final word: the offensive had been postponed. The word indefinitely was not used, but everyone understood: the Roer River, under the scientific and desperate management of the infernally clever Germans, was in flood.

The Roer River is a winding little stream hardly bigger than a good-sized American creek ordinarily. It is often only some seventy-five feet wide, not more than knee deep and flows only some four to five miles per hour. Once it was a wider, deeper, swifter stream; so it is today as it is brawling this minute from its rolling hills in the south on up until it joins the Rhine at KOMING.[131] In the intervening years the Germans had changed the character of the river substantially by industriously building a network of large and small dams in the southern hills where the river curves crazily back on itself in a series of some nine hairpin loops. The two biggest dams were set at the northern and southern ends of this curlicue. The Urfttalsperre, the southern dam, holds when full about forty-five and one-half million cubic meters of water. The Schwammenauel, the northernmost, has a capacity of some one hundred million seven hundred thousand cubic meters. The First American army had been sporadically attacking toward the dams since October, striving to get control of both dams and American strategists feared that the Germans would blow up the dams and that the resulting sweep of water would smash American river installations and damage bridge sites beyond easy repair. But the Germans were cleverer than that: years ago they had built a conduit from the lower Urftalsperre dam to the upper Schwammenauel dam so that water could be passed directly across the peninsula between the two dams without having to go through all the middle dams of the curves like a series of locks on a canal.

On the afternoon of February 9, while the Americans were polishing up their rifles and as American tanks prepared to rush straight across the knee-deep Roer, the Germans blew up the penstock gates of the conduit at the Schwammenauel dam. In only a few hours the Americans realized what this would mean: the Roer River would flood to a high stage and stay that way for an indefinite period of time, until all the water in the two big dams had slowly drained out. The Germans had been playing for time; with one brilliant stroke they had won a thirteen-day recess before the Americans could cross the Roer. Their timing had been perfect: if the Americans tried to cross this spreading flood the units on the opposite bank could easily pick them off in local counterattacks.

General Simpson acted swiftly. All the decisions were his. He never gambles unless all the odds are in his favor. Coldly and angrily he called off the offensive and sat down with Colonel Nicholas to find out when the blankety-blank river would be bridgeable. For the offensive plans and objectives on the opposite bank need not be changed; but the difficulty of getting that army across had been increased many fold.

The engineers had a helluva problem. First they had to calculate exactly how much water was in the dams. The Germans are great statistic-keepers and had figures going back for many years. They know just how much water was in the dams, just about how long it would take to flow out, and just how fast and deep approximately the river would be. In short, they could tell within hours the earliest moment at which the river could be bridged.

The American engineers were thrown back into a maze of the most complex calculations. Some of the studies they made are literally classics of incomprehensibility. But General Simpson grimly waded through them day after day, searching for the sparkling nugget of hope in the flood of data. By not sleeping very much, Colonel Nicholas, a tall, stooped, grey head who has been an army engineer for thirty-eight years, and his staff finally got some presentable figures heavily qualified. Some of the facts they needed they found in a cellar in Aachen by some brilliant detective work. They got more facts from British scholars working in the libraries of Brussels. And they got some of the facts they needed most by the hard way: they fought for them. The Americans desperately needed to know how fast the dams fell every day, especially the Schwammenauel, the big one, which held some sixty million cubic meters behind its earthen walls. The only way they could get any reliable facts was by sticking a painted measuring stick out in the waters of the dam and then watching to see how far the water dropped in a certain length of time. At night the engineers would paddle assault boats out into the dams and drive down the marked gauges. A number of expert engineers were lost this way as the Germans flare-lit the area and then spotted the boats repeatedly. But some gauges were left by daylight which the engineers watched through field glasses from their side of the shore. Day after day the Germans amazed themselves by shooting out these gauges; night after night the cursing engineers would plant new ones.

All this time the water was rolling merrily out of the conduit and on down into the Roer River valley, spreading out over many acres of the flat cabbage land. About fifty-two cubic meters a second were discharging from the Urft dam, the engineers figured, and about two hundred cubic meters a second from the Schwammenauel. This created a flood that in some places was more than twelve hundred and fifty feet wide, some fifteen times as wide as the original little stream. But most important, the current was flowing at the rate of about six miles an hour.

The swift current would merely pile up more casualties in boats, equipment, etc. as well as in men.

Another complicating factor that almost drove the engineers and General Simpson crazy was that melting snows and fresh rain water were constantly draining into the dams from surface run-off out of the hills. Again this was something the Germans could guess out of years of experience and observation of the dams. The Americans finally were able to calculate the probable amount of water in the dams. Then they made guesses on how long the new rains would take to soak off the grass roots and into the watershed. Then Colonel Nicholas, one week after postponement, guessed on February 17 that the river would be bridgeable before the 25th. He told General Simpson that the big Schwammenauel dam would be empty much like a bathtub which goes down slowly for some time and then suddenly the last third of the tub-full runs out swiftly with a great gurgle and splash.

The weary Colonel's last guess was only six hours off the exact moment that the dam emptied itself. The dam had been falling at the rate of about two or three inches in twenty-four hours. Then on the night of February 24 the dam suddenly fell seventeen inches in six hours. But by then American troops were well across the Roer; for the engineers' most important prediction had been that the river current would fall to bridging speed early enough to permit an offensive some time the night of the 22nd.

General Simpson had long ago decided to cross at the earliest possible moment. He set his new H-hour for the early morning of February 23 and then briefed his colleague generals on the decision.

Everything had been made ready so many times that the assault troops, after umpteen boat rehearsals, complained that they might as well have joined the navy and be done with it. His decision made, his desk clear, General Simpson arose at 7:00 a.m. to hear the early newscast at

Combat Daily, his favorite radio program on the overseas forces network. Then he went down to breakfast in the generals' mess, making his invariable remark: "Well, I guess I'll just have a light breakfast this morning." Thereupon he ate his invariable breakfast of a large glass of fruit juice, a dish of cereal, two scrambled eggs, a big rasher of crisp bacon, three stove-lid-size army pancakes with syrup, toast, jam and four cups of coffee. He went about his work with a light heart after the grim week of waiting and plowing through engineers' reports five times daily. After dinner that night he went to the movies, seeing Bing Crosby in "Going My Way," which he enjoyed as always (he denies liking Lana Turner, never heard of her, doesn't know one movie babe from another, fyi). At midnight he drank a highball to success and calmly went to bed. At dawn he was awakened by telephone calls from corps commanders with the results.

All that evening the American troops, working quietly and skillfully in the bright moonlight, had carefully lugged the heavy assault boats down to the muddy jump-off sites, then had dug in on the banks to await the vast barrage that would start the offensive. The scene was memorable from the quiet early twilight hours when American ack-ack sent streams of red hot tracers directly into the moon, searching vainly for the German jet planes on reconnaissance, on down to the quiet groups of American boys sleeping or mumbling or just silently smoking in their foxholes or dugouts. Some of them trembled: you could feel it if you stood near them as they lay curled in their blankets. But perhaps it was the chill in the spring night, a chill that came not only from the gleaming mist-hung river but from the empty stomach feeling you always got when the enemy is near and can shoot you if he thinks it worthwhile.

After the barrage had torn up the sky and German communications for miles and miles back from the fronts, the Ninth and First Armies jumped off. One footbridge was built in fifteen minutes flat. There doughboys raced happily across without casualties. But most crossings were more like that at the vicinity of Julich, the toughest crossing of all which had been given to the veteran 29th Division. (Calhoun: Please leave the 29th in. I have guidance asking me to plug them and the press agrees that they had the toughest spot.) There the Germans had zeroed in all the bridge sites and plastered the bridges with heavy-mortar fire hour after hour. When dawn came the 29th had only been able to get across two companies of troops although they had hoped to get two battalions over in the dark.

In the "Big Picture" the casualties were light. But any casualties you see strikes you as a heavy casualty and a number of fine young American boys were killed that night in the brick dust that used to be the lovely little ancient city of Julichena?, the town named Julia Castrarum because Julius Caesar once fortified it. (please check).[132]

The use of some hundred movie cameras up and down the front that night would give some idea of the complexity of the operation and the narrow margin by which a river crossing succeeds. That night the Ninth Army had thousands of engineers and engineer officers, hundreds of trucks, bulldozers, moveable cranes, and road graders. These represent the engineers only yet they involve thousands of American families all over the States, the mothers and fathers and sweethearts everywhere that were sitting down to dinner about that [time] or going to the movies wondering about their boys.

Figure any engineer would have to be multiplied a censorable number of times to get the total of American troops involved in the action that night from the goggled couriers motorcycling furiously through the night to the bored ack-ack crews sitting it out in a muddy clay gun pit in the Roer areas on down to the combat troops in the Mae West belts, their clothes hung with little grenades, who swirled across to the other bank directly into the bite of machine gun bullets.

By noon things picked up: the reports flowed in; a footbridge and a treadway tank bridge were in near Merken. Another footbridge, another treadway bridge for tanks was in the vicinity of Schophoven. Two foot- and one heavy pontoon bridge were in near Julich. No, one of them was knocked out by a direct hit at 3:30 p.m. But at 4:15 the bridge is back in operation and the fire is lessening as the dough feet dart from house to house hosing the cellars with their guns or pegging grenades into trenches and wall holes. A jet plane swished through the morning haze to damage two bridges. But the bridges are repaired and the troops keep moving on and on once they are over, bypassing strong points and seizing high ground. Before them, where there is time, go the sappers, the mine-sweepers, who cheerfully do one of the war's dirtiest, most hopeless jobs.

By afternoon Julich is pretty well in hand. Some of the other divisions are going much faster against lighter opposition. By now the engineers are constructing air strips for Cub planes to use for artillery observation and building prefabricated roads while the bulldozers push the rubble aside to disclose the once fashionable streets. The engineers are happy: they have captured a gravel pit of one hundred thousand yards capacity in "good condition," two anvils, one of two hundred pounds and one of two hundred and fifty pounds, both in "fair" condition.

Tanks are rolling over; whole regiments of infantry are set across; flame-throwers move over for stubborn points and the MPs are long since directing traffic calmly amid fire.

From this campaign General Simpson has been daily drawing conclusions about the changing character of the enemy resistance. Only later actions will show what those conclusions are. But certain things can be noted as part of the basic material apparent to everyone. For one thing, the German resistance is generally lighter and less fierce than it has been heretofore. Despite all the time gained by delaying actions since last autumn in this area, the enemy did not mine the area heavily. This is puzzling. At first rumors had it that there was a German shortage of mines but huge captured stockpiles of mines disprove that. For another thing there has been little or no attempt to evacuate civilians. This seems to reflect lack of transport but even so represents graphically the enemy's inability to defend the Reich as the people are the first asset of the State. One conclusion easy to reach, particularly after touring numerous prisoner cages: the Ninth Army just has not been up against anything like the real *Wehrmacht* in this campaign.[133] The fight cannot be minimized: this has been a real fight. But the fact remains that the Germans have not been able to cope with the enormous force that the Americans have sent over in just one narrow front. Despite the Rhine, despite the bitterness with which the Germans must defend their industrial *hartland* of the Ruhr, which lies just beyond the Rhine—it is now clear that the end is in sight this year. It may come in June, it may not come until September, but it is coming steadily and surely. Toward that end General

William Simpson, who will by then have made another crossing, will have contributed one of the most perfectly handled operations of the war—the crossing of the Roer River in February, 1945.

3. THE GERMANS ARE BECKONING US ON

SIDNEY OLSON CABLE 28
FROM HOLLAND TO DAVID HULBURD
SENT MARCH 2, 1945; REC'D MARCH 3, 1945

For Battlefronts[134]

This afternoon two doughs of the 83rd Division went across the Rhine at Dusseldorf. They didn't come back. But that was only the more proof that all traffic over the Rhine is one way.

By now Simpson's pattern of attack should be clear. While the German strategists and American press gave great play to the attack as a drive on Cologne by the 1st American Army, General Simpson's 9th Army, beefed up into one of the most powerful aggregations of men and fighting equipment ever put together, struck almost directly north, swerving sharply left to cut to the Rhine at Neuss, across the river from Dusseldorf. There tonight we control the approaches of a great bridge and have been registering artillery fire across the river all day.

I have been at the front for some time without much sleep now, so this will be an extraordinarily straggling collection of sleepy notes before I return to the bridge tomorrow. But some of the most important points for *Time* and *Life* editors follow. The mainest [*sic*] point is controversial and punditical: to some of us here it almost seems as if the Germans are beckoning us on with only token resistance in hopes that we reach Berlin before the Russians. This may be the sheerest moonshine but some factors about the present battle are almost inexplicable otherwise. True we have won a most important campaign, crashing some twenty-plus miles straight through the vaunted German defenses to reach the Rhine in seven swift days. But what has been the outstanding characteristic of that resistance? Every day experts have been forced to admit that the resistance has [been] "light" or at most "light to moderate." We have captured and will capture more of some of the Germans' most historic and strategically important towns, yet we cannot honestly claim to have crushed any important German army in the field. We have smeared numerous nondescript and spare parts regiments but we have (not) found in mass any really distinguished German divisions, although we have encountered here and there some traces of them. There have been many bitter little fights but the numerous defense lines dug by those eager German beavers have never had a strategic chance against the power of the 9th Army offensive. The general tactical progression was as follows: On the first day the battalions took the bridgeheads and held them while the engineers built bridges over which the regiments passed; on the second day division bridgeheads were gained; on the third day these were consolidated and sharply expanded into corps bridgeheads; on the fourth day these corps bridgeheads were expanded and beefed up, as base for armor and on the next day General Simpson committed his armor from the tip of the corps bridgeheads. The tanks went cautiously but powerfully for one day and then roared and smashed their way straight across country to the Rhine, by-passing real strong points and smearing all else while utterly crushing all Nazi communications (except by carrier pigeon) possible. The whole operation has been as pretty as tactics textbooks, pictures and charts. From the air in a Piper Cub the tank drive was a thing of the sheerest military beauty: First came a long row of throbbing tanks moving like heavy dark beetles over the green cabbage fields of Germany in a wide swath—perhaps more like a horizontal row of locusts moving steadily in a military plague—many, many tanks in a single row abreast. Then came a suitable distance behind another great echelon of tanks even broader out of which groups would wheel from their brown mud-tracks in green fields to encircle and smash fire at some stubborn thorn in the side, and behind this came miles of trucks full of motorized troops maneuvering perfectly to hold and mop up by-passed tough spots, and then came the field artillery to pound hard knots into submission and from the flanks in swift swoops sped clouds of tank-destroyers cutting across the landscape in wild swoops that hit the enemy and cut off communications with bewildering speed. And always overhead swung and looped the Thunderbolts in fullest air-cover, keeping the tanks under absolute safety umbrellas and from time to time diving to knock out trouble points several miles above the front.

Above them rode farther-roving P-47 missions to dive-bomb and strafe every moving truck, self-propelled-gun or railroad train for many miles beyond, while way up above them came the steady rumble of the great silver Fortresses in the topmost sky, purring distantly on to knock out the deep-most reinforcement areas and supply points and marshaling yards. This was one of the war's grandest single pictures of united and perfectly functioning military machines in a supreme moment of pure fighting motion. And the tanks rumbled on and on halting to fire then rolling and clanking ahead in this enormous swath that gradually cut through all German resistance. In their wake was left the not-so-grand rubble of war, both buildings and human beings: thousands and thousands of the loyalest Hitler subjects but all oh-so-helplessly thankful that at last the war was over for them.

I went in with the 29th division to take München-Gladbach yesterday in one of the weirdest actions of the war. The resistance consisted mainly of isolated detachments of nondescript troops who fought briefly at street corners. Those who were left surrendered quickly and with relief. This is the way it would go. A tank passed us and went down the absolutely lonely and deserted street through the ranks of neat and excellent two-story stone buildings, the kind of street that gives you that terribly lonely nakedness feeling of snipers and trouble around you, the kind of street out of which you back your Jeep at top speed without trying to take time to turn around, the kind of street down which you strain your eyes vainly for the sight of familiar doughfeet uniform peeking out of doors up the street with rifles slung for action. The tank went on up the street clanking and rumbling in the quiet. No, not a head stuck out of a window to watch. The tank went around a corner out of sight. Almost instantly there came a single shell crash. Pretty soon the tank crew came around the corner all safe but disgusted. An 88-SP had drilled the tank cleanly with one shot, stopping it cold. Then the SP ran off. The aim was perfect. No one was injured but the tank so powerful and impressive only seconds before was now just so much dead steel. The shell had drilled a hole through the armor, cutting an oil line. But that was all the resistance on that street, and pretty soon the GI's were making their way casually from house to house while the stolid German families sat quietly in their bunk-furnished candle-lit air-raid basements, their children and old folks about them. In one grocery store, doughfeet played store, selling each other butter and eggs across the counter. One of the great finds of the day was the Nazi auditorium and theater in Rheydt with *Gestapo* offices and officer lounge and movie theater.[135]

When night came the 29th Division was not allowed to button up for the evening, but told to carry on through the whole town which they had taken frontally from the south, street by street abreast. That night was eerie in München-Gladbach, which is the biggest German city yet captured and once a vastly important textile center. The silence seemed absolute, broken only by the occasional crashing exhaust of a jeep, which sounds as if it were strafing the roads. Under the rainy moon the city lay mackerel dead. But as you went through the blocks you would suddenly come on German soldiers standing still with their rifle. The moment they saw you they would put the rifle on the sidewalk and march up to surrender. The weary GI's, vastly outnumbered by thousands of civilians, would merely tell them angrily to stand there and then go on mopping up. As a result some Germans surrendered literally scores of times before someone had time to take them off to a battalion command post. Some stood for hours; others wandered off in disgust; some who lived near-by went off to change into ill-fitting civilian clothes in order to surrender next day.

The happiest people we met were occasional groups of forces of labor prisoners, including scores on scores of Russians and Poles, and some Italians who tried to be very friendly and scores of Frenchmen who were so unreservedly, demonstratively happy that it was difficult not to be maudlin with them. I talked to five who had been prisoners for five years in my meager French which was the first non-German guttural French they had heard in all that time, and they begged me again and again to say some more so that they could weep with delight at my American accent. They and all the residents of München-Gladbach swore that even London never could have known the terror that American and RAF air power has been to Germany: how many nights they had trembled along with the Germans as the bombs fell endlessly again and again. And München-Gladbach, which is the least clobbered city yet taken by the Allies, is so strikingly beat up that it's easy to agree that even London never took this much of a clobbering. Incidentally, all Germans and French prisoners and anyone in a position to know surprisingly agree that of all bombed German cities, Berlin, Hamburg, etc., the worst hit is Coblenz. They point to piles of smashed bricks and shake their heads and say "Coblenz."

When GI's kicked in the door of a big bank at one place we were greeted by a bank officer who spoke excellent English and had visited America twice. I asked him what he thought of Hitler now. He was an obviously sensitive, well-read, cultured citizen used to dealing with the upper ranks and obviously deathly afraid of the laconic, steel-eyed doughfeet who would have loved the chance to shoot him or any other German who seems a wrong gee [sic]. But this obviously intelligent man said sadly: "Hitler is a much misunderstood man." I said: "Yes, for one I misunderstand him." He said: "Ah, yes. You are ironic, but you will see, history will bear me out, he is one of the world's greatest leaders. It is merely that he has been badly advised, very badly advised, by swaggering louts with pistols on their hips, brutes and beasts, the Gestapo. That is how he went wrong; now he is *kaput*; but still his twenty-one points of 1927 make a great document." This seems to be the almost invariable attitude according to Major John W. Hall, of Orlando, Florida, who arrived in München this afternoon to begin the enormous task of managing 63,000 München-Gladbach inhabitants plus 20,000 Rheydt inhabitants with a fourth assistant burgomaster and eight policemen as his force. In the street little children, boys especially, wave as gladly at the Yanks as if we were conquering friends not foes and even women and older men constantly smile and essay tentative waves. Usually these meet stony responses and sometimes all over this front you will see German civilians in the streets offering of schnapps to gruff infantrymen who drink a few gurgles and then pocket the bottle and march off without backward looks. They will tell you that saying thank-you to the Germans is fraternizing. A great joke with them about the German girls is when they ask themselves out loud as a hot number goes by: "Well, is that worth $65 or not?" (The fraternization fine is $65 at least.)

The only pertinent fact in answer to the query regarding the Erft Canal is that the terrain is not so flat and thus not such perfect tank country as the Cologne plain on which the 2nd Armored Division is now powerhousing for the 9th Army near Dusseldorf. The terrain is low and flattish but with slight rolling undulations not quite hills which silhouette tanks coming over them as artillery targets. But since the Americans are already over the Erft Canal farther down, the whole question is unimportant, especially if Battlefronts will study the large-scale terrain map and note the direction of the 9th Army offensive. I personally do not regard Cologne as an important objective. If we cross the Rhine soon, Cologne becomes a rear area situation almost as unimportant militarily to the front line as shall we say Paris. Cannot say more through censorship.

My plans are to return to the Dusseldorf front tomorrow from which I may not be able to file until Sunday night, copy reaching you about 5 p.m. Sunday. This would include data on the front.

March 2, 1945[136]

Sidney Olson
Care of 9th Army Press Camp
Holland

Just to say wish we could have a cup of coffee and hoping you are feeling top hole

Harry Luce

SIDNEY OLSON CABLE 29 [I][137]
FROM HOLLAND TO DAVID HULBURD
SENT MARCH 3, 1945; REC'D MARCH 3, 1945

For Battlefronts:

The Germans blew all three of the bridges in the Dusseldorf-Neuss area today. Above those three bridges are five big bridges up the Rhine before you reach Canadian territory; two at Duisburg, one at Rheinberg, one at Uerdingen near Krefeld and one at Wesel. Some 20,000 Germans are in that pocket, backing up to these last escape hatches. Only three of the bridges probably can take anything but foot traffic, the one at Rheinberg, the one at Wesel and one of the two at Duisburg. The Germans were ferrying armor across on barges all day today in this sector. Unfortunately, the weather socked in all around the Rhine marshalling yards on the German side where enormous troop movements are reported today. There were drizzling clouds from 5000 feet all the way down to the deck which makes pin-point fighter bomber work difficult. The junction of Americans and Canadians is interesting this morning, but not strategically significant.

In studying the direction of the arrows of the Ninth Army attack, it must now be clear how constantly General Simpson has moved in a giant leftish swivel up the map, striking northeast, then north, then northeast, then north again, while the First Army merely protected his flank, and feinted at Cologne where the Germans concentrated their defenses. If ever there was a time when the phrase, "according to plan," was justifiable, it is this time. We weren't ever allowed to hint that Cologne was not the primary objective, but only incidental. The First Army in strong force is across the Erft river, and thus behind the Erft canal all along the corps front today, thus ruining any chance the Germans might have of using the Erft canal as a defense line.

SIDNEY OLSON CABLE UNNUMBERED[138]
FROM HOLLAND TO DAVID HULBURD
SENT MARCH 4, 1945; REC'D MARCH 4, 1945

Attention Harry Luce:

The coffee here is terrible, but all else is fine. I most seriously suggest that you and Roy Larsen consider getting a *March of Time* crew here if possible for a short which might be titled, "This is Germany."[139] The revenge for London and Coventry has been taken a thousandfold. The script could include a few clips from old shots of lovely German towns, and then all you would have to do is to mount a camera in a car and move slowly through Aachen, then into Julich which is mere brick dust, and then into München-Gladbach which has had no artillery damage and has not been a main RAF or Eighth Air Force target, but which has been completely clobbered. The point is that München-Gladbach represents probably the best-looking, least-clobbered city we will find in Germany if what captured civilians and all say is true. Such a documentary would not only be a record for history and most horrifyingly impressive, but could achieve a weird beauty of its own.

Again, I wish someone like Cecil Beaton could photograph this Daliesque scenery by moonlight, searchlight, dawn, or in garish daylight.[140] It should be done by a sensitive artist as the rough and tough war photographers would rather shoot battles, which is actually easier. I don't know what has been done so this suggestion may be untimely or impracticable, but I guarantee that such pictures are better than thousands of words, and certainly would be a gasp-maker in theaters. Also, in München-Gladbach we now control a populace of some 80,000, the largest body of Germans yet, utterly docile and uneasily friendly. I believe pix of these, their clothes, and some interviews with some of them on the screen might be excellent stuff. The Military Government story is now getting so big that I think it is almost time for you to plan on having some correspondent over here devoting fullest time to developments, as the problems are only beginning. Fluent German, of course, is the first requirement. Or it might be worth sending someone like Willi Schlamm here for a month's trip.[141] Put another way, it is none too soon to start whoever is coming to head the Berlin Time Inc. bureau on his assignment, as he should be grounded thoroughly in Military Government problems as they develop, and they only now are really beginning to be a big headache.

Barring developments, I expect to leave the Ninth Army in a few days to continue a briefest tour of other American Armies and the French Army and then recuperate in Paris. Since I personally believe that the Ninth Army will reach Berlin first, I believe the replacement should be a top rank Time Inc. war correspondent and that he should reach here soon. I do not know the situation of *Time* Magazine, but I believe the story is made to order for Roy Alexander. Harry, the crossing of the Rhine will be the most memorable military engineering feat, and it should be most thoroughly covered in a *Life* pictorial essay, done by a team of writer and photographer. I daren't lallygag around here too long for fear I'll get caught up in the fascination of war and press camp life; so figure I'd better push on. I will appreciate advice on this. I am steadily gathering material for an epic *Time* press story on war correspondents which I guarantee should be a homer hit. Or I could send copious notes from which some *Life* editor could write a swell text and pic piece on how war correspondents live and work in a fabulous atmosphere of fakery, laziness, danger, boredom, drunkenness and hard work. Sincerest regards.

MARCH 5, 1945 [LETTER TO ZEMBRA]

Dearest darling B.G.

I can't imagine what's happened to the mails again; I haven't had a letter from you since one dated January 24. I've had several from the folks, the last one dated February 23 (be sure to tell them) but none from you. I suppose they're caught somewhere dammit because I'm sure you're writing me when you know how I hunger for the slightest word or news from you. This interchange of letters just can't be a correspondence because you just have to keep on writing without getting answers to questions until a month later. For heaven's sakes don't wait to write me until I've answered your last letter.

I'm finally sick of it at the front here and now that we've reached the Rhine I've wired Luce, Hulburd et al. for an okay to go on with my trip which is lagging behind schedule anyway. But I've seen the war and know now what it's about—and I don't care if I never hear another bullet fired in my life, even in a shooting gallery. There just aren't any safe places in a war, even for generals; so I'm backpedaling into the rear areas now that I've had my full share of narrow escapes. And I'm plenty pooped after weeks of riding in an open jeep in snow, rain and icy winds and then sleeping in two blankets on the wood floor of a bombed out house with the rain pouring in on you. And that's lots better than foxholes, where some of the boys live. But don't get the idea I'm dispirited or anything because I'm not; I feel swell and the life actually agrees with me. Even at its toughest it's not as hard on me as that damned *Time* week. I've been a very good boy, not gambling with the poker playing crowd when we're back at camp, but playing chess with several Britishers, or gin rummy with Max Lerner, who is my roommate, and turns out to be a heck of a nice guy, although we disagree on politics, of course. But we've been through a lot together. And when they passed the liquor ration around I didn't put in for a case of cognac as the other boys did. I don't even drink as little as I did in Larchmont. And I don't chase the women as the others do constantly: for me you are the only one in the world, and I hurt monstrously to see you again and lay you like a tapestry.

Living like this changes all your values: the things I'm desperately interested in always are first food; second a warm place to sleep; third, a warm bath; and four, enough cigarettes and a light to read by and work by.

For instance I went in with the troops to München-Gladbach as they cleaned it out street by street and watched them loot it. But what was the wonderful loot that I returned with? A desk lamp, with an extension cord and two bulbs, out of a German soap factory. To me that was the find of the day. But I did pick up a few little things at Schloss Rheydt,[142] the castle belonging to Josef Goebbels. I was the first reporter on the scene. It had been fairly well stripped by the Germans, but I picked up two very cute brand new unused baby blankets, two big new blankets, a picture off the wall, and a couple of books. I also got some small silver trinkets, I'll send all this stuff if and when I can: you may or may not get it depending on luck and whether I can wangle any wrapping paper and string. Everything like that is impossible to get in Holland, where they actually only have buttons and little pieces of crocheting to sell in the stores.

Anyway it's ho for Paris for me as soon as I get the okay which may be today or tomorrow. Keep on writing to the same address, beloved beautiful darling darl, and I'll warn you when to shift over and start writing to my next address which will be Italy. At the moment I'm so terribly homesick for you that it's all I can do not to call the whole trip off. That's why this letter is so dull, darling darling darling darling darling darling; I miss you frightfully, horribly, enormously, terribly, awfully, suffocatingly much. And Whitney and John too—already they seem like pretty little strangers to me.

Did you ever get the packages I sent for your birthday? I suppose I won't know for months and then it'll be too late to start a search party after them. In Paris I'm going to try to take an absolute vacation and just relax and read and walk about. You should see me eat—and yet I don't gain the shadow of an ounce. We get a ration of four or five candy bars a week and I eat one every night before I go to bed, and all the others I can lay my hands on. That should surprise you for you know I've not touched candy in years. I drink coffee, but never more than one cup at a meal. I smoke about the same. Right now, sitting in this dusty little dutch hotel room—it's raining lightly as usual outside, and I've taken the day off from the front—I'm wearing British battledress, a uniform which I scrounged from the Canadians, my field jacket, and slippers. I'm eating peanuts and drinking a coke—both of which we get in our rations each week or two. This funny old dutch town is very dull; the only amusement is a movie that gives one show a night to the GIs at the same time that we eat dinner, so I never see a movie. There is also a Red Cross doughnut corner where you can buy coffee and doughnuts very cheaply, and read the *Stars and Stripes*, the only newspaper we ever see; and an officers club, which opens every night and where you get a ration of two drinks of cognac or two cokes or two beers and listen to a stock of eight worn out records (the newest is *White Christmas*) and watch officers dance with WACs, nurses, or Hollanders, all of them plain as a garage door. That's why I stay back and play chess, at which I'm coming along fine, as I'm playing against marvelous players now. One of them Alfred Lee is an ex champion of middle England, and he just toys with me, but he says I have one thing most beginners don't and that's chess imagination, with which you see combinations far ahead.

In Paris I'll see Les Midgley.[143] The grapevine said he was to arrive there last week, so I'll see him all right at the Hotel Scribe, where all the correspondents stay. Saw Eddie Folliard the day I was there in January.[144] He hasn't been to the front. Please give my folks all the news if any from this letter—tell them I'll write soon and that I love their letters as it's so very wonderful to get mail when you're away. And write me, darling goddess, please write me lots and lots, just little notes every day, and an occasional big one, lots bigger than V-mail. When I told you and the folks to write V-mail that was just to get you started: I want real letters, too. Still your humblest slave, S.

SIDNEY OLSON CABLE 29 [II][145]
FROM HOLLAND TO DAVID HULBURD
SENT MARCH 6, 1945; REC'D MARCH 6, 1945

For Foreign News:

Today Winston Churchill went through the Siegfried Line and into captured Julich which the press covered heavily. I send only this true story which the rest of the press is apparently skipping, but which should be covered for the benefit of historians.

Near Aachen the old tank-track teeth of the Siegfried Line march around the curves of the low hills and down along the valleys like an extraordinarily regular cemetery in which all the tombstones are exactly similar—rhomboidal cement blocks gray-green in color about three or four feet high. The party included the following besides Churchill: General Simpson of the Ninth Army, Field Marshal Montgomery, Field Marshal Sir Alan Brooke, General Raymond S. McLain of the Ninth Army's 19th Corps. They wanted to make quite a ceremony of Churchill's first trip through the Siegfried Line into Nazi Germany so newsreel men were all set on the banks of a declivity when the cars stopped.[146]

SIDNEY OLSON CABLE **30**
FROM HOLLAND TO DAVID HULBURD
SENT MARCH 7, 1945; REC'D MARCH 8, 1945

With the Third Armored Division in Cologne, March 6th—

Perhaps the best way to tell this is just as I saw things today without trying to wrap it up in a strategy piece.[147] So please excuse the use of the word "I." But don't call me Quentin.

We reached the city limits of Cologne at 1:30 p.m. after some 50 odd miles in a topless open jeep in the chill drizzling day. The city is almost a half-moon in shape, with the flat side on the Rhine. We entered on one of the radial boulevards just off center. Nearly all the main axial streets focus down to the great cathedral which is at the very hub, hard on the Rathaus (city hall), the railroad station and the approaches to the great Hohenzollern bridge. At the city limits stood a sign: "You are entering Cologne, courtesy of the spearhead division—the Third Armored." The doughs had anchored the sign very heavily so that the later occupying divisions would have great difficulty in uprooting this reminder.

We went on in. The first impression was that of silence and emptiness. When we stopped the jeep, you heard nothing, you saw no movement down the great deserted avenues, lined with empty stone boxes. In the city of 800,000 people no one now seemed alive. This was an illusion. Perhaps some 30,000 people still live there. But they live underground. You have to know where to go. We looked vainly for hotels, cigar stores, wine stores, jewelry stores, for people. Occasionally there would pass some pale German walking carefully and slowly with a white handkerchief in his hand which he would wave to show that he had surrendered. The pallor was not necessarily fright—it came from living underground, safe from the terror of allied air power.

For there is not much work left for the heavy bombers to do in any parts of Germany that I have seen until they invent a bomb that digs 50 feet deep before exploding. For the people of Germany have gone underground where they live and work in a long series of cellars, "mouseholes," from one house to the next. When the bombs smash up the empty stone boxes above them, they merely shrug and go to the cigarette store three cellars away, through the long winding caverns to get tobacco to smoke in their lamp-lit whitewashed stone basements. Perhaps in all Cologne there are some still living upstairs by day; but I doubt if any of them slept upstairs by night. The beds are downstairs in the shelters, and they have been there a long time. This changes a city's habits: when you live underground, you don't have much need for streets any more, so you just let the rubble from one bombing after another choke up the streets until they are fantastically impassable. The military made them clear up any number of main communications streets in order to let military traffic flow, but hundreds of the side streets are mere piles of rubble, more than a story high.

The Germans we saw, hundreds of them in their caves, were universally pale, indifferent, adequately to well-dressed, and glad that the war is over for them. In travelling day after day to some two score cities large and small that we have conquered in the past two weeks, I have the strongest impression that the Germans aren't fighting for Hitler or Nazism, but are under the delusion that they are fighting for the *Vaterland*. When you talk to them, whole groups will join in denouncing Hitler in the dirtiest German phrases, most often calling him "*schatz und dung*." You may think that this is merely another German trick which they do to curry favor with Americans, but I don't believe you would think so if you had seen it. Many of them seem to loathe Hitler although many others regard him as the Japs are said to regard Hirohito, as someone god-like and above all this, who is merely saddened by the sad past his "bad advisors" have brought his beloved country. But they all love their soldier boys frantically: you have never seen such passionate, loving cheers as they sent to truckloads or a marching German column of prisoners shambling past.

The other thing you notice is how they creep upstairs now when the heavy bombers pass, watching with shrinking relief from doorways as they see the bombers sailing on past, but shaking their heads over what is in store for the Germans over the Rhine. The fear of air power is so deep in them that you will see little children with their heads buried in their mothers' aprons shuddering, or peeping fearfully from behind her skirts up at the terrible skies. The children also are generally well-dressed, but pale and apparently undernourished. The main business aboveground of the Cologne population apparently was the twice-daily trip with two great pitcher cans to get water, and usually the strongest remaining male or female was assigned to do this for his cellar group, much as the western pioneers used to send out their best scout to kill buffalo for the caravan. The eerie, dead, flat silence was broken as you went deeper into Cologne by the occasional thump of guns somewhere up the dead streets.

Then we came on Major General Maurice Rose of the Third Armored, slick and polished, tall and confident. He invited us to follow his jeep to the various fronts through the town. Although following generals in this war is a good easy way to get killed, it is hard to refuse. On the far left of the town the Ford factory, politely untouched by American bombers, had been captured and the troops were on the river almost down to the end of the semicircle there. General Rose's Third Armored was driving straight into town from the southwest with the Cathedral and bridge as objectives. On the left fringe of his front we parked flat up against some houses to look down a street to an underpass. "The underpass is the front," said the general softly. "Stay in these doors as they keep opening up with machine guns along here." Here the General ordered doughs to work their way down through the park and pinch off the machine guns so that the tanks could roll through about a mile left of the Cathedral. Then we left for the main attack axis, down the Venloer Strasse right at the river.

There is a feeling you get to know very quickly in war: that of menacing loneliness. You sight down the long empty street as your jeep rolls slowly ahead, listening and looking. If you see a GI in a doorway ahead, you feel relieved and happy: "among friends." If you don't see anyone, you don't stop or turn around as plenty of that gives someone plenty of time to sight on you; you just roll the jeep quickly to the nearest wall and duck into doorways until you are sure it is okay ahead. Gradually we rolled on down until we could hear our tanks shooting at something and occasional bursts of German and American machine guns. I was with Max Lerner of *PM*. We had been joined by Howard Smith of CBS (*Last Train from Berlin*), his handsomeness obscured by a three-day black beard. Here the General told us that rubble more than anything else ahead was holding us up from reaching the Cathedral. He ordered a bulldozing tank into the attack supported by a couple of heavies and four light tanks. We waited until things would clear up a little. I went over to look at a dead German. He had been lying flat on his stomach, spang in the middle of the street, firing his machine gun at the doughs flitting from door to door when a tank burst had hit behind him. He seemed to have no wounds and wasn't bleeding. He was now on his back about ten feet away, both hands clenched very hard, lying easily on a pile of bricks, his green uniform brilliant in the grey afternoon. A potato masher lay near his hand.[148] Howard Smith found a Czech who needed three or four consecutive haircuts and some little German boys and talked to them; Max Lerner found a Jew who had lived underground for six months. I talked to the American tankers. Out of the street ahead which was supposedly jammed, suddenly dashed a press jeep. In it were Frank Conniff, the brave cheery *Hearst* feature reporter and Everett Walker, the slim, grey-haired *Herald Tribune* writer. They had been up to the Rathaus, about 200 yards from the Cathedral, having moved up crouched alongside a tank until they could see the Cathedral plainly. They said that there were quite a few snipers about and then left on the long ride back to do their stories in time. We decided to go on up. Three blocks up the lonely street where doughs still crouched quietly in the doors we came on Morley Cassidy of the *Philadelphia Inquirer*. He had stopped there, because a sniper's bullet had ricocheted off the pavement nearby a few minutes before. Nearby was tall, grey, able Hugh Schuck of the *New York Daily News* who had walked alongside the first American tank with Conniff and Walker. We decided to go up some more as snipers are as bad one place as another. After another block we left our jeeps and walked along pretty fast. We passed the concrete memorial with the huge wolf on the top, with the three bas-relief heads of Trajan, Hadrian and Antonius Pius on its side. Opposite it stood the once-great red-brick building which was the *Rathaus* of Cologne. Four American tanks were in line along the street. The battle was on just above, in the square before the Cathedral, two short German blocks of about five houses each up the street. Here we found some British reporters clustered with a few medics in one of the auto entrances to the Rathaus. An American tanker lay wounded there on the pavement, his leg smashed.

For the tank, beside which Conniff, Walker and Schuck had walked, had suddenly been smashed wide open in front by a German bazooka. This boy had been brought out under direct machine gun fire by a red-haired American medic, whose name no one had gotten.[149] The tanker kept smoking and trying not to cry. Soon a medic stretcher truck came up, and he was lifted up and started off on the long journey back. Lieut. Robert Cook of the Charley company of the 36th Armored Infantry of the Third Armored Division organized a little rescue party to get a tank lieutenant who was believed alive in the tank although his legs were gone. Six men started up the street when suddenly off ran Meyer Levin, the short pudgy little novelist (*The Old Punch*) who is now a reporter for the *Jewish Overseas News* and has more guts than life expectancy, his rosy cheeks grimly set. I admired his courage, but told myself it would be a pity to get shot after coming all this way without getting into the Cathedral. Lerner and I then found by talking to the doughs that they had some civilians in the cellar and that one of them claimed to be a Belgian. We went downstairs into the air raid shelter and wound through the usual pitchy caverns into the usual central collection of bunks around a candle-lit table. There sat three women and an old man. The man and one woman were German civilians, happy at being captured; the two younger women were Belgian girls, captured by the Germans in the Bulge and imprisoned by the Gestapo for being friendly with the enemy. We pricked up our ears at that word Gestapo and soon she told us that the Gestapo HQ and prison for the area was only one block to the rear. I asked how much they had to eat. She said two slices of brown bread twice a day and water, plus a pail of water-soup twice weekly. She took us through a labyrinth of caverns under the Rathaus to the Gestapo building, a neat little, three-story, grey concrete house just like any other town house. Down the cellars were nearly two stories of concrete cells about thirteen by eight feet in size. She said twenty-four men were kept in one cell usually, not because there weren't plenty more cells, but because that involved less watching and also pleased the Nazi sadists more. She and three other girls had lived in one tiny cell and had been allowed to work as charwomen. Upstairs we went through the offices. There I found a *Waffen SS* helmet which I gave to Lerner as he is going home.[150]

Outside, in a bomb crater, were still smoldering the Gestapo documents and papers in a great heap. Flimsies and vital papers had been burned first; only Nazi law books and propaganda material were still unburnt. Beyond, near a wall, the Belgian girl showed us where the Gestapo had hung ninety-four male prisoners a few days before when it was clear that the Americans would take the town and they didn't want to bother evacuating them to the rear. As we came out of the prison, the Germans sent over some screaming meemies, their deadly rockets, and we all, doughs and correspondents, flattened against the walls, and one, the muddy street as the rockets exploded nearby, shaking loose bricks in clouds of dust.

Back in the *Rathaus* we wandered upstairs with some doughs who had just been ordered by the Colonel to get for him the *Burgomeister's* flag of Cologne.[151] The great hall is all smashed: it had obviously been used lately as an officers' quarters. The doughs' search was fruitless. One reason perhaps is that Lerner and I already had been given the only two Nazi flags captured in Cologne, and those flags were safe in our trench coat pockets. In the main lobby on the stairs had been a granite pillar, topped with a bronze head of Adolf Hitler with bronze letters tacked on the stone saying: *Ein Volk, Ein Reich, Ein Fuehrer*. Some dough had given the pillar a burst and had knocked off Hitler's head, on which numerous doughs apparently had then committed a nuisance. The bronze letters were loose: I picked off the letter H.

Back in the street things were still stalled. Most of the correspondents had gone back to press camps to meet their deadlines although a few had followed Meyer Levin after awhile up to the smashed American tank to find that the wounded lieutenant had bled to death. Occasional rocket bursts were hitting near the street, but the prisoners were beginning to file back in a steady stream of about 10 at a crack, middle-aged men mostly. The doughs in the doorways asked as they always do: "Why the hell do you do this when you could be back home?" "Oh, things are tough all over," I always say and talk about the cigarette shortage, etc. back there, but they know I am kidding.

After awhile we got impatient. That's how people get killed. I remember one minesweeper I talked to about his work, and how he said that after awhile he got sick of bending over his mine detector, watching the dial every time it registered a nail or a piece of shrapnel. So after he would get tired of bending over, he would just put the mine-sweep on his shoulder and walk straight through a mine field with a what-the-hell feeling, and then tape off his path as the cleared route. But it was getting on in the afternoon and the battle was pounding steadily ahead without moving. Our tanks were still stalled where they were behind the first smashed tank. The doughs were having lots of trouble clearing the German bazookists and burp-gunners out of the cellars around the Cathedral Square. We walked up, ducking from tank to tank, Lerner, Cassidy, Levin and I. As we reached the last house beside the Square, a dough said from a doorway: "Keep way over to the right as you try to cross as the Germans are using bazookas against guys." I didn't like that phrase "try to cross" but I asked him: "What do you mean, bazookas against guys?" He said that they want to use up all their ammunition before they surrender, and they can't get over here where they can hit any more of our tanks.

As we came out into the Square we could see at last the brilliant blaze of a Nazi tank burning. It had been hit about fifteen minutes before, and clouds of smoke had drifted up against the tremendous height of the Cathedral from it. Now we could see it plainly about ten yards to our left. Nothing burns like a tank except possibly an airplane. They burn for hours, brilliantly. Just before we crossed, some prisoners came back with a dough. One of them was complaining that his watch had been taken. Lerner asked him: "What did you do in Russia? in France and in Belgium?" Another Nazi, obviously punchy, his eyes dazed, lunged toward Lerner. One of the doughs raised his rifle, his trigger finger itching. Another one kicked the Nazi back into line and they lurched on back. One dough said: "Go ahead, shoot the bastards." He said it quietly. The itchy-fingered one raised his rifle and sighted it while the prisoners looked on helplessly, and the other doughs leaned casually, watching. I tapped him on the arm and said: "If we act like Germans, we are no better than they are." He dropped his rifle and said angrily: "They shot my two best buddies when they were captured. I saw it. I was a prisoner for forty-eight hours in the battle of the Bulge, and they shot my lieutenant and sergeant." He was sweating, but not really angry. He was just helpless with frustration. He had been brought up too decently to shoot anyone in cold blood and he knew it—but he wanted to get back at the Germans somehow. Just as we crossed the Square our tanks finally rolled ahead so we crouched beside them as they make wonderful cover, unless they are hit. Ammunition from the burning tank was exploding, but there was no firing from the left side of the Square. The Germans, except for the snipers, had been driven to the outside left rear corner of the Cathedral which is a couple of hundred yards from the river. We and the tanks crouched snugly against the right wall of the Cathedral. From farther on our right, a machine gun opened up towards us from the rear, but a quick snapshot from the lead tank silenced it before things got uncomfortable. Then the tanks nosed on around the rear of the Cathedral to begin a steady thunderous barrage against the German positions just to the rear of the Cathedral.

Here we were at last, standing in a welter of captured Lugers, bayonets, officers' hats, empty Champagne bottles from secret hoards, opened by the first GIs, and the two newsreel men who had been there for about an hour were trying to start four small German cars, three of them the smart little Opels. Lerner and Levin wanted to go downstairs into the famed basement hospital and air raid shelter underneath the Cathedral. Cassidy and I wanted to go into the Cathedral itself. Cassidy who is steady and careful went out into the deadly open and tried to get in the front doors. He came back swiftly to grumble that the doors were jammed. He went on downstairs with Lerner. I asked Levin about the side doors just above us. He said that the third one would open if you kicked it hard—that he had stood inside for a moment. I ran up and kicked open the door of the Cathedral of Cologne.

The Cathedral dominates all of Cologne and all the plain about the great city for miles. No matter where you approach, you see always two great spires looming dark with age against the sky. They gave me the prickly feeling I get when I see something I think is beautiful. I had watched the church longingly from down the street as the smoke of battle drifted in blue puffs against the black-brown weathered Gothic curlicues that had been restored sometime in the last century. But the Cathedral is another tremendous testimony to air power's accuracy. For these towers are especially unique in that they are there at all in the miles and miles of roofless desolation wherein no tall buildings stand. All around it everything has been smashed as the rail station, rail yards and bridge approaches have always been a most prime target. Inside, the Germans had sandbagged the heavier statues and then carefully bricked them in almost impregnably. The Cathedral has suffered somewhat from blast concussions. There is no glass in the windows although I suppose that the Germans long ago removed that. But the window frames are still there except for one or two on the right rear near the river, and the great vaulted roof is almost intact. The floor is a mass of minor stone rubble where pieces have crumbled from the pillars under the concussions nearby; the benches have been gathered together in groups. The confessional boxes are pretty well smashed for some reason. The altar has been removed, but the little pulpit near it is only scarred. Our doughs had had orders not to fire a shot at the Cathedral unless absolutely necessary.

Entering the Cathedral was almost my last entrance. Two doughs had just kicked in the front door, and one of them raised his M-1 to take a snapshot at me until I yelled: "Hey! Stop it!" They came over; both were very nervous; one of them with a walkie-talkie on his back, trembled so that the little aerial finger on his instrument trembled all the time. I told them I was scared too, which was no lie as the Germans were just through the wall to the left of us, firing at our lead tank. I told them that this was one of the most famous buildings in the world; that all the papers in America would carry the story tomorrow morning, March 7th. They said: "Yeah? Whaddaya know? Ain't much of a place right now though, is it?" We stood silent looking around. The tank guns outside shook the place. Little green lamp shades hang in the Cathedral on cords hundreds of feet long from the dim-distant recesses of the roof. When the tank guns spoke, the green shades would dance in order down the long main aisle. After awhile we left; the tanks had moved farther on. We went downstairs to see the hospital where the fresh wounded crew of the Nazi tank had been brought. Then we rode back in the night; six of us in a jeep in the absolute dark. Our jeep had no cat's-eye crosses on the headlights, and in combat zones you can't use the big lamps so Cassidy had to hold a flashlight over the windshield top, focused on the road all the way back, some 50 odd miles in a rain that came down harder and colder, it seemed, each mile. But some of the way was lit by burning factories, burning homes, and burning haystacks.

One or two other reporters said that they had been in the Cathedral too. I don't doubt it although the doughs on the Cathedral steps said no one else but Meyer Levin had been in. But this war is full of misinformation.

When we got back an RAF friend told me that of all the bombed cities he has personally investigated for the RAF in Africa, Italy, France and Germany, this was the most-perfectly scientific job. I was prepared to agree although both Julich and Duren seem to me the most absolutely flattened and powered cities of all the clobbered places I have seen. He said: "What did you think of the railroad station?" I said blankly, "What railroad station?" "Aha," he exclaimed triumphantly, "that's the perfect answer."

SIDNEY OLSON CABLE 31
FROM PARIS TO DAVID HULBURD
SENT MARCH 10, 1945; REC'D MARCH 10, 1945

For Battlefronts
Attention Mr. Walker:

As possible aids to Zinder research for the Dempsey cover, Wert suggests I send afterthoughts on the Rhine crossing difficulties supplementing my *Life* piece on Simpson in which the engineering problems were discussed.

What follows is personal strategy only after map-study. The first thing is to find the juiciest possible military objectives within quick striking distance once past the Rhine. If you look along the Rhine from Nijmegen all the way down to Coblenz you will find that the most major objectives within fewest miles are Essen, Dortmund, Mulheim, Bochum, Becklinghausen, Gelsenkirchen, almost in that order of importance. All these are concentrated in the Ruhr heartland within a few miles of each other and within a few miles of the Rhine and all are substantially north of Dusseldorf and south of Xanten and Wesel where the Nazis are making the fiercest last stand of all the Rhine pockets in a prolonged bridgehead maintenance. Solingen and Wuppertal south of Dusseldorf also seem the primest easily reachable targets once the Rhine crossing is achieved. You can write your own strategy whether the American or British armies will cross the Rhine south of the Ruhr and slash north or cross north of the Ruhr and slash south. All this I base on the personal view that the upper Ruhr is the primest primary objective with Berlin secondary as its capture would apparently wreck almost instantly the German war-making capacity no matter what the stockline program has been. Another thing to bear in mind in taking the opposite view, however, is that bridging the Rhine is slightly easier from Cologne southeast to Bonn and Coblenz et al and north of Dusseldorf. Particularly north of Duisburg the Rhine gets the fullest effect of rainfall and fluctuations in the watershed from the upper reaches naturally so the difficulties I described in an earlier cable of bridging with fullest allowance for variance in stream depths are increased proportionately. Strategists in Army groups, however, have long since made their decisions and even now the fullest preparations are under way along all the chosen bridge sites. As I have reported before part of the Rhine crossing stockpile of boats, bridge materials, etc., was used necessarily in the Roer crossing when flood made the Roer a substantial barrier, but this is already replaced for (by?) the heaviest stores so that no Army engineers are now lacking equipment.

In the map-study, Editor Walker and Bob Chapin might closely ponder the rail and road networks on both sides of possible crossing sites to consider the strategic advantages to both sides. For example, what seems to me personally an excellent crossing site and (omission—checking) but it has some strategic disadvantages such as the fact that five main roads center in Wesel on the German side while on the American side the Venlo-Goldern road crisscrosses only the Neuss-Rheinberg-Xanten road so that in effect the Americans would have only two supply routes while the Germans would have the flexibility of five such roads. That this can only delay and hamper operations while not precluding them was most strikingly illustrated in the recent Ninth Army push from Julich north to the Rhine. There actually was only one main road north running through Mersch Garzweiler parallel to the Erft near Grevenbroich and then north to Neuss. For several days parts of this road had to be used to supply both the Second Armored Division as well as the Twenty-Ninth Division to name only two. As the Second Armored is practically beefed up to small-army size, this meant day and night hub-to-hub, hood-to-tail traffic in both directions just to get the attack moving. Two generals separately told me they could have reached the Rhine three days faster if they had had three roads instead of one, and I cite this in detail only to illustrate most simply the background of the Rhine crossing site selection problems. You can just as shrewdly project the mile by mile advantages and disadvantages of other sites up and down the river in both directions as far as you care to. Having been with the Ninth Army I am naturally prejudiced in the unit's favor as regards territory and fighting capacities and hope this will be helpful in what I regard as a very tough cover-writing job. I discussed this with Zinder yesterday in Brussels and he generally agrees with this analysis of the crossing problems.

[1945] [DIARY]

    Mar 11 arr Paris.

    Mar 12 Scribe, bad cold. Jack Parker.

    Mar 13 Move Lanc.[152] Scribe.

    Mar 14 Wed Lan[c]

    Mar 15 Thu

    Mar 16 Fri Rodgers Mme [?] Pelgrin [?] Bigart[153]

    Mar 17 Sat Thibault Champrosay,[154] _____ [?], Therese

SIDNEY OLSON CABLE 32
FROM PARIS TO DAVID HULBURD
SENT MARCH 17, 1945; REC'D MARCH 17, 1945

For USAW, attention Welch and Alexander:

I think the projected USAW story about Cologne most excellent; I am very sorry I am not on the ground personally as it would be a wonderful eyewitnesser, but I left when Cologne fell and am recovering from a bad cold in Wert's fur-lined foxhole with a champagne fountain playing afternoons, but am returning to the front when Wert rings the bell soon. Throughout eight weeks I worked regularly with military government types in Aachen, Alsdorf, Rheydt, Munchen-Gladbach, however, so the following points may be useful.

The first thing to realize is the magnitude of the Job. Several thousand Gis in a city, all working at war jobs, simply cannot keep eyes on thousands and thousands of civilians in the wilderness of ruins. The main initial task of MP officers is to keep the Germans off the streets, but that is no particular control in cities where the Germans long since mouse-holed their way from basement to basement for ease in underground life, often for stretches of blocks. There is nothing to prevent a German from going cross-country at night to turn up as an inhabitant of another town, for the Rhineland from Wesel to Krefeld to Neuss to Cologne is one vast stretch of farmland, flat open country criss-crossed with countless ancient farm roads and bypaths. The second main fact is that thus far, despite possible ease of sabotage, etc., the Germans are utterly docile, utterly subservient—even more, eagerly cooperative. They are conquered and they know it; their great desire generally is to forget the whole thing and return to the most peaceful possible existence. Goodbye to all that, is their heartfelt feeling as they watch the bombers carry the old terror on to cities beyond them. This lack of sabotage, this utter quiet is so contrary to the expected Hitler underground that AMG[155] officials frankly cannot believe their senses. When the Nazis occupied France apparently every good French husband clipped at least a few communication wires every night on his way home from work and after dinner joined the fellows in killing a few Nazis. But so far as can be found out thus far no German has tampered, interfered with or shot at any American or American installation. The only arrests have been of some youthful types who made faces—honestly—at some German cops who were too obsequiously currying favor with Americans. The law's dignity must be upheld. This is a great fact in the history of this war; apparently the Nazi ideal is something you fight for until you are licked—but not after that. Just consider the Norwegians, still blowing up their own fine buildings and bridges years after occupation. The MG characters are perfectly prepared to be stern and severe as need be and won't be caught napping if an underground gradually emerges. But the great fact remains that there are no signs of its emergence yet, while all signs point to the opposite attitude among the Germans. And always remember that at the front the captured Germans will always tell you that they hope we reach Berlin first, before the Russians. In short, you have perfect conditions for sabotage in a great conquered area difficult to police, and you don't have any of that sabotage.

[1945] [DIARY]

Mar 18 Sun. Party for It Trib[156] at Lanc & Maison des[157]
Mar 19 Mon
Mar 20 Tues Lan Fr, Ballet
Mar 21 Wed Walks to Quais.
Mar 22 Thurs
Mar 23 Fri
Mar 24 Sat. Lancaster: Pere Lachaise

RESTRICTED

Supreme Headquarters
Allied Expeditionary Forces
Main, APO 757

MARCH 24, 1945
Subject: Orders
To: Mr. Sidney Olson, (US) (War Co), SHAEF Reg. No. 940,
    Public Relations Division, Supreme headquarters, AEF.

Richard Stokes, (US) (War Co), SHAEF Reg. No. 451
Public Relations Division, Supreme Headquarters, AEF.

You will proceed via military aircraft, government motor and/or rail transportation on or about 25 March 1945, from present station to Headquarters, Twelfth Army Group, to carry out the instructions of the Director, Public Relations Division, Supreme Headquarters, AEF.
By direction of the Supreme Commander,

Hilton H. Ellison
Captain, AGD
Asst. Adjutant General

SIDNEY OLSON CABLE UNNUMBERED[158]
FROM PARIS TO DAVID HULBURD
SENT MARCH 24, 1945; REC'D MARCH 24, 1945

Part II

Harry, I strongly suggest that you should write a piece sometime during the next two months which would update from your Days of Wrath piece in *Life* at Pearl Harbor time.[159] The text might well be your own belief in the marvelous recuperative powers of men which will now undergo an extraordinary test period. I am still betting on Simpson's army reaching Berlin before the Russians, and think Lang an excellent choice for this story. I hope to open the Berchtesgaden Bureau personally (and am already picking my staff from the ranks of the *Comedie Francaise*).

To: Mrs. Sidney Olson
Bear River City
Utah, U.S.A.

From: Sidney Olson
War Correspondent
P.R.D. SHAEF
A.P.O. 757

MARCH 25, 1945
Dearest darling:

    I left the First Army right after the Fall of Cologne and went to Paris, where I have been for nearly two weeks. In that time I didn't do one lick of work; I didn't even write you a single letter; I merely recovered from a very bad cold, and sat around on the terraces of Paris cafes, usually in Montmartre, playing gin rummy with Leslie Midgley for a franc per point. I was quite low and bedraggled to be honest; I'd stayed at the front or very near it working very hard from my work with the air forces in England during December all the way through January and February and part of March.

    I was very tired. I just missed pneumonia, it seems, but the army takes very good care of you, and stood ready to load me with penicillin in case I got it. Now I'm well and feel wonderful, honest. Paris did it for me just because it is the most beautiful, the most perfect city in the world, and is probably where we will settle down to spend the rest of our lives. The pneumonia thing was all around: the day Mitch Davenport got to Paris for the *American Mercury* he went off to the hospital with pneumonia, even before he'd been to the front. He's getting better though now. The only work I've done is to study my French and I've now gotten so I can carry on fairly well with taxicab drivers, hotel waiters, etc. I can also understand quite well most conversations, but have so little vocabulary that it's difficult for me to answer correctly any intelligent question. This is infuriating, and I'm working at it at least an hour a day from now on.

    Wert took very good care of me in his apartment, a fur-lined foxhole if ever I saw one.[160] But I'll write you all about Paris in a long letter soon.

This letter is from the Twelfth Army Group headquarters where I arrived today, full of beans. How Les laughed and laughed at my misspent youth when he saw me wolfing candy bars just like you and Whitney—after sneering at candy all these years. Les is fine. He got five letters from Jean yesterday. Hmmm. My last one from you was dated about February 24, darling dear. It can't be just the mails; everyone all around me gets letters dated March 14; and I've had letters from the folks right along. The last was only a few days ago. What's wrong, BG? You must have been getting my letters. Have you gotten the Brussels packages I mailed before your birthday? The Paris office will mail some more stuff for you tomorrow, it includes two blankets (baby), a picture, some ashtrays (a set of six); all liberated pieces from Joe Goebbels castle in Rheydt (liberated by me); a pair of galoshes the Canadians gave me; and one of the only two flags captured in Cologne. I ripped it off the Gestapo wall myself. I love you. Your slave.

[1945] [DIARY]

Mar 25 Sun Goodbye to Paris
Mar 26 Mon the ride from Paris
Mar 27 Namur

[1945] [DIARY]

Oberstein, Germany, March 28, 1945

Twelfth Army Group Press Camp
McGowan, Redding (chess, bds)
Yarborough, Despuys[161]—the lighter
The phone records
Capt Jimmy Campbell
John Hall[162]—The British brdcasters
Dave Anderson
Dick Hottelet. The briefing
The chateau. Namur. Gilland.
The spelling of dissipated. Authority on spelling or dissipation? B-l-o-w.
The flight to Luxembourg. (Bastogne)
The sick lieutenant.
The airfield—clobbered planes, K-rations, Iowa—those to whom its still an airplane ride, his father in Iowa.
To Trier: to Oberstein: the look of the mountains.
The road: the crater filled with horses. The walk around the town with Jack Fleischer.
Dinner with Maj. Owens.
Bob Wear . . . Evelyn Irons . . . Pete Huss [?] & Zeppelins . . . Giant . . . Ed Ball
The worship of Patton . . .
Maj. Quirk[163] Capt Drake Capt Lamb

[1945] [DIARY]

March 29 interview with Patton. Hacker [?] newspix. Col. Codman of Bost__ [?] Pattons aide. Sheahan of Chi Trib, artist. Louis de Roche Robt Richards bc brit. The two Lucys of press camp.

[James Quirk, General Patton's public relations officer (PRO), set up Olson's interview with Patton. Quirk wrote to his wife on March 29:][164]

MARCH 29, 1945

I am busy with a lot of things. General Paton's [*sic*] Picture will be on the cover of *Time* for next week and Sid Olsen [*sic*] of *Time* was here for the story to go with it. I gave him a lot of material, gave him hell about some of the previous articles in *Time* long ago, and took him over to see the general this morning. The General was as interesting as usual and Olsen was duly impressed. The session had a couple of interesting things purely from my stand point. We were chatting about one thing or another when Olsen said, "The Major said this morning that the Germans will probably quit when they have lost the last piece of high ground." The general looked at me with a somewhat surprised expression and said, "That's a very intelligent remark. Very intelligent . . . and quite true." He seemed surprised that such a remark should come from a PRO.

SIDNEY OLSON CABLE UNNUMBERED[165]
FROM GERMANY TO DAVID HULBURD, *TIME* MAGAZINE
SENT MARCH 29, 1945; REC'D MARCH 29, 1945

Attention: Luce, Matthews, Longwell, Hulburd

Unpublishable:

I suggest Adolf Hitler as the cover two weeks hence.[166] There is plenty of bloody fighting going on but it's very much like Joe Louis circling a groggy opponent looking for the exact spot to produce a quick kill and it's very hard to realize that this is finally it but, to put it personally, this is the first time I've been optimistic since the Spanish Civil War in 1936 and the terror is on in Germany as the armored divisions roam with seeming wildness, but actually according to plans, sealing off great pockets of bewildered, bedraggled, transport-less troops who are either too young or too old and thousands of docile civilians who smile hopefully, but without drawing return smiles from the stony-faced doughfeet. I'm sure you've already planned it in great detail, but want to go on record in favor of one *Life* issue devoted to V-Day pictures from all around the world with main text pieces on London and Chunking. The London piece could be a tender masterpiece as those ineffably weary Britons realize they can unkink their stiffened backbones at last. And for the Hitler cover, in case war is not ending in another two weeks, I believe it could be a swell piece of description of contemporary Germany, the fruits of Hitlerism. I believe Percy Knauth's arrival well timed as he saw Germany before and should be able well to evaluate the differences. And I believe Lang, Zinder and myself might also be helpful. I also want to stress the absolute docility of the Germans and the utter lack of any underground or even minor sabotage so far, despite such baloney propaganda on this subject, and this atmosphere is weird; I'll try to describe it in an accompanying short piece.

Attention: Walsh and Walker:

I arrived at the Third Army press camp by sitting on a lieutenant's lap in the single rear seat of a Stinson L-5. When an army's on the move you can't find anything, even the enemy, let alone a pinpoint Piper Cub airstrip. The lieutenant got airsick and stayed airsick. But times are tough all over I guess. Hope to see Patton tomorrow and will file something every night this week although how good I daren't predict, and will cut loose about Saturday to try to catch the Fourth Armored Division for the action end of the story. But the war may be over before I can catch them at the rate they're going.

Sidney Olson Cable 34
From Germany to David Hulburd
Sent March 29, 1945; Rec'd March 29, 1945

For Battlefronts for background on Patton Cover:

Here are merely some highlights of one typical day's operations of some of Patton's rampaging divisions as they casually and smoothly perform incredible military feats. One division smashed eight miles east through fairly tough opposition. Another advanced eight miles over two intact bridges it had captured. Another advanced four miles. Another division crossed the Rhine after midnight, and then crossed the Main at 0300 hours to enter Wiesbaden whose peacetime population was 170,000. In short, they made two major river crossings in force within three hours. Another cleared a hardhead town and smashed into Frankfurt. Another cleared towns. Another crossed the Main in force. And the beautiful 4th Armored went 27 miles in one direction and 13 in another and has no intention of stopping for tea. This is only part of the picture, and this is only one army of the six which are all crashing on into Germany. The above operations were for today, Wednesday, incidentally.

General Patton's troops have recently overrun many beautiful little German hill towns in the Rhineland. The first flower buds are just changing from pale green to white on the pear trees that line the little valley roads that wind among the carefully forested hills. The blooms make the valleys shine with a pale shimmer of white in the stretches of fresh green along the purple hills. At intervals along the roads at alternate strategic positions are the shattered remains of German concrete pillboxes set cunningly to command all approaches. The ruins are irony at its prettiest. The pillboxes are the fruits of how much labor, how much skillful defensive design, and how incredibly much expense! Yet they were blown by the Germans as they retreated from one of Patton's traps only to fall into another farther down the road. Perhaps they blew them so that when they make that imaginary recovery someday, they will not be defensively useful to us. Anyway there they stand, melancholy memorials among the pear and apple trees to the New Order.

Along the little valley roads are the junk of war, the crunched helmets and the equipment thrown away in panicky retreat, the charred hulks of tanks, guns, trucks and automobiles.[167] The windshield wipers and seat cushions have already been stripped from the trucks and autos: the doughfeet like to be comfortable. Dead horses line the roads too although one enormous dive-bombed crater smack in the middle of the road is now partly filled with 12 dead horses which the efficient Germans were both burying and using as road filler at the same time. But they didn't have time to finish filling the hole, and neither does the 3rd Army which just shoved a bulldozer around one side of the crater to make a new road. Farther along the road at regular intervals are groups of German civilians working steadily and phlegmatically at unrooting the earth-filled double row of log roadblocks which perhaps the same men put in place only weeks ago. These blocks are built of two rows of massive pointed tree trunks stabbed into the roads tightly together with 3 to 4 feet of packed earth-fill insulating the wall against artillery. But what good are such careful defenses all the way back through Germany if enormous tank columns are far behind them, stabbing swiftly between and around the strong points? The little hill towns are only slightly damaged by bombing as they were never strategic targets. It seems odd to see a German town in which housewives are actually washing windows. Usually there are no windows, of course. As a matter of fact, the whole is difficult to capture. You want to stay in the doorways or skulk swiftly along the walls of the houses because you know you are in Germany, and there may be snipers. It takes time to realize that this is actually far in the rear.

The civilians stroll the streets as civilians stroll any streets in the world except that these duck out of the way of the rolling trucks and tanks with a nervous realization that the Americans don't give a damn whether they run over them or not. The French, Dutch and Belgians long ago lost this traffic timidity, and many Americans are happy to drive along roads where the people skip out of the way. The teen-age girls saunter along giggling as teen-age girls always do, obviously anxious to strike up an acquaintanceship with the good-looking casual GIs, but uncertain of their reception. They are all quite well dressed, without style but comfortable and with clothes of good material. The shops are quite adequately supplied, and many a Briton who has lived for years on utility imitations would love to have a crack at these stores. Occasionally along the street will come dispossessed Germans whose house has been commandeered, dragging their belongings in two-wheeled carts. But the general tone is one of business as usual, which is somehow infuriating to see although we have nothing to complain of in their absolute docility. But if you talk to a German, pretty soon you'll find him invariably grumbling at those Nazi brutes who forced him to join the Party, and then subtly changing to a little delicate grumbling about the discomforts of wartime living. This is really infuriating, but a people so thoroughly without real honest news for so many years cannot be expected to appreciate Lidice, Oradour-sur-Glane or Maidanek.[168]

I am too tired now to carry this on. But I intend to keep cracking at this German atmosphere until I am satisfied that I get across some of its unreality.

SIDNEY OLSON CABLE 35
FROM GERMANY TO DAVID HULBURD
SENT MARCH 29, 1945; REC'D MARCH 30, 1945
Datelined Third Army Press Camp

Attention Welch, Walker:

In reading the following research in my Number 35 on Patton please bear in mind Beedle Smith's absolute rule against quoting American generals in stuff sent from the field except for selected quotes in addresses to soldiers. In short, I had a swell interview for a full hour with General Patton, despite war pressure, but you won't know until next October what he said.

As the research will show, I was enormously impressed by Patton. I suggest you read the research as USAW reads reports of the President's press conferences as regards quotes. Under the rigid rules of censorship I may not say what he says regarding any subject or indicate what he thinks. In this case it is a bitter shame as the whole salty quality of Patton shows best in his wonderful mixture of language. The piece will follow this dispatch immediately in transmission to censors but it may be held there for some hours.

I plan to go tomorrow with either the Fourth Armored or other divisions and plan to file to reach you by Sunday morning.

Are you aware that General Gaffey, Patton's great right hand, has been promoted to command of a corps? You might query Graebner re. Gaffey if you want a fill-in from him on Patton.

If Knauth reaches here tonight I will suggest he stay on the ground to clean up and follow queries while I go forward as he will need a brief rest after an intolerable jeep ride, all the way from Wertenbaker to the Twelfth Army Group to here.

For Battlefronts:[169]

General George Patton will be 60 years old next November 11th. That will make 53 years that he has been a military man because he decided on his career when he was seven years old. He remembers the occasion very well, naturally, as men remember the real milestones in their lives. It was on a pleasant day in his California home town in 1892 and he was riding in a carriage with his mother. You should understand that until then he had been strictly a Navy man and believes he may even have had on a sailor suit. But suddenly the decision sprang clearly and fully made into his mind and he has been an Army man ever since.

Some Americans may not yet appreciate the position George Patton holds here, not only in the American Army but all over the continent. Only Eisenhower's name is as familiar to the people of England, France, Belgium, Holland and Germany, of all the American generals.

You notice it first in England, where Patton's name is as important in table talk as that of Montgomery. Other generals may win big battles and the English headlines will read First Army Crosses Rhine or Ninth Army Does Such-and-Such. But when the Third Army moves the headlines avalanche the words Patton Strikes Again. This is exactly the case in Belgium, Holland and France and Germany. But there is more to it than this: The real argument that goes on at dinner tables among civilians of these nations is in effect and endeavor to answer finally the question, Is Patton the greatest general this war has produced? If not, why not? If not, who is?

I have had civilians of all the nations mentioned bring up the name of Patton. They all have great confidence in him, even the reserved British, who regard him as something of the same kind of showman as Montgomery. When they meet an American occasionally who has reservations about Patton they are frankly puzzled. They regard him as clearly and obviously the ablest American field commander and wish we had many more like him so that the war would be over sooner. The other nationals mentioned all just plainly adore him. He could spend the rest of his life making triumphal parades through Europe if he wanted to. This phenomenon of absolute confidence, of hero worship, I found first with the R.A.F. in England.

They always wanted to know if I had met Patton. They were keen to find out at first hand what he was like. They thought he had great style. Speaking now only of military men and correspondents at the various press camps, I have found almost none but Patton admirers with the British and Canadian armies and the American Ninth and First. His only detractors were never military men but correspondents who had never served with the Third Army and they always quickly subside under the heat waves of enthusiasm of the other correspondents. Other generals shake their heads with admiration. Some of them imitate him as best they can.

I sketch this background as essential in appreciating the truly towering position of esteem he holds. The slapping incident is dismissed as forgotten water over a blown-out dam.[170]

The first real shock I got was when I learned that Patton's Army has the fewest casualties. That makes you think. The Patton personal theory of warfare, which he believes is as old as any hills in Europe, is about as follows: If a certain objective must be taken and it's going to cost 40 tanks it is better to lose the 40 and get the objective on the first day rather than lose four a day for ten days. I would guess that he believes in letting the Germans know that they are being hit and being hurt; that shock is one of the most primary things in the art of warfare. I would also guess that his flair for those superbly dramatic, quick, slashing strokes might also come from a strong humanitarian streak not usually associated with him. I am sure he wants to save lives.

Some day perhaps the casualties will be reckoned by Armies. At that point it can be confidently predicted that Patton's name will shine brighter than all the rest. The difference is greater than you could possibly guess. Yet no one can say that the Third Army has fought any less than the other armies. Take today, for instance, March 29: One Division gained six miles, another struck 19 miles to move across the Autobahn between Limburg and Frankfurt. Another struck five miles north, another cleared Frankfurt up to the outskirts. The Sixth Armored Division struck five miles to the vicinity of Bad Neuheim, another struck six miles northeast and the fabulous Fourth Armored (whom I try to catch tomorrow) shot 20 miles east into Lauterbach, some 31 miles from Giessen. Another chunk of the Fourth Armored went a mere ten miles east into Ulrichstein. Patton's Third Army is now 140 miles into Germany, the penetration of all American Armies. It has captured 8,790 square miles of Germany as of today. On March 19 alone Patton's Army captured

950 square miles of Germany in one day. Today SHAEF announced that the Fourth Armored Division had received a Presidential citation.

George Patton is much bigger than you expect. He is very tall, very urbane, very polished. He bears himself very much like John J. Pershing once did, very squarely, erectly, with a somewhat smoother dignity than Pershing's gruff stiffness. In fact, he is courtly. These are his company manners, all gracious Southern courtesy. With women, whether WACs, nurses or civilians, he has a special manner of close, courteous attention that thrills them in tingles to the toes. At such times, to speak impressionistically, he is a composite of fine khaki smoothly pressed, of silver-haired urbanity, of a clear, smooth polish that is very impressive, if you follow me surrealistically. He has as many other manners as John Barrymore and some of them are the same kind. For he has one of the absolute requirements of field leadership: whether he has a stomach ache, is depressed or gay, he can instantly sense the attitude that a situation requires of him and then act it out to the bloody hilt.

He is a great actor. I say "great" seriously. He feels his audience quickly, chooses his moods and then runs through them from A to D or even to Z if necessary. No other general is his equal at calling down offenders, but it must instantly be added that no other general even approaches him in inspirational leadership. I can speak only of the armies I have been with, but I have discussed this with correspondents who have been everywhere. It is no joke that the doughfeet would stand up in their foxholes to salute George Patton. Personally, if it were a good time to be in a foxhole, I wouldn't stand up for George Marshall, but that may give you some idea.

Something that would give you a better idea would be the actual total of Americans killed in the Third Army yesterday. The figure is taboo by censorship, but I can tell you that it was unbelievably small. Yet at that slight cost, a veritable tithe of casualties in other armies on a normal day's operations when they are merely shelling the enemy and getting shelled back, Patton's Army had another terrific field day.

What is it? Is the quality of the troops against him any less than that against other armies? I only know what I see, and the Third Army prisoners I have seen are infinitely huskier, younger, stronger, smarter specimens than the conglomeration of streetcar conductors, retired policemen and teen-age kids I saw fighting the Ninth and First Armies throughout February and early March. And remember that Patton is the *bête noire* of the Germans; that their prisoners would (omission—checking) . . . that German soldiers are often said to consider it more honorable to be captured by Patton than by armies they have never heard of; that they always beef up the front opposite Patton very heavily. Patton likes this because the more enemy in front of him, the more he can kill and capture, and thus the sooner the end of the war. Obviously one reason he can go so fast now is that he has repeatedly encircled enormous blocks of Germans, and the Germans cannot forever keep reinforcing only the Patton front.

What he always likes to do is to have someone else hold down the enemy by frontal attack while he slashes him to ribbons with kidney punches. Many years back he said this in a phrase that is hereby twice euphemized: You hold them by the nose while I kick them in the rear. This phrase it is believed has been translated into all languages. (Remember to read this as USAW would handle prex press conference notes.)

I have just been interrupted by the flash that the Fourth Armored Division took 8,000 German prisoners today. If that isn't proof that someone in Time Inc. who chose Patton for the cover is psychic, I don't know what is. Anyway all honor to the cover chooser. As Patton begins to sense what kind of a listener he has, he imperceptibly relaxes and adapts himself. I must admit that he charmed and attracted me as I have not been attracted by a public figure since I first met Franklin Roosevelt in 1930 in Salt Lake City at the Governors' Conference. He is utterly engaging. He put on a marvelous show of military erudition, mixing up exact references to the battles of Alexander the Great with quick monkey-grinning remarks disconcertingly apt in knifing through the tangles of thought. When he found out that I had read the military wisdom of Sun Tzu, the great Chinese military philosopher, courtesy of Roy Alexander, he went off in a literally dazzling burst of military conversation that left me far behind, as he ranged easily from the Battle of Fredericksburg to the battles of Frederick the Great. One of his favorite anecdotes as earlier research may show is the discovery of the cuneiform tablets of the Hittites in 1913. The tablets recorded the solemn agreement by the Hittites and two other groups whose names escape me, but didn't him, never to have wars. But if one did become the aggressor, the other two were pledged to join against the law breaker. As he recalls, with his quick grin, the reason that the tablets were well-preserved is that the other two nations of that earlier Big Three joined up and wiped out the Hittites, somehow overlooking only the tablets. From such anecdotes you might conclude that like all readers of military history, he may be naturally pessimistic about this war ending all wars. I would guess that he was although I am certain that he would say that this is the last war for him.

Incidentally he doesn't want to be called Old Blood and Guts. This was the first thing I was told when we were introduced. His reason: the troops have never called him that.

Another thing to remember about Patton in assessing his stature as an American general is that most of the time he has been operating with the smallest or next to the smallest of all American armies in this theater. You can best assess the importance of that fact in New York. One most important thing is this: with both the Ninth and the First Armies I tried hard to study tactics, and watched with admiration as they carefully made river crossings by companies and then battalions, then joined the battalions to make division bridgeheads which were then carefully linked up and in two more days became corps bridgeheads as they were beefed up. Finally beyond the corps bridgeheads, the troops got some more extra elbow-room and set up what is called the base for the armor. Then the armored division was turned loose and it went like hell.

Now consider the case of George Patton who I would guess doesn't like to stand still for a month ringing a bell to let the Germans know he is coming. He threw an infantry division plus one regiment across and then, when the commanders often take time out to build up, he had the division stand aside while he slammed his power through and beyond the Rhine. Then it went straight on through, by-passing strong points, and going on and on and on while the bridgeheads were built up far behind them by the infantry divisions who then went like hell to try to outdo the armor. It is no secret now that when Patton decided to cross the Rhine his army was not ready in the sense that other generals get their armies ready and then lay down artillery barrages etc. But he set a time 48 hours hence and told his Chief of Staff to get cracking. Orders buzzed and throbbed all over the army furiously as divisions uprooted themselves and loaded up. There was the varying against (exact cable reading) seismic spectacle of an army getting itself off the ground and getting mobile. Then George Patton took another look at the map and at his inner crystal ball and calmly told his Chief of Staff that he was giving the whole thing up [sic] 24 hours: the armor was to cross the Rhine that very night. Where others would have merely fainted away or sweatily argued that it was impossible, Patton's men just grunted from one end of the army to the other and said affectionately: so the old such and such wants us to go tonight, hey! Well, we'll go—and tell the Russians to watch out for us. And they did it; and the operation was another Patton special that will be studied with admiration by military students for generations.

It must be remembered that Patton does not brood and ponder and sweat over the maps. I would guess that he would say that it would make him nervous. He is much more like a quarterback who doesn't stop to think how far it is to the goal line, or how desperate is his own plight, but has suddenly observed that the opposing left tackle is getting tired and hurt and begins pouring plays through left tackle until suddenly he busts through for a touchdown. (omission—checking) . . . thinks the chess instinct too, and Patton used to play chess because I would guess that he had read that many generals had studied the game.

It is the instinct of leadership. He is full of that. That is what accounts for his instinctive showmanship, and is what makes duller greyer souls deplore his knack of the dramatic. Frankly I would guess that he deplores those stiff self-conscious Americans who are allergic to the real dramas of life and perhaps considers himself an American in the less self-conscious tradition of great Americans. It must be remembered that if some American general knelt in prayer today at a battlefield called Valley Forge that there would be scores of cynical littlings who would sneer that such a thing was an obvious publicity stunt, and in very poor taste. For Patton is not the least self-conscious in the sense of having learned to act. He acts naturally; it is a part of him. I personally believe that he is genuine and agree with the English and the Continental who know when to enjoy a great show put on with living people. I harp on the English because I respect their own still reserve; they are the first to deplore the phony. But when they believe a gaudy character is genuine, they admire him in all his peacocky brilliance, and though they might not want to live with such a spectacle, they are the first to throw their hats in the air as it passes by.

Another Patton favorite is the anecdote of the historian researching a Civil War battle who finally found one of the survivors of that battle and asked him the question he had wanted the answer to for so very long: Where did general so and so place his artillery? Was it along this ridge or that? What did the general have in mind after studying the terrain, the supply problems etc.? Said the old coot deliberately: The General set up his guns where he could kill the most Yankees. That kind of simple but profound military truth attracts Patton enormously: always he seeks the quickest way to hurt the enemy the most. He is greatly interested in pocketing Germans where he can kill them at greater leisure and with greater safety.

One way of judging generals by what their officers and men say about them. Another is by what the war correspondents say about them. Without drawing invidious comparisons it is my observation that both groups around General Crerar respect and admire him; both groups around General Simpson ditto, perhaps even a little stronger; both groups around General Hodges just don't discuss him much. But the Third Army is one almost hysterical wave of absolute Patton enthusiasts. I haven't found anyone here yet who doesn't regard him as a great man and this group includes people who have served in all kinds of places and all kinds of armies. If you were to take the testimony of his staff alone or of the doughs alone you'd have something in the most startling contrast to the views, however favorable, that are held in other armies. And the correspondents almost without exception become his personal publicity agents, avidly seeking new adjectives of praise for his army and his methods. They get no more favors here than other places; there is no effort even equaling that at other press camps to get favorable publicity. But what the correspondents do get day after day, week in and week out, are swell action stories of war, of Germans being killed, of towns being taken, of heroism beyond the call of duty by Patton-inspired doughboys.

He is an unswerving devotee of air power. No army has closer liaison than the Third with the air forces. Fighter bombers anxiously watch the roads far beyond the bomb line because they know that Patton tanks and troops will be much farther down the road than the latest dope had it. He has airmen near him all the time as personal friends and his conversation is larded with hearty tributes to the airmen.

Somehow, by the magic of leadership, Patton has developed whole teams of unique commanders and specialists, soldiers and officers who are literally wild men when compared to the discreet commanders and quiet doughs in some armies. They all worship him. When a Patton division is moved away to another army for strategic reasons the division always groans and complains and wangles until it gets back. Someday perhaps *Time* can tell the story of how one armored division pinched out five infantry divisions and sealed off a terrific pocket of Germans in what gossips say was not actually part of the plan but merely an effort to get back to Patton's army.

In gauging the probable continuance of the Patton dashes into Germany you might remember that at maneuvers he used to work armor for 200-mile dashes and that if he has his way perhaps one of these days one of his divisions will simply peel off for Berlin or Berchtesgaden or Czechoslovakia and will run around everything between. Actually American, meaning Patton, armor could probably slash all the way across to the Russians if they got the go signal and there was no careful tactical thought about reinforcing that corridor. But I would guess that Patton is not interested in Berlin or Berchtesgaden but in the enemy; I'd guess that he is merely sitting behind his desk with his cavalry boots cocked on the glass top, with his white Boston bull terrier Willie (repeat, Willie) snuffing in happy sleep on the rug; slender, groomed, erect in his chair, his groomed hands in his lap, not thinking consecutively but letting his mind leap or idle about until suddenly the killer's instinct stirs and he will call someone in and tell them when and how and in what new direction to strike. One more thing: Patton's armor recently performed an impossible military feat. Two armored divisions, each of whose spearheads was actually in combat with the enemy, crossed through each other at right angles. In looping through a big pocket the two armored divisions came across each other at right angles on two highways. This could have become one of the great tragic pileups of the war with contact with the enemy lost by both armor until it was untangled. You must remember that such an armored division is a great flowing mass of steel at least forty miles long on a road. Instant action was taken. At the crossroads the two lines flowed through each other at 120-yard intervals steadily until the boys had passed on, still fighting the fleeing enemy. That is one for the history books too. If you can imagine traffic at Broadway and 42nd Street being passed through each other, one car from each road at jog time at exact intervals with no stalling and no confusion, you will have some [idea] of the spectacle.

This ends this part of the Patton cover for me. I will go with the Fourth Armored tomorrow and since I am unable to get a plane forward from here I must jeep, so will courier the stuff back from corps headquarters. No sign of Knauth yet. Expect more by Sunday noon. I hope this take is helpful.

TIME
THE PRESS: GETTING THE STORY[171]

In Europe's "fluid fighting" last week, such rearguard baggage as censors, press camps and corps headquarters jumped about almost as much as the front did, or were left far behind. *Time* correspondent Sidney Olson, who interviewed Lieut. General George S. Patton Jr. for last week's cover story, cabled this description of his trials and tribulations:

"To reach the Patton story I jeeped from Paris to the Group, flew a Piper Cub to one airfield, flew a Stinson to another, slept on the floor, saw Patton, wrote the piece riddled by censorship rules, slept on the floor, jeeped to the XII Corps Headquarters, slept on the floor, changed jeeps for a 125-mile ride through spearhead territory, slept on the floor, jeeped back to Corps Headquarters through towns that exactly 20 minutes later were reoccupied by 5,000 Germans in a moving pocket, reached Corps Headquarters to find I had only 35 minutes in which to write the piece, on a German typewriter with letters in the wrong places, in order to catch the courier airplane back to the Army press camp.

"In three days I missed five meals, was strafed by jet planes twice, narrowly missed capture once, was kissed by at least 500 Russians and Frenchmen, was absolutely lost in Germany twice, ate four candy bars in one afternoon after not eating candy for 15 years at least, got myself three pairs of German binoculars and found a champagne factory, which a general commandeered next day after tasting some of my loot, was waved at by bevies of German civilians as if they were happy at being liberated, saw at least 5,000 German prisoners and flew back from Corps Headquarters in weather so rough the Piper Cub pilot's sweat visibly rolled down his neck, while I counted the wings to see if they added up to two. When we 'crabbed in' for a landing the pilot said: 'If you ever have a rougher flight you'll never write about it.'"

Mar 30 [1945] [Diary]

Jeep w Lawrence Wilkinson to Mainz, sandwich lunch w. Maj. Clarence G. Martens, real estate dlr (Mt Vernon, New Roch). The complaints about negro rapists. The pol. Sta. for binoculars, cameras. Over the Rhine Over the Main. To 12th Corps HQ Capt Potter.[172] Lieut Murray.[173] The__ [?] damp [?] tax bldg. Room 35—Rooms 29–30. To Frankfurt for Champagne. To dinner with General Eddy.[174] His staff. Chateauneuf de Pape 1934.

Mar 31 [1945] [Diary]

Sick—Wire off re. atrocities story.[175] With Cambridge driver in jeep following Col. Anderson of Sig. Corps. To Lauterbach, strafed by jets. To Bernshausen, 90th Div. Coffee with press corporal in kitchen. Dinner at officers mess with Col. Scheppes. Houses—Col. Boswell. 87 dresses, food, linens etc.—marmalade.

4. A VIOLENT CONTRAST

SIDNEY OLSON CABLE 37
FROM GERMANY TO DAVID HULBURD
SENT APRIL 1, 1945; REC'D APRIL 2, 1945

The accompanying story is written on a captured German Mercedes typewriter in 45 minutes in order to make a courier plane that will fly it the secret number of miles back to Army Headquarters. I haven't bathed for a week, but otherwise feel fine. Hope it is some good. I was unable to catch the Fourth Armored Division and still get back here in time to get anything off this week.

The long steel fingers of the armored divisions along the whole front are now hooking into the vitals of Germany, thrusting and stabbing furiously about searching for the still-pumping heart.[176] This is a mighty spectacle, compounded of all the power of the Allies directed skillfully in a coordinated series of enormous amputations. It is also a long series of little scenes, like shots from a movie that have not yet been glued together into a dramatic whole.

If you follow one of those steel fingers into Germany, it looks like this:

You cross the Rhine through the artificial white fog, listening to the whine of wood saws and the coughs of the red-eyed engineers who have been living in this fog for days as they throw bridge after bridge across the smooth fast-flowing waters. The fog is punctuated here and there by the unbearable blue light of the acetylene torches cutting steel. Your jeep rolls quietly over the gently bouncing treadway on the pontoons. On the other side as the mist lifts, you pass through the familiar phenomena of big captured towns in Germany: mile after mile of smashed industrial sections, of ruined homes, of great old buildings broken and broken over and over again into brick dust, with only a piece of an arch or a chunk of a statue or a graceful iron gate to identify the buildings' one-time beauty. Then suddenly you are past the last stretch of rusted junk that used to be a railroad yard, and you begin winding over the superb wide brick roads that sweep on into the German uplands beyond the Rhine.

You thrust past the huge road blocks, of logs sunk deep in the road in rows with earth piled in between, where the Germans had hastily improvised defenses against the surge of power over the Rhine. Around these lie the old familiar signs of another lost German battle, the scattered helmets that covered heads now shattered or standing bare inside prison cages, the ripped off pant legs and coat-arms where wounds were dressed, the golden sprinkles of ammunition scattered on the ground, the smashed machine guns and the still smoldering trucks overturned in the ditches.

But after the armor had broken through this last crust, it had merely taken off in wide swoops over all the great road network. Patton's famed Fourth Armored Division, commanded by the fabulously tough team of Abrams and Cohen, as one of the American armies' most veteran outfits in this type of war.[177] In operations such as this fantastic penetration toward the German heart, the armor actually moves like a cross-country skier, sliding swiftly down roads diagnosing the terrain on the fly. If an obstacle appears too difficult to slide over or through, the armor skids around it in a series of sashaying loops. The armor always works with two fingers at once, each of them acting in this alternately skittish and power-driving way.

The results along the road are obvious. As you follow the armor you sail along easily for several miles. Then suddenly you come to debris of war again: a bend in the road where the fleeing Germans turned for a delaying action. You can see the tank tracks where the tankers hurriedly tore out into the fields to hit the Germans from several sides at once. Then you pass the bend where the smashed trucks, guns and equipment are scattered colorfully over the fields, the scene at first glance much like a littered picnic ground, where the picnickers will never yawn awake again.

You go through scores of little German country towns. They are untouched by war. All the glass is in the windows; the pansy beds are trim and fresh with purple and yellow blooms; the big beds of straw-covered beets are carefully protected against the weather in regular brown mounds. From each house flies a great white banner. When the Americans first go in usually a few houses show a strip of white bunting. But one of the first things the military police do is to tell the villagers that they must really show that they have surrendered by flying big white flags. Then the houses quickly blossom with white, from bedsheets to table cloths. This is good psychology: it teaches these Germans that they are conquered. But it has another use: it relieves the Americans of any responsibility. If any sniping is done from a house flying a white flag the Americans then treat it as they would a military obstacle. Here and there down the road you come to one house that has been completely smashed and whose timbers are still smoldering. There some German foolishly tried to heed Josef Goebbels' call to all Germans to resist to the death—and got it. For when the armor is moving fast there is no nonsense about opposition. If resistance comes from a house there is no dickering: an armor merely blows the house apart with a few tank bursts and then rolls calmly on. After a few such examples the word seems to get around. Anyway you roll for miles through the German uplands with no signs of fighting. But far below some five miles to the right of this steel finger there is a whipping cloud of smoke and flame rising in the light wind. There at an unmentionable town there was a real cluster of resistance. The armor skirted it and the great field cannon carefully set themselves in position to demolish it at leisure. The motto of the armor is: if they want any war they can have it.

As you whip through the little villages the townspeople are in the first of the three stages of submission. The three stages, according to Major Clarence G. Martens (repeat, Major Clarence G. Martens) of the military government in Mainz, are: 1) they are stunned and whipped; 2) they suddenly realize they are free and are not being massacred; and 3) then they begin to complain and whine that they haven't enough coal or the light system isn't working, etc. Their complaints get short shrift, it should be added. In a village you will see a little girl sucking her thumb while the white handkerchief of surrender floats in the wind from where her mother has pinned it to her sleeve. You will see the sour, silent German elders staring helplessly at the enormous accumulation of tanks and troops flowing endlessly past; occasionally shaking their heads in obvious sour awe. And here and there and always you meet streams of the newly liberated.

Down the road they come singly, in couples, in dozens, and then in great clusters of fifty and one hundred at a crack. These are the slave laborers of the Germans; these are the people responsible for the carefully cultivated beauty of the German farmlands. They are so happy it makes you happy. You get happier by the minute as they flow on by, liberated at last, all of them beginning the long walk back to the homes that may not be there and to the families that may be dead—but happy, happy, happy. They crowd around you and shake hands and try to kiss you, ten of them at a time. Here are Russians, scores and scores of them, with the SV [*sic*] daubed hastily on their backs for Soviet Union. Many of those I talked to had come from Stalingrad and had been prisoners for three years, they said. There were many Russian women, strong and heavy-set, smiling with broken teeth from ear to ear. There were French from all the provinces of France; some of them had been prisoners for five years. One of them found I had been in Paris recently. He asked if the azalea (repeat, azalea) was in bloom and when I told him it was but only in the flower stores he began to cry and so did I. The exhilaration of this scene endlessly repeated as we went mile after mile down the steel finger and met Poles and Italians and French and Russians gradually uplifted you until you felt like bursting with pride at even being a spectator to this liberation. All of them were eating K rations that the Americans had hastily tossed off the tanks and many of them had bicycles that they had commandeered from the Germans. In the country they had eaten fairly well but they had only pity for their comrades in the cities.

APR 1 [1945] [DIARY]

Sunday, Easter, breakfast

Jeep through Ravolzhausen, Gelnhausen to Hanau, across Main to Offenbach.

Writing story—Wade Werner of AP.

The bath we didn't get

First hot meal in 5 meals—n.g.

drunk cook: blonde "spies."

APR 2 [1945] [DIARY]

Monday: in jeep w T Sgt. Looking for airstrip:

Lt. Taflinger: the pocket of Germans

The flights, off & on; the weather

The flight—Looking for the field. "Crabbing in."

The rain. Waiting for the jeep.

Lt. McHugh. Lt. Durante.

Press camp. The stink. My cold.

Champagne with Wilkinson.

APR 3 [1945] [DIARY]

Breakfast. No coffee for thermos.

Jeep in rain through Trier and Lux

Lunch at chateau, gin rummy with Capa & Wert. Bed early

APR 4 [1945] [DIARY]

Breakfast earliest one:

Briefing

Ride in with Dave Anderson.

Yarborough & Bob Myers UP

Lunch—work in aft.

Stroll w Yarborough

Arturo Despuys: his play—his song [?], clock of horses hooves.

Oh Leo, you're hurting me with your monocle.

Drinks bef dinner: to officers' clubs.

Impromptu jazz concert—Maj. Bob Shackleton singing.

SIDNEY OLSON CABLE 38
FROM GERMANY TO DAVID HULBURD
SENT APRIL 4, 1945; REC'D APRIL 4, 1945
Dateline Twelfth Army Group

For International or Foreign News:

The following notes in the attitudes of Germans may be helpful in amplifying Knauth's close studies. The first thing to remember is that very obviously many many Germans apparently do look on Americans as liberators on first entry. This is very puzzling; very difficult to evaluate. If you enter a town the first day of capture scores of Germans wave, smile and offer Schnapps. This baffles the Americans, usually entering on a cold wave of hatred of the enemy that has forced them to leave their homes and endure much for years in a war they didn't want. Americans almost invariably preserve a stony-faced, business-like, chill attitude. It is a rare minority of combat-exhausted troops who get drunk and seek sexual relief, although I have seen some extraordinary sights. By the second day usually the Germans relapse into timid docility, although many go on smiling and trying to be friendly for weeks thereafter until finally they understand the Americans are almost anesthetized against them. The Americans want nothing from the Germans except absolute obedience. Many of the Americans would just as soon shoot a German as argue with him. Even cute German children, who are impervious to rebuffs in their complete fascination by American equipment and chewing gum, are usually regarded sourly by the dough-feet as the little bastards who will be killing their own sons in the next war. Since this attitude is so deep and prevalent, any doughfoot who seems soft in treatment of Germans is soon brought sharply back into line by his tougher colleagues and meekly conforms.

Personally I have had great mental trouble in seeking the right attitude. As with any Christian it is very difficult for me to hate other people except in abstract masses. When you confront actual people you are required to hate, it is difficult, especially when a great many of them are attractive children, attractive young girls and helpless elderly people.

Then you think of the Gestapo or see a Gestapo jail or Gestapo graves or get authentic eyewitness stories of atrocities. You talk with doughfeet who have lost their buddies to German viciousness or who have been captured by the Germans and you boil with vindictive rage. When that simmers down there is still a residue of at least distrust.

Then you talk with Germans and ask them about Hitler. They always begin by agreeing he is *kaputt* now. They invariably say they were not Nazis and are hurt when you patently disbelieve them. They always eagerly try to prove that until the great party membership drives were put on after the war had begun, their names had not appeared on party membership rolls. But they do think of Hitler as a great slum-clearer, great make-work man who solved unemployment, and a great prophet of a United Europe against Bolshevism.

They admit they are frankly puzzled and honestly hurt by the American non-fraternization policy. They have no conception, you must remember, of the degree to which they have been put outside the pale of the human race. They begin to complain and they are great complainers. They complain of being ousted out of their homes by billeting American soldiers. This makes the Americans positively fume with rage in a red haze of anger. You say, "You are complaining of being ousted out of your homes? What about the people of Lidice, of Ouradour sur Glane and Maidanek, etc.?" Then it dawns on you that they don't know what you're talking about and wouldn't believe such atrocity stories anyway. That leaves you helpless while they go on complaining that there is no coal or water or food or something.

But something inside you always wants to believe the best and you wonder if some of them perhaps are not good people who were helpless in the political clamps of Nazism. You thrust this thought aside. You wouldn't dare voice it before any group of correspondents or military men because they would take it as complete proof that Americans are soft, decadent democrats who will win the war and then feel so sorry for the Germans that they will give them their country back again with plenty of loaned money to build a bigger, better war machine. All levels of American soldiers are so cynical about this that it is possible to predict a solid body of opinion among returned soldiers some day which will insist on being everlastingly harsh on Germany; will insist on military training for the next generation; will insist on a powerful navy, army and air force. Incidentally I have nowhere found any optimism that this is the last war; all soldiers merely hope that this is the last war for them.

Back on the Germans: they are all surprised that the Americans let them keep their radios, on which they can freely get German propaganda broadcasts. Some of them try to turn in their radios first thing in an effort to be impressively cooperative. American policy in this, I am convinced, is most shrewd. For instance recently Goebbels broadcast a speech that he was disappointed in the lack of resistance behind American lines. The Germans of Mainz where I heard about this merely stared in awe at the endless columns of American troops and tanks rolling on through the city day after day and wondered what could Goebbels be thinking about. One German said, "I was very much impressed the first day or two with American power, but here it is two weeks and still my house shakes all day and all night with trucks rolling past. *Gott in Himmel!* That Hitler!" Forays into the German mind, handicapped as I am by lack of the language, are most unprofitable but I feel better about it when the reporters who lived and worked in Germany for years all report absolute futility in their efforts to get explanations of the events of the past few years. In short, the only sensible conclusions I can draw which I feel are solid are that almost to a man every conquered German is damned glad it is over, and two, he is perplexed and dismayed at the grim sternness of the American attitude, and three, if he has a home he is lucky and had better stay there minding his own business for years to come. Many German women complain of being attacked and raped, usually by rear-echelon colored troops. Only a few cases have been authenticated so far, however, and punishment has been severe with, I am told, hanging having been used as a sentence though not carried out so far. (This last not red check.) Perhaps also of interest relief in Germany is that in little farm villages which I saw in the wake of the Fourth Armored Division many well-to-do Germans had moved in from bombed cities. These little towns of fifty or so houses were untouched by bombs or war. Slave labor had kept them in perfect condition. In a typical three-story farmhouse a farmer would live in the bottom floor while the upper two floors were remodeled into de luxe apartments, and I mean de luxe, filled with fine paintings, expensive furniture, silver, glassware, linens, clothes, trunkfuls of supplies and cellars crammed with foodstuffs. In one woman's closet I counted 87 dresses, no fooling, and three pairs of boots and 17 pairs of shoes. Drawers of lingerie etc. correspond in quantity and quality although (cable reading:) no pairs labels. One whole drawer was crammed with tightly-packed, unworn silk stockings which a major had commandeered. GIs in these little villages were living the life of Riley, sleeping on modern blond wood featherbeds with great billowy down comforters over them, and after carefully checking henhouses, etc. were averaging three eggs each for breakfast with chicken for dinner. Incidentally chicken dinner is the absolute number one favorite meal of the GIs I have seen with eggs for breakfast as a close second. Spinach and carrots are wasted on them and to a man they loathe marmalade, which Washington keeps assuring them is the soldier's favorite preserve. You should hear them talk about the Sunkist orange monopoly and about strawberry or raspberry jam or plum preserves while they pass around the hated marmalade, gingerly spreading a dab of the stuff on their bread. These little farm villages apparently all through Germany were the resources of wealthier German families either bombed out of (?) or as alternate refuges.

APR 5 [1945] [DIARY]

Luxembourg: Bob Myers, Gault MacGowan, Jack Fleischer, Arturo, Redding, Brightman, Yarborough, Capa, Wert.[178]

SIDNEY OLSON CABLE 36[179]
FROM GERMANY TO DAVID HULBURD
SENT APRIL 5, 1945; REC'D APRIL 5, 1945

Dateline: With the 12th Corps, Third Army

For USAW, Attention Roy Alexander:

Over the *Chateauneuf de Pape* (repeat Chateauneuf de Pape) 1934 at dinner one night General Manton S. Eddy of the 12th Corps of George Patton's Third Army brought up the problem of *Time's* USAW story of February 26th on what women think, a story titled *They Think of the Moment*. General Eddy suggested gently that it might be a good idea to check into what the men of the 12th Corps thought of their American women at this point. A veteran newspaperman, Captain Merle A. Potter, who is the PRO of the 12th Corps went off that night and devised a questionnaire to be submitted to 100 men of all ranks representing the Corps in an effort to get a true cross section of the American Army.

The questionnaire began by rehearsing the *Time* story and then said that "it seemed pertinent to get the angle of service men thinking along similar lines." The filling out of the questionnaire was purely voluntary and no signature was necessary. It was stipulated that all questions should be answered with utmost frankness, honesty and sincerity. The results are in today and Captain Potter has submitted them to me for transmission to *Time*.[180] Other newsmen taking down the score have agreed to hold the release for both London and Washington until next Thursday, *Time's* publication day. I believe the questionnaire and the results are fascinating and submit them in high hopes that USAW will regard the story as a valid response to the sincerity of *Time's* original story.

APRIL 5, 1945 [LETTER TO ZEMBRA]

Dearest darling b.g.

This is a cool but pleasant spring evening; I am in a beautiful old chateau quite a way from the front; I have had a hot bath three feet deep; I had two gins-and-grapefruit juices before dinner and white wine with dinner; I have plenty of Camels and a Hershey bar handy; I have clean clothes on; I'm writing this in the twin-bedroom of one wing of the chateau, wearing my British battle jacket and my dark green trousers; I have just had two great steaks for dinner, canned peas, mashed potatoes, spinach soup, with pineapple upside-down cake for dessert and two cups of coffee. When I finish this letter I will go down to the Blue Room of the chateau and listen to the BBC give the day's news, will have a small cognac with the other correspondents, will play a game of chess with one of them, and will go to bed at 10:30. The bed unfortunately has no sheets or blankets so I use my bedroll.

I go into this great detail because it is this violent contrast that makes this war correspondent's life so interesting. I got back yesterday from nine days at the front with General George Patton's Third Army, where I chased the Fourth Armored Division, toughest of all tank outfits, up one of those steel fingers that are stabbing into Germany. In those nine days I didn't have a bath although I was terribly dirty and sweaty much of the time. I slept on the floors of various basements five nights. Two nights I slept on a cot on the third floor of a huge gloomy tax-collection building in a German town near Frankfurt. One night I slept on the featherbed of a wealthy Nazi who had moved his family to the country to escape the bombing of the cities, slept beautifully under a great down comforter that billowed over me about two feet thick, but kept sliding off the bed like one of Mammy's ice-cakes. One night I didn't sleep. In three days I missed seven meals, living on occasional boxes of K-rations, which is like eating a can of deviled ham and four soda-crackers and then chewing some dried raisins. One morning I had two fresh-laid eggs, which makes five times I've had fresh eggs since December 16. And every night I did two things, only one of which will surprise you: I dreamed a sweet short dream of you, and I said a long prayer for the safety of you and Whitney and John and our folks; as Whitney says: "For all the good people and the dear people and all the good children and all the dear children."

But now I've had a night's sleep and a wonderful bath and am living in superb comfort and the stretch at the front seems like a dream that happened to someone else. That's the curious thing about this life, darling dearest most beautiful b.g. You go into all kinds of danger—without looking for it: war's too unpredictable for it to be safe anywhere in the world—but you never worry much or think much about it and suddenly the danger's over and you're comfortable and forget all about it. I lost a very good friend the other day, when Maj. Gen. Maurice Rose, commander of the Third Armored Division, was killed by Germans from ambush.[181] He was the general who I followed around the streets of Cologne; absolutely fearless; tall, blonde, good looking, Jewish, I learned later with great surprise. He's a great loss to the Army and everyone who knew him. He used to say that nowhere is safe, so you might as well go anywhere. I still don't agree with him. I had a lot of exciting experiences. I was strafed—I say but I mean the troops I was with of course—by German jet planes twice. You can't hear them coming except that the ack ack in the sky is popping at them. As they pass overhead, they make a kind of screaming whistle like a shell does when it falls nearby—that's all. They're the fastest things you ever saw—in fact they're unbelievable. One of them went overhead only about 1,000 feet up and it gives you a queer feeling to know that only 1,000 feet away is a grim-faced young German ducking his plane through the flack, dressed in green, thinking of his wife, too, perhaps. War is damned silly, I think. I do a lot of flying, myself, but usually in those little Piper Cub planes or Stinson L-5s, which are wonderful little things that just skim over the trees and can land on a highway or an open lawn or anything. They save a lot of time and save my fanny too, from the thousands of miles I have driven over shell-holed roads in an iron-bottomed wide-open jeep, which is just like driving somewhere with a refrigerating fan blowing very hard all over you, chilling you to the bone, while someone keeps hammering you right on the bones of the fanny as hard as you can bear for hours with an iron paddle. When you finally step out after such a ride you're absolutely dazed and bruised and numb and chilled until you can't really speak or think. But then again, as

I've said, the next day you're lying around napping on a great featherbed with nothing to do between meals.

I have been with the British, the Canadians, the Ninth Army, the First Army and now the Third Army. Now I'm leaving the Twelfth Army Group as they call it and going to the Sixth Army Group, which consists of the American Seventh Army and two or more French armies. I am going to this sector to see if we can finish off the war. I am not going to try for Berlin, or for the meeting with the Russians: what I want is to go to four cities: Stuttgart, Nuremberg, Munich and finally Berchtesgaden, where Hitler lives and where he may make his last stand. That's my story. In the meantime I'll see the wonderful German country of the Black Forest, and will travel along the fringes of the Alps with the French, studying hard on my French. Since I was in Paris—did I tell you?—I am resolved to learn French, most seriously. Even at the front I take my little book and practice for one full hour a day. I have only studied a couple of weeks but am encouraged very much already. The German. Then Russian. Then the piano. Haw! [page cut off]

SIDNEY OLSON CABLE 39
FROM GERMANY VIA PARIS TO DAVID HULBURD
SENT APRIL 6, 1945; REC'D APRIL 6, 1945

Battlefronts Shorty:

As of today the Allied armies have nine more bridges across the Rhine than the Germans had one year ago (exact number censorable).

SIDNEY OLSON CABLE NO. 40—VIA PARIS
FROM GERMANY TO DAVID HULBURD
SENT APRIL 6, 1945; REC'D APRIL 6, 1945

For Battlefronts:

In the strategy piece this week I would personally advise to hold way back on optimism of the early end of the war. If the general characteristics of German resistance thus far continue—and there are no signs they will not—this war, at a minimum, has at least four weeks to go and the likelihood is eight or more.

Reading down the front from left to right, the Germans are fighting a most expert and skillful battle in the north against the British and Canadians with very adroit use of tough terrain. Here there are no signs of weakness or of breakthroughs although the quality and quantity of enemy troops is not very high. Again personally guessing, it looks like the British have another slow hinge job, as they had at Caen and Falaise in Normandy, and as they had in eastern Sicily. Moving south, the Ninth is also against stiff to moderate resistance but is moving smoothly towards its objectives. A breakthrough by armor may come, which would help unhinge the stubbornness of German defenses in the north. I would guess that Zinder will get to cover the liberation of Amsterdam, Rotterdam and Denmark, plus the capture of Kiel and Wilhelmshaven. Unless Lang has moved south, I would also guess that he would reach Berlin first, as per my predictions since very early.

The problem of *Time* and *Life* battle editors this week must largely be one of guessing how long liquidation of the giant Ruhr pocket will take as it obviously is tying up a considerable number of powerful and experienced American divisions of both the Ninth and First American Armies; my own guess is that while liquidation may take a week or ten days, the renewal of a really massive offensive of all armies eastward across Germany will not await a clean-up of the Ruhr pocket but will coincide with the earliest moment that it is obvious the pocket is well in hand. That moment does not seem to have arrived yet from a look at the map and situation reports showing constant German counter-attacks and showing stubborn resistance all around the perimeter. I would watch developments on the map closely today and Saturday for a tip-off as to the length of time the pocket cleanup will take. In short, if American divisions begin knifing easily through the pocket, I would begin to look eastward at armored columns' positions thrusting into Germany; if not, I would sell optimism short for another week's issues of *Time* and *Life*. Points which you are already aware of but which bear reiteration are that the northern area of the pocket are highly industrialized areas of cities lending themselves to house-to-house fighting and secondly, that the entire pocket area is literally pock-marked with ammunition dumps, gasoline supplies and equipment. FYI—I am unable to discover that any famed German generals are still in the pocket but believe at least two ranking corps commanders are therein, directing the expert resistance thus far shown. In pondering the pocket problem I would handle it this way: for every geographical chunk ripped out of the pocket I would count that as one more division freed for eastward German assault. You can best make your own guesses as how much space to allow per each division but you can safely guess that pocket cleanup has high rank in the Eighth Command's priority list of military tasks.

In guessing as to which Army will meet the Russians first, I would personally choose between the First and Third Armies, with my own money going down on George Patton's fabulous 4th Armored Division. One reason is obvious: The 4th Armored has now clanked and burned its way through the nastiest of terrain it faced and now is poised on the edge of two consecutive flat basins that run right over indescribably tough terrain in Czechoslovakia. When Patton turns that 4th Armored Division loose I would guess that the leading elements will be shouting "Tovarich" to Russian friends within two or three days. Probably the security blackout will descend on the Third Army at some point and when it lifts you will find the 4th Armored drinking vodka and trading coffee and Postum for samovars. In studying strategy on the map, I believe it will be obvious that Patton, as always, is ahead of the other armies geographically. Another point perhaps worth making is that tactically in future operations he may have another great advantage in that he has cleaned up his own smaller pockets very speedily so that his forward elements might be considered a little more rested and farther advanced in regrouping and in the supply situation. In saying smaller pockets, I mean only by comparison with the Ruhr as only yesterday the Patton cleanup was, as always, far ahead in speed and size of other armies'. Of the total of twenty-six thousand seven hundred ninety-three prisoners taken, the Ninth Army took seventy-four hundred, the First twenty-nine hundred, while George's boys captured a whacking sixteen thousand four hundred fifty-four.

Regarding the Russian front, there is apparently good evidence to support the Russian claim of having knocked out eleven German divisions around Vienna, as you will see in the continuing speed of the Russian advance thereabouts.

I hope this will be helpful in assessing the prospects. As always, I welcome questions, which please shoot soonest.

APR 6 [1945] [DIARY]

Won at gin rummy from Redding.

APR 7 [1945] [DIARY]

Jeep to Eagle Tac Airstrip;[182] flight with Cregar [?] to Kaiserslautern. Cooling for Landstuhl; the hell field; chow near airstrip; flight to Heidelberg; apple blossoms; landing; jeep to H. Lt. Col. Levien, Lt. Hartley, Lt. Cargill [?], Ed Bowan, Charles Stewart, chow at Europa, jeep through hills looking for Lauda, no map, wrong password, ret to Heidel (that path by ruins, through thickets)! Bed at Europa.

APR 8 [1945] [DIARY]

Jeep along beautiful Neckar river to Tauberbischoffheim & Lauda. Filed piece on Sunday feeling. Bedded same room w. Vincent Tubbs, *Afro-American* papers.[183]

SIDNEY OLSON CABLE 41
FROM GERMANY TO DAVID HULBURD
SENT APRIL 8, 1945; REC'D APRIL 8, 1945
Seventh Army Press Camp

For Foreign News or LIFE:

Not—repeat not—all of Germany is in ruins, rubble and misery. Old Heidelberg today slept in the April sunshine in a cloud of apple blossoms, as tranquil and placid as the mirror-smooth Neckar—repeat Neckar— River and here the war seems something far away,[184] a mere memory of pain, an irritating but unimportant thought, to be brushed away like a fly from a sleeper's nose. No bombs have fallen here to break and burn the ancient town. The sunny, crooked streets wind peacefully along the river and the hillsides; the curtains blow their lace through open windows which still have all their glass; the strolling villagers walk gravely or merrily over streets cleaned by the Street Department, not swept by engineers for mines and cleaned of rubble by bulldozer-mounted tanks.

On this Sunday, the first after Easter, the people of all the towns in the Neckar valley were out in force for the great weekly business of Church-going. The big men of the towns were richly dressed in tailcoats and high hats, their great stomachs resplendently vested in oyster white or French gray. The women were soberly dressed—German women are either mainly in mourning or they have no talent for fancy dressing—or both. Everywhere scores of little girls, ten years old or less, were dressed for some special rite of the day, in frilled long white dresses. Each wore a floral wreath on her head and carried a two-foot-long white candle, which was also wreathed. The little girls skipped happily along the streets, their shrill chatter sounding much less throatily guttural than the clobbery German speech of their elders.

Around and above Heidelberg and the other river-valley towns were woven the apple trees, now coming fully into bloom, the blossoms just at the stage where the pale green has turned to white. In a few days the white will be pinkish. But now the effect is such that the two rows of purple mountainside are clouded in a great white mist, out of which the castles and church spires rise softly, something like the lost Atlantis will look perhaps as it rises from the sea one day. Below the waves of blossoms moves the beautiful Neckar River, like a broad, rich green stripe painted in a smooth series of curves. I have never seen so beautiful a river. It has no trace of muddy color; it flows brimful to its banks so exactly that you cannot imagine it ever being an inch higher or lower. Perhaps beautiful is not the exact word—pretty may be nearer the secret. For it is like an imaginary stream painted by an artist who wanted to paint a pretty picture and so arranged to have a dark green river flow perfectly glassily between two banks of stretching lawn for many miles, with flowering trees and houses that can only be called quaint picturesquely mirrored on its surface.

To find the war in Heidelberg you must look for it. When you look for it this is what you find. Occasionally good-looking solemn young German girls hurry by; they have Red Cross arm bands on their left sleeves. A little procession passes: first march two German boys aged about six and eight, holding each other's hands tightly; then comes a little wheelbarrow, pushed by their mother, a young woman of about thirty, her fair face red with exertion and her brow furrowed with anxiety about the little ones ahead in the complexities of traffic. Such a sight is no novelty: in all Europe misery is commonplace. You ask yourself: where is her husband, their father? Was he one of the pale dead on the Cologne plain, lying stiff on the yellow clay churned by the tanks? Was he one of the millions sent to death in Russia? Or was he one of the bastards who laughed each time he sent off a V-bomb at Antwerp or London to kill women and children? Or is he still serving in the Gestapo, at this minute whipping or torturing some helpless prisoner whose offense is being Jewish?[185]

I mention this range of thought only because it is typical of that in the American army today. A thousand times the gentle Christian upbringing of American soldiers make them want to be gallantly friendly to German civilians obviously in distress: but a thousand times the impulse is stilled by the memories of American soldiers shot in cold blood by German captors, of American fliers murdered by Nazi mobs when they parachuted down from a bomb raid, by the belly-stiffening rage at the atrocities of the SS troops and the Gestapo. At present the non-fraternization policy is an adequate compromise between a tradition of Christian chivalry and the desire for revenge. But that policy is no solution, and the time for a clear-cut American attitude is soon at hand.

The signs of war are present, all right. Back from church come not only the hale elders and the happy youngsters but the mutilated young generation of Germany: the wives walking very slowly so that the men with the steel crutch legs can keep pace with them. And on all the roads through the valley pour the powerful columns of American armed might: the dusty tanks printing their steel treads endlessly in the German dirt, their huge motors rattling the windows of the little towns as they clank on and on and on. Again and again as you travel with an armored column you see the women and little girls put their hands over their ears, deafened by the giant roar that never seems to end, while awe-struck little boys goggle with boyish admiration, and most significantly you catch again and again the hopeless looks that the village elders exchange, as if to say: how could we ever fight against all this? Let it be no secret that the doughfeet enjoy this tribute: there probably never was a tanker who did not race his motor extra loud as he clanked through a conquered German town, and the jeep drivers always rip along the streets with motors wide open, exhausts popping as if they were strafing the roads, driving with twice the break-neck skill they show on the quiet open roads. But even the Martian-like intrusion of the steel monsters did not shake the unbreakable placidity of the Neckar valley sleeping in the Sunday sunshine in the clear blue and gold day. Fishermen drowsed over their poles by the water; along the banks American troops napped with a copy of the *Stars & Stripes* over their faces and here and there sat little colonies of Poles, of Russians, of French, the husky, beaming, escaped slaves of Naziism, each dreaming mile by mile along the roads out of Germany of some little far-off home town, even as the dozing GIs dream of Manhattan, Kansas and Beloit, Wisconsin and Savannah, Georgia.

SIDNEY OLSON CABLE UNNUMBERED [A.][186]
FROM GERMANY TO DAVID HULBURD
SENT APRIL 9, 1945; REC'D APRIL 10, 1945

Part III
Attention Henry Luce:

I would appreciate your reaction to my present outlined plans, which, in effect, mean watching the finish of the war here and then proceeding through the Balkans, Near East, India, as a tourist, before joining with the Jap war, which I, incidentally, bet will finish this summer too. In short, is that okay with you?

One point you may be interested in: I find that it takes some time and experience to be a good war correspondent; it isn't an easy matter of describing things. This accounts for terribly bad books written by people, like John Steinbeck's *Bombs Away*, etc. Steinbeck had turned *Mice and Men* and *The Red Pony* and the *Long Valley* material over for a long time in his mind. This war, in short, has been too much described by expert rewrite men such as myself and other journalists without proper familiarity with troops and things they work with and tasks they perform. I have studied hard these five months and thought quite a lot and maybe I will surprise you and *Life* editors yet with a piece that gets inside instead of describing the color of the outside, which is what they all do and I mean Ernie Pyle too.[187]

John Hersey's first book was in the right direction.[188] But maybe there is more to be done.

Incidentally I never did see *Life*. Is it possible to send me copies as I haven't seen one since the January issues.

All best to you. If Clare is in the neighborhood anywhere I would much like to see her.[189]

Wish you were here. X marks my foxhole.

SIDNEY OLSON CABLE UNNUMBERED [B.][190]
FROM GERMANY TO DAVID HULBURD
SENT APRIL 9, 1945; REC'D APRIL 10, 1945

Seventh Army Press Camp

Attention: Henry Luce:

A few points from down here some 50 miles north of Heidelberg.

I wish you would personally read my Cable number 40 on strategy background. Therefrom I suggest you turn the word Berchtesgaden over in your mind.[191] I well remember when you asked a Battlefronts Editor where Truk was and he had never heard of it. The point is that *Life, Time, Fortune* or *March of Time* might well prepare some acts on *Festung* Adolf, where the last set will be played in fullest Wagnerian style.[192]

It is my personal belief that wherever possible all S.S. troops are being pulled back from all over Germany in a great ring so that the northern breakthrough across, through Berlin and to the meeting with the Russians will still leave vast circular defenses protecting *Der Fuhrer* from all sides. Without pretending to be able to gauge American sentiment from here, I fear that the capture of Berlin and the meeting with the Russians may be taken as an indication that the war is over, with a resulting letdown as it drags possibly for weeks through fanatic fighting up Alpine country, similar to the Italian campaign, where a few madmen with an 88 can stop armies a long time as the terrain is unsuitable for tanks.

No signs whatever that I regard as valid that the hard Nazi core will cease resistance following the American breakthrough across Germany, which I personally expect soonest. One more weary time I believe we should nip possible over-optimism in the bud. I am wiser than I was in a cable for your attention several weeks ago although I think the Hitler cover[193] soon would be an excellent opportunity to draw attention to this last *Festung Gotterdammerung*.[194] I also believe *Life* might look over all Berchtesgaden pictures ever taken for a possible spread.

My own objectives, as outlined before, are Nuremberg, Munich, Berchtesgaden, in order, but I draw your attention and that of *Time* and *Life* mapmakers to the city of Regensburg, whence a superb road network extends in all directions.

Perhaps now justified is Hitler's keeping 25 divisions in Italy, most of them resting much of the time. I personally believe that Berlin long since was stripped of its great communications corresponding to our own Pentagon Building and that one further move has now been made to Berchtesgaden, which is the combined Pentagon and SHAEF head-quarters at last rather than a White House to which information was incidentally channeled.

APR 9 [1945] [DIARY]

Lauda, day off; no luggage!

APR 10 [1945] [DIARY]

To Geldersheim to watch bombing of Schweinfurt. How now brown cow! The steeple. 88s. P47 spraying town. 42nd div.

APR 11 [1945] [DIARY]

To Schweinfurt, after stop at Div.

entry in town. Explosion behind us.

My driving Redferns jeep back.[195] Wine from Wurzburg.

SIDNEY OLSON CABLE 42
FROM GERMANY TO DAVID HULBURD
SENT APRIL 11, 1945; REC'D APRIL 11, 1945
Dateline: Seventh Army Press Camp

For Battlefronts:

Today was hot, clear, blue and still. Plumes of dust swirled up to hang above the net of roads north of Wurzburg as the Seventh Army rolled over the flat-lands, snuffing out the military life in scores of some of the most ancient villages in all Germany. The Seventh was closing in on Schweinfurt, famous as the ball-bearing center of Nazi industry, and for many years hence to be remembered by many American families as the town where the American Eighth Air Force won its first huge Pyrrhic victory on March KOMING 1943, when fifty-eight out of one hundred eighty-eight Flying Fortresses were shot down.[196] Within twenty-four hours after that black day, under the general press outcry and amid threats of Congressional investigation, General "Hap" Arnold was forced to issue a statement justifying the 33% loss as unavoidable and necessary or whatever it was he said. After that as the Nazis patiently rebuilt Schweinfurt and fought furiously to protect it, the RAF and Eighth Air Force hit it again and again until the town sank so bottomlessly into a pile of rubble that it ceased to be a top priority target and the Nazis depended more and more on Sweden for ball-bearings.

Today the front had come at last to Schweinfurt. The famed 42nd Division, the Rainbow Division of World War I, had closed in on the town, working carefully over the wide sweeps of green flatland.

The landscape changes subtly as you approach a frost laid out over such flat open country. The grass is just as green, the little clumps of trees along the horizon stand as prettily, the little streams ripple just as calmly. But there is death in the calm air. The menace makes the land ugly. Through the glasses if you look carefully along the farm fields you can pick out a low clump of brown clay in the distance, not far from a clump of woods. If you watch long enough you will see a crouching German running swiftly along the communication trench. The low clump of dirt is a machine-gun outpost. And always as you watch you know that

German eyes are watching you through their field glasses, ready to call down fire on any target big enough to justify the risk of counter-fire.

Today all movement toward Schweinfurt stopped at 11 o'clock in the morning. The armor swerved off and halted. The soldiers of the 42nd inched carefully into the barn-lofts of the cow-smelling little German towns and pried small holes in the shingles on the Schweinfurt side. Some of them climbed into the little church spires and hacked open observation posts. Others inched around the stone houses or sneaked forward under the apple trees to low ridges. The big show started at noon, and most of them wanted to see it. Those who didn't care stayed close to the buildings and stared upward.

At five minutes to noon the first wave of the silver medium bombers sailed into sight, flying close and pretty, the big black flowers of heavy flak breaking open slowly around them. But after one look all eyes watched Schweinfurt. Men who knew what bombing is like shivered in the hot sun.

Suddenly all of Schweinfurt was blotted out of sight. In the clear blue distance the thick white clouds of smoke boiled up suddenly. The bombers came on steadily, wave after wave of them. There were two hundred and eighteen bombers in three concentrated attacks. When they finished, the terribly broken, beaten city was only a mass of broken stones.

We watched the beginning of the bombing from a church steeple, after a climb up a series of creaking ladders. The cloud grew and spread and became part of the filmy horizon, its lower edges shot with pink. The cloud grew and grew and then merely hung in the sky. We were a little more than two miles away from the town. But there was nothing to be seen now but the cloud. Suddenly came the great smashing crump of two bombs very nearby and then the stomach-churning roar of a plane diving directly on us. We ran desperately for the ladders but the plane had pulled out low overhead and was pouring strafing shells through the village. In five minutes we had four different versions of the plane attack. One tanker swore it was a German jet plane. Another dough said it was a British plane. Two said it was a Thunderbolt. Another said it was a British plane with German markings and that our ack-ack had shot it down just beyond the village. (The truth: It was one of our own Thunderbolts escorting the medium bombers which had somehow gotten off course.) I went out along the street to see the damage. The bomb damage was too close to a German machine-gun nest to be looked at carefully. But the trail of the strafing was plain. In the quiet, sunny street, where the rough-handed German farmers and their old hausfraus were beginning to peep out cautiously again, there lay a freshly killed brown cow, who kicked her last as I approached. How now brown cow? In the house opposite a neat row of great bullet holes had ripped across the front. I kicked open the door and went in. There were no Germans there; perhaps they were still cowering in the basement. The bullets had smashed two old family photographs in their frames along the wall; both of them stiff, last-century poses of stolid-faced Germans in their best *fin-de-siècle* finery. On the neat dining room table, around the plaster plums and grapes in a wooden bowl, stood plates still spread with the noon meal of potato pancakes and ersatz honey. A medic in the street asked me if I wanted a cup of coffee. We drank it, boiling hot, in a barn doorway. An old German lady came out with some sugar. We didn't need it but she was so old and looked so disappointed that we each took some. Some other medics came up. They talked shop. One of them asked: "How's Red?" Another said: "If there's any circulation in his foot tonight they'll be able to save his leg." We all drank some more coffee and then one said: "You remember Blank? He got hit in three places last night, right hip, right rib, right thigh. Each wound is just a clean, deep nick." Another said: "That's too close."

I walked on down the street with a soldier going to the forward observation post. After about four short blocks the lonesome feeling came on very hard. Without saying anything we stuck very close to the walls. We passed under an old archway. The date on the arch was 1618. Over a little crossroads, in a long brown house was the forward post. This was the absolute front. As we peeked through the arch a soldier standing on the safe side of the house waved us back, so we didn't cross the road. On the left, hung up in some apple trees was a dark-green Focke-Wulf plane.[197] It had a big hole in the fuselage and I thought I could see a dead German in the plane. The soldier thought there were two. Looking past the house we could see we were on the edge of the big airport that separates the 42nd Division from Schweinfurt. At this point we were about a mile and a half from the burning town. But you couldn't see anything—the great cloud of smoke still hung there in the sky on the horizon. We turned back, talking about 88's. The Germans have a heavy ring of perimeter defense around Schweinfurt, which they got by merely depressing their ack-ack guns and using them to fire 88's on the flat. We had learned that many of the guns are manned by German children whom the Nazis bribe with candy and cigarettes to stay and pull the lanyards while they duck into shelters. We agreed that those German children are wonderful marksmen for their ages. It was then that their 88's opened up. We had gotten back by the little church when there came the flat whistling smack of an 88, and all of us, soldiers, townspeople and officers dove for basements, doorways, windows, anything. Overhead there was a crash, a ringing sound and then the shatter of tiles and glass and the slow fall of stones. One shell had hit directly on the church steeple while several soldiers and correspondents were in there. There was one casualty: A soldier had a deep wound in the ankle.

But still the day was fair and blue and hot and still. The young German country girls walked in giggling twos and threes along the street, pretending not to eye the soldiers. The German children pushed each other forward to ask for chocolate. An old man came up to ask us if he could take away his hand-truck on which we were sitting. It was a crude and ancient wooden version of the kind of truck baggagemen use in railroad stations. He patted it and said sarcastically to no one in particular: *"Deutscher Panzer."*

We just looked at him. There wasn't anything to say. But he looked down the street at the American tanks huddled close to the houses and back down at his old wooden handcart and decided he liked his own bitter joke. *"Ja, ja, ja,"* he said loudly, chuckling. *"Deutscher Panzer, Deutscher Panzer."* And he wheeled it off down the sunny, cow-smelling street, the wheels inevitably tracking through the long trail of blood from the dead cow.

SIDNEY OLSON CABLE 43
FROM GERMANY TO DAVID HULBURD
SENT APRIL 11, 1945; REC'D APRIL 12, 1945

For Battlefronts:

Early this morning two patrols of the 242nd Regiment of the 42nd Infantry Division poked out of the little houses of Geldersheim and began feeling their way in the dark across the airport (see my research in Cable 42 for locations; in case, by any chance, you are looking at large scale maps, the airfield I refer to is not the Schweinfurt airport, south of the town, but the main fighter field directly west). Very quickly they bumped into machine gun nests. But they kept zigzagging slowly forward and suddenly noticed that they were nearly in Schweinfurt without drawing fire. They had found a small rutted cart path beside the airfield which was somehow not covered by German fire—perhaps because the little road led almost directly from the American positions in Geldersheim straight into Schweinfurt and smack into whole clusters of 88 positions. Of course, no one would be fool enough (omission—checking). The two patrols acted quickly, sending runners back to regimental headquarters with the good news. By five o'clock in the morning the 242nd had two battalions down that road and into Schweinfurt. On the way they had captured twenty-eight 88 gun positions. They were into the positions before the crews could sweep the little road. After that it was too late: other German gun crews dared not fire into the melee in the dark until they knew what they were shooting at. Thus the battalions cleaned out the twenty-eight gun positions by daylight.

They had broken cleanly through the heavy defense crust of one of the most fiercely defended towns in all Germany. The breakthrough was wide enough to make it fairly safe to keep pouring troops into the town through the breach. Tank destroyers heaved over the humps of the cart path that threaded around the enormous bomb craters that had ruined the airfield, and went on in to help the doughs who were house-to-housing their way down the streets. The unnameable colonel of the 242nd sent one battalion down six streets abreast to cut a wide path straight to the river. Sniper resistance was very heavy; but the careful German defense plans had visioned a gradual shrinking of the whole semicircle of their defenses, rather than a breakthrough right through the middle. Before they could effectively reinforce the center from the sides, the regiment had broken the center cleanly, splitting the Germans in two big wings without communication.

The armor that had come up from the south to hit Schweinfurt from the rear had gotten stalled several miles back so the Germans were not at first hopelessly pinned. But back at division headquarters another regiment had been passed around to the north to filter through some woods toward Schweinfurt's northernmost outskirts. Word came that the northern wing of the two German remainders was marching in a column along the river road, trying to withdraw northeast. The officers smiled grimly. One of their battalions had reached that road on the riverfront before noon, and was lying in wait to ambush that wing. And behind the retreating Germans the 242nd was rapidly spreading through the center of the town, knocking out snipers as swiftly as (omission—checking).

A main feature of the resistance here and throughout southern Germany is something *Time* & *Life* editors should be aware of: the Nazis are manufacturing thousands of *panzerfausts*, the short, lightweight hand-bazooka that even children can operate. They are dropping these off trucks at little towns everywhere for the use of the home folks. With each *panzerfaust* comes a short, simply worded booklet of instructions. Even a little girl can knock out a tank by pointing one of these out a window. After a few bursts the civilian merely surrenders, reminding his captors instantly that he was never a Nazi himself and has two relatives in the American Army. This is one reason why so many Americans shoot first and ask questions later. But it should also be reported that there are several instances where townspeople, usually indignant housewives, have flatly refused to countenance local Nazi last-ditch measures and have even dug up and removed roadblocks themselves.

When we came into Schweinfurt this afternoon, the city was still smoldering here and there from yesterday's bombing. We did not get very far in; the snipers were too thick. The road along which we came was the cart path of the night before, so we could appreciate very clearly how the town is being taken. This road runs exactly along the fence line of the vast

VKF (repeat V.K.F.) and Kugelfischer ball bearing plants, the factories which made more than 50 percent of the ball bearings for the whole German war machine.[198] Many of the acres of low-spreading buildings looked like mere mud holes from over the fence, but we were told that the real factories, still in production until yesterday, were underground. Since the doughs had not gone through the labyrinthine tunnels yet, I cannot say how much of a plant they still have here. We may get down inside them tomorrow when Schweinfurt is declared cleared.

Apr 12 [1945] [Diary]

Into ballbearing factories at Schweinfurt. The sniper. The Russian slave laborers. Prex died.[199]

Apr 13 [1945] [Diary]

To 10th arm. for reaction to Prex death.

SIDNEY OLSON CABLE 44
FROM GERMANY TO DAVID HULBURD
SENT APRIL 13, 1945; REC'D APRIL 13, 1945

For Battlefronts:

There may be controversy for some time to come over the actual efficiency of air bombing. Take this testimony:

There was still scattered sniper fire and the occasional bloop of a *panzerfaust* in Schweinfurt today. We entered as before from the west, accompanied by a guide, as casual wandering about the streets was not yet quite safe. The first thing that impresses you about Schweinfurt is dirt, plain grey dusty dirt. In the great cities, such as Cologne, Aachen, Frankfurt, Mainz and Wurzburg, you are conscious mostly of broken stone and steel; the metal tubes of the insides of buildings are strewn about like entrails among vast masses of broken stones and shattered brick walls; always, steel and stone. But Schweinfurt (literally pig ford) was a middle-sized town of 44,000 population at the highest figure, and it consisted mainly of low buildings spread over several miles along a loop of the Main River; modern two-story housing developments planned for light and air and accessibility to the great ball bearing plants: the *Kugel-fischer* (repeat *Kugelfischer*) (this is the correct spelling) and the *Vereinigte Kugellager Fabrik* (repeat *Vereinigte Kugellager Fabrik*) better known as VKF, presumably some relation to Bill Batt's SKF plants in the United States.[200]

When enormous bombs repeatedly hit low broad buildings, the buildings merely disappear into great dirt craters. That's what most of Schweinfurt looks like: huge round pits at the bottom of which will be the usual collection of twisted rusted metal, broken children's dolls, sodden rags that probably were clothes, and some splintered wood. As you stare over the town, you look over a long succession of such enormous craters, some of them abutting each other and try in vain, no matter how powerful your imagination, to guess where once ran the line of buildings and in which direction ran the streets. Then suddenly you can figure it out: looped into the air and hung there, like the first part of the Indian rope trick, is a steel bar curved in the shape of a question mark (repeat question mark, not quark). The curved steel bar is obviously part of a streetcar railway. Both the railway and the street itself are gone, but here and there out of the acres of craters, you can follow the line of the bent steel bars and suddenly your mind puts together little pieces of evidence in a quick picture, and you can visualize the street much the same way you put together a jigsaw puzzle.

Let us have no more articles anywhere in the American press about the bombing of London. Let the *New Yorker* series on the bombings of Wapping cease and be forgotten. (In fact let the *New Yorker* writers suffering bravely at the Savoy in London be forgotten, too.) The Londoners have exactly the correct attitude about their past travail, which is, briefly: "Let's forget all about it." For as has been said before, the revenge for London, Coventry and all others has been taken a thousandfold and then a thousandfold. Only by the use of Professor Kasner's (repeat Kasner's) word "googol" denoting the figure one followed by one hundred zeroes, can you assess the revenge that has been taken on Germany. In Schweinfurt the grey, gritty dirt of a city pounded smack into the earth floats in a light haze, settling in a grey film like a volcanic ash alike impartially on food, on faces, on clothes. That is the testimony to the power of air bombing that is first apparent.

The reason for bombing the town into irregular heaps of dirt studded with snaggle-toothed brick walls that once were modern homes and apartments was the ball bearing works. I frankly shrink from describing the Kugelfischer works in a quick dispatch like this. One way to do it is this, perhaps. We had been told proudly by the brave infantry men of the 42nd Division—and by their 49-year-old commander, Major General Harry J. Collins—that the factory had been in production right up through yesterday, despite all the bombings, and that production did not stop until the infantry men came in the front doors. We found the manager, one Otto Schaefer, a rather greasy, youngish businessman about 35 years old, and asked him for some facts.[201] He spoke excellent English. He told us that production had never been hampered by bombings before the great Eighth Air Force raid in August 1943, the raid which was so costly that General Arnold issued a statement justifying the cost in lives. Well, General Arnold was right. For that first daylight bombing knocked the plant's production down from more than 100 percent to a little more than 30 percent. Despite furious efforts to rebuild the plant, and evidences of the intensity of that effort were visible everywhere there today, production never came back higher than 30 percent. Then repeated attacks almost snuffed out production. In the last few months production had never gone higher than 10 percent of what it was when Hap Arnold's bombers hit it in August 1943. So help me, I will never argue with (omission—checking) about anything as long as I live. Yet there were at least several thousand superb machine tools in perfect order, greased and ready to go, spread through the hundreds of yards of basement and one-story underground workings. The secret is the same as that in a two-day Detroit production strike: modern integrated production must be kept flowing in all parts equally like the circulation of the blood. A perfectly good right hand cannot function if a lung is missing. So it is with the two great plants at Schweinfurt. Essential parts of them were hopelessly smashed and when those parts were replaced, some other part was smashed—and always the railroads were being cut or vital parts or needed tools were smashed in bombings of railroad yards somewhere else, or military traffic took priority, or essential men were put in uniform for the army, or a fleet of trucks was caught on the road by fighter bombers, or too many slave laborers were sick on the poor food. When the infantry walked in, the manager said, he was down to a few hundred workers who had not worked for more than two weeks. The slave workers, mostly Russian women and girls, corroborated this; and the Italian and French men talked about how they would sabotage a machine "just a little." In evaluating later more careful testimony on the exact production status of Schweinfurt factories, *Time* & *Life* editors should beware of pictures showing acres of machinery in perfect condition, as after a hurried trip through the factories, I can assure you that even in my minimum experience of Detroit production lines,[202] that these machines were as useless as anything designed by Rube Goldberg, because some other part of the factory was ruined. But G.I.s without production-line education were happy in the belief that production went on until they got there. The VKF factory is not nearly as hard hit. It was a somewhat healthier area, however, as a sniper's bullet hit a brick wall near the captain who was guiding us as he turned a corner. With my usual good sense I had stopped to interview a high-breasted young Russian girl worker, age 20, named Inna Krschwiskaja (repeat Inna Krschwisknaja) [*sic*], from Vitebsk who had been a worker for 16 months. I interviewed her until the captain said things were all right, which seemed much too soon.

I realize that I am over-sending Schweinfurt now that I have heard the Berlin approach news, but we hadn't had any news here for days. I will cut this off now, but welcome any questions if information is needed as I have packs of untouched notes. Add items of interest: German SS officers hanged eleven soldiers who wanted to surrender in the last two days. One was not cut down till noon today.

PART II

As a wandering *Time* editor, please let me make two observations. Please hold down hardest war-end optimism, if any in America, over the approaching fall of Berlin, as that is just another city, and apparently insignificant except sentimentally. I am sure you are doing this anyway, but am just chipping in this observation with a No. 8 iron. Secondly, I believe the greatest story in Europe today politically and emotionally are the thousands of liberated slaves streaming down the roads out of Hitlerland. This army alone has liberated some 190,000. What I described in the Patton research, the long columns of weirdly mixed refugees from all lands, blackening the roads in all directions over the hills endlessly, is now true of all Germany. There are immediate political future complications of enormous potential as they add a back-breaking food and transportation load to the strained Allied resources, and are literally crazy to fight the Germans or to go home. Please watch most closely.

SIDNEY OLSON CABLE 45
FROM GERMANY TO DAVID HULBURD
SENT APRIL 13, 1945; REC'D APRIL 13, 1945

For Battlefronts:

I spent several hours today talking to men of an armored division fresh out of the line after a bitter battle with the Krauts. I am convinced that foxholes reaction stuff is actually phony. If I had been with the boys in German basements last night when they first actually heard the news and actually watched their jaws drop, I might have a legitimate piece.[203] But next-day stuff is considered judgement rather than actual reaction to news. The best quote of the day, for example, was one boy who drawled: "It's a rugged deal" which is good army slang understatement which they use à la Hemingway for everything from lack of toilet paper to eating cold rations or getting heavy shellfire. Actually most boys I talked to were worried about the future as summed up by one who said: "Well, the Big Three will look kinda funny now. Truman will probably be in the middle, like lucky Pierre."

Content Peckham knows that story.[204]

Other than this I have nothing worth sending. I suggest that *Time* in handling the story consider me as a typical audience since literally thus far at eleven o'clock Friday night I have heard nothing beyond the barest announcement of the president's death and the briefest bulletin in *Stars and Stripes*. I am keenest for those beautifully exact details which *Time* only can supply, and await most keenly the copy of *Time* which I'll get in about two or three weeks with all the fresh news of the circumstances in it. So will all the troops. For instance, one major said today: "Well, *Time* will tell me all about it in a month, and until then I won't know whether to worry or not. Meantime, I got a job." In short, *Time* and *Life* editors, please tell me everything and I don't mean an obituary because I know that by heart.

Albest luck to USAW and *Life* editors in an excruciating week.

Apr 14 [1945] [Diary]

To Heidelberg. Claire, the English g of who married a German, Capt. Hincley, Charlie Stewart, Prof. Martin Dibelius,—Devers for dinner w Syd Stoen, photog: Clare Boothe Luce, Henry Cabot Lodge, Henry J. Taylor, Gen. Harrison, et al. The villa, food, talk, dancing. Europe Hotel as a V.I.P.

APRIL 15, 1945 [LETTER TO ZEMBRA]

[This undated letter was most likely written on April 15: Olson refers to Roosevelt's death (April 12) and dinner with Clare Boothe Luce (April 14). He also mentions the anticipated fall of Nuremberg (April 16–20). Page 1 is missing, and page 3 has been cut off.]

Italians, Czechs, Yugoslavs, French, Belgians. After all, I thought we must have a lot in common; they were slaves under the Nazi boot, and I am a slave under your boots—although my kind of slavery is a lot more fun, of course. We were sniped at once, or rather the Captain who was taking us around was, but we never found where it came from. I talked to quite a lot of German prisoners, trying to find out what they think of Hitler. They always say: *"Schatz und dung,"* which means "s . . . and corruption." Even young girls say that, and very bitterly. But you don't know whether they're acting or not. But one weak young prisoner we took was typical of many: a trembling thin fellow of about 30, who had been a soldier for 8 weeks, four of them as a chauffeur and four as an infantry man, after being nothing but a grade school teacher all his life. If he's a soldier, or if any of those 13-year-old boys I've seen are soldiers, then I'm MacArthur. Most of the women correspondents are a lot tougher characters.

Friday I took off to do some writing work, and to get some reactions to the President's death from GIs. Saturday I went back to Old Heidelberg the Beautiful, to try to interview some German professors on the history of Nuremberg, in preparation for when we take it, and thus got to make that beautiful drive along the Neckar river valley again. Most interesting I met was a young ugly English woman now working for the American Military Government. She had met a young German in Heidelberg when she was studying there in the summer of 1939, had married him and had stayed there through the whole war. He's missing, prob. dead somewhere in Russia, of course. She hadn't heard from her English family until a couple of weeks ago when she learned that her mother had died in 1942 and her father had been bombed out of two houses and was living with friends in England. Her three brothers were in the Canadian army, the RAF and the British Army, and two of them are missing. That's quite a lot of news to get all at once, hey? She acted as interpreter while I talked with some German professors. She said that she's been caught by the war with only some summer clothes and one pair of shoes, which she was still wearing. She'd had to make these clothes do for six years.

Just as I was getting in the jeep to go back to Press camp, a messenger caught me from General Devers, who commands this whole army group, asking me to dinner. They gave me a VIP (Very Important Personage) room at the big hotel, a toothbrush and a hot bath and put me in a car to go off to this villa which is quite a ways off. When I walked into the magnificent, really out of this world, house, bowed in by colonels, etc., it was to find, having cocktails, none less than Clare Booth [sic] Luce and Lt. Col. Henry Cabot Lodge. I was in battledress and combat boots and everyone else was spit and polish as only the Army can be. But we had three quick beautiful dry martinis, my first since last December, some canapes, also my first; and talked for almost an hour. Then the Gen. came with some others Gens. and we all had our pictures taken on the terrace, and went into dinner. Also there, traveling with Clare, was that superjerk Henry Jay Taylor of Scripps Howard—remember him and wife at that foreign policy dinner in the Waldorf last fall?

But it was a wonderful evening; and Gen. Devers and Clare were both in great form. She had on an army nurse's uniform with yellow scarf, and really looked swell; with puffs of grey, really grey hair on each side of the blonde, in front. She was really delightful this time, with Prince Ali Kahn, son of Aga Kahn, on one side, and Lodge on the other, with Devers opposite with me on one side and Gen. Harrison on the other. We had soup, roast perfect beef, etc. with a superb red wine, then champagne and topped with 80-year-old brandy. In the evening much bourbon was drunk. Clare was in great form, and gave some wonderful mimicry imitations of certain political characters absolutely exactly, until everyone laughed to the point of weeping. She wasn't a bit chilly this time, and of course, as the only woman there, which she thrives on, she was something. After we danced, and she taught the Gen. to rhumba, jitterbug and tango, while we laughed some more. Then we went off to our homes, and this morning they sent me back up here to the front in one of the Generals' cars. Riding on those soft cushions in a closed car after bouncing on the absolute bony point of my fanny in an open topless jeep through the whole winter was such a dream of comfort I was almost killed with pleasure. Anyway now I'm back to work, and will watch the fall of Nuremberg.

5. THE LAST DAYS

Apr 15 [1945] [Diary]
   Ret to Lauda in Generals car.

Apr 16 [1945] [Diary]
   Old Heidelberg with Choclett, the courier, no shock absorbers:
chow at Europe, Bowan, Stewart, Gen. Harrison, Capt. Chico, Col.
of G-3, Stewart, LeVien,
   jeep back after interviews with Prof. Hoops, prex of Heidelberg U.

Apr 17 [1945] [Diary]
   Jeep with Argo [?], Plambeck,[205] Klein [?], to Burkenbuhl[206]—the flat
tires, the weasel over the mine to 3rd Div.

Apr 18 [1945] [Diary]
   Burkenbuhl.

Apr 19 [1945] [Diary]
   To 45th Div. CP & down to 180 Inf Reg: Nuremberg Stadium. Ret
to Lauda alone with Argo [?]. Kitchen—werewolves.[207]

Apr 20 [1945] [Diary]
   Day off in Lauda—the Yugoslavs.

Apr 21 [1945] [Diary]
   Back to Nuremberg—Lochner, Pat Lockridge: Kitzingen, Neustadt,
R__ [?], Num.
   The hunt for Schwabach. Sleep at 157th (Battn CP) of 45th Div.
Katzwang.

Apr 22 [1945] [Diary]
   To Nurnb. Back to Lauda.

Apr 23 [1945] [Diary]
   Lauda. Wrote Darl.

APR 24 [1945] [DIARY]
Lauda. *Life* piece.

APR 25 [1945] [DIARY]
Lauda. *Life* piece. Bought German portable from Tubby Abrams. Wrote AE Holmgren. Sent package to Darl.

APR 26 [1945] [DIARY]
Dillingen move (on a Sat.)

Cable 46: Some Background

Between April 17 and 22, 1945, Olson went into Nuremberg several times, as it was being taken and immediately thereafter.

On April 23, he typed "Notes for Nuremberg Piece," which helped him write Cable 46 on April 24 and 25. He cabled his dispatch from Seventh Army press camp to New York on April 26.

Olson sent a second, slightly different version of Cable 46 called "K-64" (mostly in capital letters) on the same day. Almost all of this dispatch is included in Cable 46.

About half of Cable 46 was published in the May 14, 1945, issue of *Life*. The article was called "Defeated Land." The magazine's editors also included portions of Cables 47 and 49.[208]

Sidney Olson Cable
from 7th Army Press Camp—No. 46
April 26, 1945

The Last Days

The Collapse of the Nazi Empire is a fantastic show. The spectacle is so massive, so rich with gargantuan ironies, with miseries, great and small, and so charged with terror and laughter that the words fail you. Surrounded by death, walking through the brick dust that once was historic, you find yourself chuckling at a drunken Russian who is solemnly trying to bicycle home to Russia (via France) loaded down with an enormous roll of fine dark worsted suiting. Many of the things you see are quite simply unbelievable. You can either clutch your Army haircut in despair or just ignore the whole staggering scene, much like the worrywart correspondent from the Midwest who goes through blazing ruins quite oblivious to the blood, the desolation, the looting, the open fornication, the drunken revelry, anxiously seeking only the names of soldiers from Iowa.

For the war is over, although there is much shooting so letter-perfect in the difficult art of war, that the story of the city's fall could have been days in advance, with a very close guess on the exact hour when the usual "fanatical resistance" from the usual "SS troops and Hitler youths, armed with machine guns and *panzerfausts*" would be "mopped up in tough house-to-house fighting."

The Seventh Army, smallest and weakest of all American Armies on the Western Front—but with the widest front to cover—has probably a higher proportion of veterans than any of the others. Its divisions have seen action all the way across Africa, they landed and took Sicily, they landed at Salerno and ill-famed Anzio and fought up the peninsula, they landed in southern-France and fought their way up the Rhone Valley and finally broke through the Siegfried Line in one of the most difficult sectors.

In such divisions as the famed Third and 45th, which have teamed together for many months of combat, there is nothing you can teach these soldiers about living and fighting. If an electric light fuse blows out in a house they know how to fix it with a cartridge. And they know how to take their time working from building to building through a German city, and they work with a grim easy smooth professionalism that is something to see. When their two expert major generals, the Third's John W. (Iron Mike) O'Daniell (KOMING—age), and (KOMING—name) Fredericks, (KOMING—age) (the youngest major general in the Army)[209] telephone the regiment impatiently to get their tails busting forward faster, the colonels and the majors and the captains merely smile tolerantly and take their time. They think the war is over, too, and they don't want any casualties. It took them an extra day to take Nuremberg but the casualties were unbelievably low. For such reasons reporting the war in terms of military action is now almost a thing of the past. The mammoth armies of the Allies are merely killing the pocketed remnants of the *Wehrmacht*, expertly, smoothly, carefully, always offering them surrender or death, and quite willing to give either. Usually the Nazis seem to prefer death, and the Americans are happy to accommodate them.

Thus the story of Nuremberg is not a military story. The city was approached from the north. First the 14th Armored Division cut straight south below the city severing its eastern communications. Then the 45th Division swung around the inside path of the Armored and attacked the city from the east and southeast, while the Third Division attacked it frontally from the north and the 42nd attacked from the west and southwest. In a few days the city was cut off and the Nazis were attacked from all sides in a steadily shrinking perimeter. Very early on the morning of April the 20th, on Adolf Hitler's birthday, the last of the Nazi fanatics were trapped in one of Nuremberg's ancient tunnels, leading from the old walled and moated inner city to the capital Berg that dominates the town. In that last hole were Karl Holz, the successor to the famed jew baiter Julius Streicher as *gauleiter* of the district, and Willi Liebel, the friend whom Holz had appointed as *oberburgomeister* (mayor) of Nuremberg. As the last Nazis were being killed methodically by the relentless Americans, Holz shot Liebel and then killed himself. This pleased nearly everyone. . . .[210]

Nuremberg was one of the great cities of Germany. It was first mentioned in the year 1050 AD. In early Medieval times it was the German terminal end of Mediterranean trade from the Levant through Italy and the Danube. As one of the first great Free Cities of Germany it became a cultural shrine, as the wealthy merchants spent their gold on the arts and the churches. Here Albrecht Durer, one of the greatest German artists, lived and was buried; here lived Hans Sachs and the singers whom Wagner made immortal in *Die Meistersinger*; here were made the first watches in Europe, the famed "Nuremberg Eggs." Nuremberg was famed for three great churches whose Construction spread over the 13th, 14th, and 15th Centuries; the *Sebalduskirche*, the *Lorenzkirche* and the *Frauenkirche*. Nuremberg was the home of bratwurst, those delicious pale fat sausages, and one little church had a bratwurst *haus* on the corner. In the inner walled city, once ruled by the Count von Zollern whose family later became the Hohenzollern emperors of Germany, were many streets that had been preserved since the Middle Ages, perhaps the most perfect collection of Medieval architecture in all Europe. In the museum by the great berg, the castle on the hill was the famed iron maiden of the middle ages, in whose spiky embrace perished many a victim of the Inquisition. Nuremberg was one of the great centers of the religious reformation, although Martin Luther never preached there. Nuremberg was one of the great toy centers of the world and its dolls had been shipped to little girls in France, England and Sweden since continental trade began. The *Germanische* Museum was the nearest thing to a central collection of German culture in all Germany. Nuremberg had been the repository for centuries of the *Reichskleinodein* (the crown jewels of the old German emperors). When Adolf Hitler *Anschlussed* Austria in 1938 he took the mantles, the great jeweled orb, the jewel-crusted swords, scabbards and scepters away from Vienna and brought them back to Germany to place in Nuremberg's *Germanische* Museum.[211] From its suburb of Furth ran the first railroad in all Germany, ten miles long, to Nuremberg.

It was because Nuremberg means all these things and many others to all good Germans that Adolf Hitler chose the place as a natural center of Nazi *Kultur*. The old city wears a halo to most Germans; millions of them feel about the city much as the French do about Paris. Very early Hitler made a majority of the city council of Nuremberg his puppets. Then all Germany took sudden shocked notice when the beautiful, historic Nuremberg, became a Nazi shrine. That really impressed Germans; white-haired, old Doctor (KOMING) Hoops (and see your morgue),[212] President of the University of Heidelberg, will tell you so today.

By 1935 Nuremberg was the great annual convention center of the Nazi Party. A special Nazi committee actually worked all year long devising ever grander and ever more stupendous spectacles with which to stun the German burghers. Here Hitler ordered built the greatest architectural monster since the Tower of Babylon attempted to reach heaven, a series of enormous arches, each whose pillars was a skyscraper, set on top of each other. The dream he dreamed, that once he would address thousands of the enslaved representatives of all the multitudes of Europe from the topmost keystone of the topmost arch set on pinnacles of skyscrapers was never realized of course. Construction of this and all related arenas, stadia, congress halls and marching fields had to stop when total war usurped materials and manpower.

But it was on this sacred Nazi soil that Hitler first began to frighten the world. One of the great stadia holds 450,000 people, and the Party faithful once filled these acres of concrete benches in a great horseshoe, beneath the 304 tall steel poles surmounted with gilded swastikas.[213] There they faced the quarter-mile long concrete platform where sat the dignitaries of the Party. Behind and around the stadium 400 huge searchlights threw light into the night in a vast Gothic arch that met over the stadium in the reaches of the sky. Across the spread of the lawn would troop the picked divisions of the Wehrmacht or the bronzed half-naked armies of the labor battalions, their steel shovels shining like knives in the swift flashing drills before their *Fuehrer*. Then the spotlight would focus on the bronze doors at the top of the dais and Adolf Hitler would come down alone to the podium, there to anoint each of the Nazi battle flags solemnly by touching them one by one with the blood-stained flag of 1923 (please check 1923).

Old Nuremberg stood fair and beautiful on its plain, they say. Hitler's theatrical additions in the southwest suburbs only added architectural excitement. Here was the quiet charm of old Germany all in one place, deepened and enriched by the blood and gold-shot tapestry of its history. To look at Nuremberg last week as it fell,[214] one needed only the sense of history and a sense of humor. The humor must be that of high comedy in the Greek sense, comedy that includes many tragedies. As a place of culture, charm and tradition, of music, art and fine food, Nuremberg is gone, gone as are all the fine cities of Germany with the single exception of old Heidelberg. Today Nuremberg looks like all the rest of them, a great waste of broken bricks. From the berg on the hill in the inner walled city the vista is much like that looking down into Bryce Canyon in southern Utah, a stretching pink labyrinth of stone broken in fantastic shapes in canyons that wind senselessly about.

We went in with a man who had lived in Germany many years, who knew Nuremberg well and had often attended Hitler's party congresses. He had his Baedeker guidebook with him to refresh his memory. From the start he was utterly bewildered. There were no landmarks to guide him: the huge railway station, the Grand Hotel, his favorite restaurants, all of them turned out to be heaps of rubble, when he finally uncertainly identified them. It was only after several hours of work, much in the manner of archaeologists studying ruins, that we could orient ourselves with any exactness. Then the shapes of buildings could be imagined from the traces left of statuary, of the iron bases of fountains, from the burned stones.

Very gingerly we entered the shell of the *Sebalduskirche*. A strong wind was blowing, and from time to time big stones fell from the shreds of the vaulted roof far above. The whole church is gone except for one huge mass of reinforced concrete in the center, where the Germans had bricked over the priceless altar of Saint Sebaldus. From the top of a rickety 60-foot ladder you could see that this modern brick sarcophagus had held firm against the years of bombings and the days of shelling, with only a few cracks in the concrete. In the *Lorenzkirche* one such altar also is safely walled up, guarded by a stone Crucifix of Christ, whose left arm was shot away. The *Frauenkirche* is utterly smashed, and the famed entrance, which had also been walled over, suffered a direct shell hit that broke the reinforced concrete in to powder. Above it there is no trace of the world-renowned *Männfeitlaufen* clock[215] where every day at noon the seven electors came out of the clock jerkily and nodded their little heads in a still bow to the seated figure of Charles the Fourth and then filed back into the church to await noon.

The massive *rathaus* or city hall is entirely gone except for the shrapnel-chipped groups of caryatids at one end. The *Bratwurst* church is obliterated; only a leaning, dusty poplar tree marks where it stood. The four famous fountains are destroyed. The Hans Sachs house is gone, although the statue of old Hans is there in the rubble. The Albrecht Durer house has vanished. The *Germanisches* Museum and the tower which held the iron maiden in the museum near the Berg are mere shells. The crown jewels of the ancient German emperors are in some vault, perhaps, or perhaps Hitler has them.[216]

Over all this sickening desolation which the Nazis (something missing) hangs the pall of a city not yet done burning, with dark smoke where some old smoldering wood has been fanned up again, and the pink cloud of fine dust, brick dust that has been powdered finer than sand, almost into talcum powder.

And throughout the city moves the smell of all such cities as they are conquered, a smell compounded of many smells, of death first, of offal, of woodsmoke, of gun powder, and a sick-sweet smell that comes from thousands of opened bottles of wine and spirits half-drunk and then smashed on the ground.

For through these ruins move the motleyest crowds that Europe has seen since the Crusades.

The greatest number are Germans. You can tell the Germans by their manner; they are stunned and tired and beaten and frightened; they start when spoken to; they smile timidly, ingratiatingly and beg information most humbly. Even a German in the greatest of distress does not stride boldly up to any American to ask for help or directions. They pluck your sleeve softly. In the ruins they stand, cooking their meals on open-hearth, improvised brick ovens, readying the food to take down below in the innumerable caves and cellars they having been living in so long. Many of them have had no electric light or running water for a long time. They live like people will perhaps when the ice returns over the earth, huddled together for warmth and comfort and against the loneliness; with someone outside in the night guarding the hole that leads down to their caves. In those caves life is exactly what you would imagine it to be: foul and pitiful, but at least warm and safe against the bombs and the terror outside. But the ones who move with cocky assurance through the ruins are the thousands of (capitals) DPs (the Army initials for the capitals Displaced Persons) who are now thronging out of Germany in a phantasmagoric pilgrimage, an endless wave of thousands of vengeance-minded slaves and war prisoners, pillaging and raping and burning their way through the towns and cities, hopelessly out of hand for days after their liberation, as the fighting troops move rapidly on and the expert but hopelessly undermanned staffs of the Military Government strive desperately to cope with them somehow.

The Germans fear their former slaves with an almost insane fear, and that fear is not misplaced. God help the German family that lives in an isolated farmhouse these days. At the very least the DPs commandeer all cars, motorcycles, bicycles, farm wagons, carts. Then they loot their way through houses looking always first for liquor and then for valuables and then for food, and then for clothing. But they will take anything. Nuremberg for two days was totally out of hand of the military. After the expert GI souvenir hunters had taken a quick look around for cameras, binoculars and watches, the DPs moved in as the soldiers moved on. Nuremberg was a city of 800,000 people once. Perhaps 200,000, perhaps more, still live there, mostly underground. Such a city naturally must have great stores of food and wine. To control this city the American Army had a picked staff of 26 officers, two warrant officers, and 21 enlisted men.

Into the city poured thousands of the liberated from the environs. The greatest number were Russians, virile, short, stocky, happy, and the vast majority of them beautifully drunk with liberated champagne, cognac, vermouth and even beer. From two days of observation in the town and three days around it, I can safely say that the Russian is a person of indiscriminate tastes. He will take anything he can lift—and he can lift anything. You ride for a solid mile past happy, grinning, drunken Russians walking, bicycling or pushing carts, all of them laden with great bales of cloth from a clothing warehouse. For two days you see them fighting and clawing, tearing the clothes from each others' backs in an effort to crowd into an already jam-packed underground warehouse where the Nazi's kept food and especially liquor. The American soldiers would order them away but the happy, drunken Russians would merely give him the old Bronx cheer with a special Russian flute-like tone. Scores of them would thumb their noses at the lone soldier, who could only grin helplessly. If he fired a shot in the air they merely clapped their hands admiringly and crowded around him to offer bottles of their stolen schnapps.

I went down several of these underground warehouses. One had been a Nazi-officers' sales store. This was actually more dangerous than small-arms fire because in the flickering candlelight hundreds of DPs were scrambling and fighting ferociously in the dark over each package, each paper carton, each shelf; scrambling like fat rats all over the floors in wales of paper, seeking they knew not what. Out of one office building basement came a dozen Russians carrying German typewriters, great heavy machines they are too, but solidly made. What earthly good could a German typewriter be to a Russian who is several thousands of miles from home and is facing the wrong way anyway? One of them had a small iron stove. One Russian girl on a bicycle was red-faced from pedaling under the weight of a mass of sausages tied together like a bunch of bananas. On her back were hung six bottles of wine. Everywhere in the ruins were the bottles and everywhere on the streets was the bottle glass. You walked in the pink dust that blew in sudden sand storms into your face, your boots crunching over glass, piles of live and dead bullets of all sizes, and past the little drifts of torn Nazi uniforms and piles of German helmets and belts and ammunition cases; surrounded by the Russians drunk and grinning and friendly, the Belgians, Poles, hundreds and hundreds of Yugoslavs, the Dutch and Italians. In the crowd suddenly you notice a man with a yellow, six-pointed star on his breast-pocket. On it is the word "Jude" (Jew). He tells you he is the only Jew left in Nuremberg; that he was unmolested because he had a German wife but that all his family long since went off to concentration camps. He lived underground for six years he said and was not permitted any ration cards for food or clothing. He lived on what was smuggled to him by German friends of his wife. He vowed that today was his first carefree day in the open air for many years, and certainly he breathed the stink of Nuremberg as if he were on the freshest peak in the Alps. Then you see a spare, thin British soldier on a bicycle, Private Sam Hewitt of the Cheshire Rifles, who has been a German prisoner since June 1940. His uniform, although faded, is freshly washed and neatly mended. He has bicycled in from the prison camp near the stadium. His reason is very British: he just wanted to see the sights of Nuremberg. He is pleased at the excellent destruction of the town, but a little disappointed too, for it looks like all other German towns.

In this fantastic end of Hitler's attempt to make an empire, that is the guiding truth: there are no German cities left, always excepting old Heidelberg where the unbombed professors somewhat smugly assume that they will naturally be the intellectual founders of the next new Germany. There are no cities. Nuremberg is no symbol of anything. We went there because it was a great symbol of old Germanic culture, and then a great symbol of Nazi ideology. But the city, symbols and all, is gone; and in the place of Nuremberg you can write in whatever town you choose, from Berlin to Berchtesgaden. Aachen, Cologne, Bonn, Coblenz, Wurzburg, Frankfurt, Mainz: all gone in one sweeping reach of destruction whose like has not been seen since the mighty Genghis Khan came from the East and wiped out whole nations all the way from China to Hungary.

All those ruins have the same characteristics: the smoking ruins, the smell, the thousands of liberated streaming happily through on their way to blacken the roads for miles and miles on both sides of the Army's traffic, heading south out of Germany. So it turns out that Nuremberg is not important. Nor will Berlin or Hamburg or Bremen or Munich be important. They are only marks on a map of a country that exists now only in books and pictures.

[1945] [Diary]
April 27 Augsburg
April 28
April 29 Dachau

CABLE 47: SOME BACKGROUND

i. An Historic Document

After witnessing the liberation of Dachau concentration camp on Sunday, April 29, Olson wanted to get his report out as quickly as possible. While the details were still fresh in his mind, he typed up "Cable 47" in the early morning hours of April 30 and sent it to New York "via RCA." The 18-page dispatch was typed entirely in capital letters, and each page bears the stamp of the field press censor.

About one-third of his dispatch was used in *Time*'s May 7, 1945, issue. The article bore the heading "Dachau" and credited Olson. The article was accompanied by several photographs. A week later, *Life* included another third of his dispatch in the May 14, 1945, issue. Olson was given a byline for this article, which was titled "Defeated Land." This article was illustrated with line drawings by David Friedenthal.

About one-third of Olson's Dachau dispatch was never published. The entire dispatch has never been seen by the public—until now.

ii. A Second Version of the Cable

Olson sent a second, nearly identical version of Cable 47 on the same day, likely through a different channel. He obviously hoped that at least one of the two would reach New York. The second version resembles the majority of his other dispatches, with standard capitalization and Time Inc. details in the upper-left corner of the first page.

What is notable about the second version is that it contains several lines of text that at some point had fallen off the RCA version (due to tearing along the crease where two of the pages had been folded).

The RCA version is reproduced below; we have added the missing lines of text found in the second version, using italics to differentiate.

In comparing the two texts, we found that in the RCA version, Olson spelled out numbers (like "2-2-2") as well as the pronunciation of pronouns (like "aye," "eyem," and "eyve"). He also spelled out punctuation, for example, "Cma" for comma, "Quark" for question mark, "Para" for paragraph, and so on. For the sake of comprehension, we have changed these to recognizable words and punctuation. The overall lack of commas in this dispatch can cause occasional confusion; however, we felt it was important to leave it "as is" to retain the sense of urgency.

The second version contains several small changes made either by Olson or the typist or the censor; for example: the word "jolliest" was changed to "wooliest."

iii. A Photograph Is Found

In his dispatch, Olson named several of the people he encountered as he roamed through the camp: General Linden; Lieutenant Colonel Downard; correspondents Cowan and Ridder; and a survivor who was discovered among the dead inside the boxcars.

Several soldiers and correspondents who encountered Olson at Dachau mentioned seeing him in their own contemporaneous accounts. For example, General Henning Linden, the assistant commander of the 42nd Infantry "Rainbow" Division, named Olson in his official report.[217]

In Sam Dann's compilation of oral histories recorded by members of the 42nd Infantry Division who were there, at Dachau on April 29, 1945, one account stands out in particular. Sergeant William "Hap" Hazard, a combat photographer for the *Rainbow Reveille*, recalled, "I believe Sid Olson of *Time-Life* asked for an Army photographer soon after he had heard that the 222nd Regiment was to 'take' Dachau." Like Olson, Hazard set out immediately for Dachau:

> After crossing a small river (the Amper) near Dachau, we spotted a long line of boxcars near the prison compound. Rifle and machine-gun fire could be heard from the general direction of the stalled train. . . . I joined Colonel Downard as he made his way toward his patrol, which by this time had radio'd their findings in the boxcars. These were next to a side entrance to the camp, itself. This is when Downard, joined by a T.D. Commander (Captain Roy Welbourn), was told that a survivor was in one of the cars filled with bodies. I asked the Colonel to wait briefly until I could get into position, before rescuing the survivor. It took me less than 15 seconds to get focused and insert the flash bulb in my 4x5 Speed Graphic. Sid Olson joined me just after the picture was shot.[218]

As the emaciated survivor was carried to the passenger door of a waiting jeep, Hazard took another photograph. In this one, Olson can be seen standing at the front of the jeep, wearing a trench coat, his spectacles shining.

In 1994, Hazard wrote about the fate of this photograph in a letter to Art Lee: "A print of Col. Downard and the live Polish prisoner was subsequently picked up by Sid Olson, a Time/Life correspondent who appears (light trench coat). . . . Olson later told me the picture arrived in New York too late to make the *Life* deadline, and was lost in the shuffle on the picture editor's desk."[219]

Hazard must have retained a copy of the print, however;[220] in 1946, it was included in the 42nd Rainbow Division's published history of World War II.[221] Olson never told his family about the photograph and declined to discuss his experiences at Dachau.[222] After his death, the book was discovered sitting in plain sight on his bookshelf.

———————————

VIA RCA NUMBER 47
TO: PRESS HULBURD TIME INC NEW YORK
FROM: SIDNEY OLSON *TIME & LIFE* CORRESPONDENT SEVENTH ARMY

Pro Battlefronts Attention Walker and Pro *Life* Attention Calhoun:

Note to Censors: Please do not hold this copy up or refer it! If it must be cut, cut it and send it on as it must reach *Time* Magazine as early as possible Monday in order to make this week. Thanks very much. Olson

I have been in Dachau today from the time the first American troops entered until the place was cleared.[223] I will tell you about it chronologically with no attempt to embellish so that you may judge for yourselves.[224] Perhaps the United States is satiated with horrors after the other prison camps; certainly there is a limit to how much horror the mind can absorb. But when all the other names of prison camps are forgotten the name of Dachau will still be infamous. It was the first great concentration camp that Rudolf Hesse [*sic*] set up for Adolf Hitler and its mere name was a whispered word of terror through all Germany from the earliest days of Nazi control of Germany. It was not only the largest of all German concentration camps,[225] it was the place where all German opponents of Nazism were sent. Here came the Social Democrats and then later the intellectuals, the journalists, the professors of all nations that fell into Hitler's hands. And here were concentrated the flower of Nazi sadists, the beasts who delighted in torture and death. This was the training school, the proving ground for Gestapo sadists who were then promoted as the New Order spread *into control of their own concentration camps. But no one ever improved on the old model. We waited outside the little town until* the woodpecker noise of machine guns had died down somewhat and then followed the 692nd (repeated 6-9-2) tank destroyer battalion into town. The Second battalion of the 222nd Infantry Regiment of the 42nd Rainbow Division was already moving past the town to join I for item Company of the 157th Infantry Regiment of the 45th Division at the concentration camp.[226]

Before we went in we talked to a company of Germans just captured outside of Dachau. For your information they all believed as of tonight that Hitler and Goebbels but not (repeat not) Goering and Himmler were dead and that the war is over, but that there is no one to issue the cease firing order but Himmler and he refuses.

In the town we found Lieutenant Colonel Donald Downard of Olympia, Washington, commanding officer of the 2nd battalion of the 222nd Regiment (repeat the 2-2-2 regiment).[227] He volunteered to take us down to the concentration camp where elements of the 45th Division's 157th Regiment were still fighting it out with SS troops.[228] We went over two bridges that had been inadequately blown (one of them collapsed before we came back tonight). The camp was easy to find: along the little road through the tall pines of Dachau were yellow metal road signs lettered with the phrase: "K (the letter K) Lager."[229] We followed these until we reached the sweeping concrete curves to the camp.[230]

Beside the main highway into the camp there runs a spur line off the main Munich railroad. Here a soldier stopped the two jeeps and said "Colonel, I think you better take a look at these boxcars." We got out and walked a few yards to a long row of boxcars standing on the siding.

The cars were filled with dead men. Most of them were naked. On their bony emaciated backs and rumps were whip marks. Most of the cars were open-top cars like American coal cars. To be accurate, I must not say the cars were filled: the average layer of the skinny half-naked bodies was two deep. But when they had been able to stand or sit up; before they died lying atop each other they must have pretty well filled the cars. I walked along these cars and counted 39 of them which were filled with these dead. The smell was very heavy. I cannot estimate with any reasonable accuracy the number of dead we saw here but I counted bodies in two cars and there were 53 in one and 64 in another and I picked them as average. There were about 15 or 20 more freight cars farther along this spur supposedly also filled with dead but there were many loose SS snipers firing from houses only a few yards farther up the line so I turned back.

I have a strong stomach: the physical spectacle of blood and death has never bothered me as a reporter. All I felt up to this point was anger.

A German civilian rode his bicycle up beside us at this point. He was crying and trembling. He said he lived in a house near Dachau, but like most Germans had never believed all the stories about the camp until last Thursday night. Then this trainload of political prisoners, evacuees from other prison camps brought here hurriedly by the SS had been brought in and left on the siding. He said they moaned and cried night and day as they died of thirst and hunger and exposure. It has been very cold here, and you can see the glistening peaks of the Alps from Dachau. But they didn't get this thin in three days. Some of them were literally skeletons. In two boxcars there were raw rib cages from which you could only deduce cannibalism, as these were only parts of bodies and they had not been cut up but torn. If this is too strong for any citizen's stomach, let me repeat I am trying only to report exactly what I saw as only a posturer would try to go beyond the facts. And tomorrow morning, April 30th, the War Crimes Commission movie men are going in to record it all exactly that it may be shown to German movie audiences in the future. Tonight we merely told the movie men where to look. The weeping German didn't even care if the angry GIs around him killed him, he was so desperately, abysmally ashamed of being a German.

Then it happened. As we walked back down to our jeeps, a soldier suddenly shrilled: "Look, for Christ's sake, one of them's alive!" Out of the mass of bony yellow flesh one figure sat up feebly.[231]

Colonel Downard jumped up in the freight car and lifted the skinny thing out to us.[232] The only way you could tell he was any more alive than the others was that he could still move slightly.[233] He could not even smile. But he was semiconscious and we wrapped him in blankets and put him in a jeep, and Colonel Downard drove him back to a field hospital. From the patch with the capital letter P on his coat we knew he was a Pole. He weighed about 80 pounds but was fairly tall. He was wearing only a short coat. We went on alone to the great gate of the prison with the swastika over the arch through which so many thousands have passed since this camp was first planned in June 1933.

Here the main entry road runs past several largish buildings. These had been cleared; but the doughs were still shooting it out from barracks to barracks and factory building to factory building a few hundred yards ahead. Now we began to meet the liberated. The first we met were slaves who had worked in the Kessel (repeat Kessel) building which actually houses two-story high very modern vats in which they cooked the thin potato peeling soup that was the main item on the camp's bill of fare. Several hundred Russians, French, Yugoslavs, Italians and Poles were here frantically, hysterically happy, many of them in blue and white striped pajama-like uniforms. They began to kiss us and there is nothing you can do when a lot of hysterical unshaven lice-bitten half-drunk typhus-infected men want to kiss you. Nothing at all. You can't hit them and besides they kiss you from all over at the same time. It's no good trying to explain that you're only a correspondent. A half-dozen of them were especially happy and it turned out they were very proud: they had killed two German soldiers themselves in the Kessel Building. One of them finally explained in broken French that they wanted permission to throw the bodies outside in the street to make the house cleaner. We—I mean Walter Ridder of the *Saint Paul Dispatch*[234] and myself—thought that was okay and so they lugged the bodies out in a wild scramble for the honor. They threw the bodies, both dressed in the paint-daubed coveralls of the Luftwaffe's flak regiments down on a railroad track and then kicked them for awhile. The Germans had been beaten to death.

On the railroad tracks here inside the camp stood a line of railroad armored cars painted the German tan. Things had gotten quiet again up ahead so we crossed a lawn and looked into one of the first factory buildings. This was a pottery factory and the workmanship was most excellent. There were many large busts of Hitler and some elegant white figures of SS commandants mounted on white horses, all of them delicately tinted at well-lighted workshops where the starving slaves must have found a special irony in being forced to put delicately handsome tints on the SS officers' faces.

For a while now things were hot outside only a few buildings down so we stayed there for a while. When the noises settled down we went on and the great size of the establishment of Dachau began to open before us. Factory buildings and barracks and big administration buildings spread on and on apparently endlessly. With us we had two men from the 42nd Division which gave us that comfortable feeling. A description of one barracks will be enough for you to get the idea. We entered very carefully because ex-prisoners had warned us repeatedly of mines and booby traps, only using opened doors and watching for wires. In one barrack which had been used as an SS officers canteen the slaves slept on straw mattresses in a long room which was filled with their defecations as they had no facilities of any kind. From beyond it came the sound of rushing water. Poking into the room we saw that the liberated had sacked the place thoroughly in their desperate rush for the food they served but which had been denied them and then had turned on all the huge water taps, which were flooding the floor. On our right was a long wooden table at which sat a Nazi lieutenant dead. He had been shot in the back as he sat eating a sandwich and drinking beer. A half-empty brandy bottle was before him. He was freshly dead and still bleeding a little. We went on past occasional dead German soldiers and finally found in the loneliness of that expanse of barracks on barracks and building on building a Czech. He was running and we thought he was a German and maybe he was but he said he was a Czech and he most cooperatively found us two ladders so that we could climb over a high cement wall topped with rusted barbed wire and down into the most select inside of the camp.

Outside the first building we saw here, half covered by a brown tarpaulin a stack about five feet high and about twenty feet wide of naked dead bodies all of them emaciated to the skeletal point. We went on around this building and came to the central crematory. The rooms here in order were first the office where the living and the dead passed through and where all their clothing was stripped from them; second the Brausebad room (repeat, the Brausebad) where the victims were given baths and third the crematory.[235] In the crematory were two large furnaces, both cool to the touch. Long grates were fixed to slide in and out bearing the bodies. Before the two furnaces were hooks and pulleys on rafters above them. Here according to a number of Frenchmen, the SS often hanged men by the necks or by the thumbs or whatever their fancy dictated. From here the victims could watch while being whipped and tortured as their comrades were slid into the furnace either alive or dead and either slowly or rapidly according to the SS mood. Behind one furnace on the walls were portions of two curious sadistic pornographic murals. Each of them showed an SS officer riding a huge white sow (repeat sow pig). This was in keeping with the SS doctrine that all opponents are swine. The figures had no heads, but curiously the officers were drawn as wearing large Windsor bow ties around their collars. This gave these murals an effeminate look. The murals are placed so that the furnace tenders can see them.

In the next room was another great stacks [*sic*] of bodies piled about seven feet high here much like cordwood, all naked, all emaciated, and many with whip marks.

Outside, a Pole showed us his right hand. The first finger had been cut off well down into the hand. He said, "SS."

We were quite tired and tense. The fighting was still very close sometimes only a few barracks away, and you could never be sure that any of the houses you passed were cleared. And always we were being kissed and backslapped and pounded by these pitiful happy starved hysterical men, each of whom wanted to tell us his home country his home city and ask us news and beg for cigarettes. The eyes of these men defy my powers of description without going off the deep end. They are the eyes of men who have lived in a super hell of horrors for many years and are now driven half crazy by the liberation they have prayed so hopelessly for. Again and again in all languages they called on God to witness their joy. In case I forget—I'm writing this at Fifteenth Corps Headquarters[236] at three in the morning of April 30th whence a courier plane will fly it far back to the Press Camp—I saw today men of these *nationalities: Russian, Polish, French, Dutch, Belgian, Yugoslav, Luxembourg, Turkish, Greek, Italian, Austrian, the Austrians of Schussnigg's day, Spanish. I saw no* British or Americans although GIs told me that one reason they took no prisoners wherever possible all day was that they had found the bodies of two American aviators who had been shot in the back of the head this morning. I did not see this so cannot vouch for it, but the soldiers swore it was true.

But though we were tired from the long all morning and half the afternoon drive through freshly fought territory where mines were sown from time to time—and nothing makes you tenser than mined roads— we were lured on and on and on from building to building. What lured us was a sound which at first we had thought was the wind in the pines of Dachau. Then after a while we knew it was cheering—the sound of thousands of men cheering and cheering again and then cheering in crescendi that rose and faded in the afternoon air. At last we came to a high wooden wall and went through the gates.

Before us stretched the great prison compound of Dachau. This must be at least one square mile in extent. A paved highway runs all around it. Then there is a small canal around it which acts as a moat; it is about twelve feet wide. Beyond it is a path clear around the enclosure with guards towers at intervals. Then there is a barbed wire fence about fifteen feet high and beyond it a great grassy ditch nearly twenty feet deep and beyond that a lower fence of wire which we were told was electrically charged. I do not know for certain. Several prisoners said that while the soldiers were fighting the SS and flak regiments here that a number of prisoners rushing to escape had been electrocuted in the very moment of liberation.

In and out of this vast stretch of open compound studded with low barracks were swarming the liberated men of Dachau. I cannot pretend to estimate the number with any exactness. But there were many thousand. Reputedly the camp could hold forty-five thousand transients between life and death. Thinking over football crowds and political crowds, I would guess conservatively eight thousand. The prisoners themselves insisted that there were thirty-two thousand men there.

As far as you could see swarmed these men, cheering as hard as their feeble strength would permit. We had already given away all our cigarettes. They tore themselves getting through the barbed wire to touch us, to talk to us. Some of them were nearly mad with joy. Here were the men of all nations that Hitler's agents had picked out as prime opponents of Nazism; here were the very earliest Hitler-haters. Here were German social democrats, some of whom I talked to. Here were Spanish survivors of the Spanish Civil War that began all this. Here I found Djun Merin, repeat Djun Merin, the Ankara Turkish Correspondent of the *New York Times* who had only been in Dachau one month but had been in German prisons some time since he had been spirited out of Turkey by the Gestapo for writing anti-Nazi dispatches for the *Times*.[237] Here was a correspondent for *Paris Soir* who cried so hard I couldn't get his name. The few GIs here were fresh out of combat and had been given the hopeless thankless task of shooing the thousands back inside the enclosure until they can be transported away. But they kept swarming through and the doughs were driven to discharging their rifles in the air. But to the Russians especially this was only amusing; a dough would shout ferociously and fire a clip into the air and immediately would disappear under a cloud of Russians and Poles who wanted to kiss and hug their beautiful comrade. One Russian got a loaf of brown bread and ran desperately back and forth gnawing on it while a score of starved liberés chased him until they brought him down and flung themselves on the bread until a half dozen were gnawing on it on the ground with others jumping atop the pile.

Over the big concrete gate that stretches between two guardhouses hung the camp slogan of the SS: "*Arbeit macht frei*" (repeat, Arbeit macht frei—Work will make you free) which was a lie that deceived no living soul in Dachau. A German Social Democrat who had been a prisoner here for eleven years told us that on the hill near the camp were six thousand graves from the days when the dead used to be buried; before the deaths became a problem warranting the great ovens we had seen. Three Belgians then came up to me; they were a committee of intellectuals[238] appointed by the camp an hour before to represent the Belgians and French to tell us that last night the SS had killed two thousand inmates of the camp at first by special selection and then in some panic as the American firing had come closer apparently indiscriminately. They had killed them with machine guns all that night and in the early morning even to women with babes in their arms. Incidentally we did not see any women and could not find the bodies of such women. This committee wanted to show us the bodies. But at the gate there was a tremendous crush of the less patient liberés to get out as many could not understand why they should not have instant liberty. Here we found General (KOMING) Linden (repeat Linden), Assistant Division Commander to Harry Collins of the 42nd Rainbow Division.[239]

We explained to General Linden that we wanted to tour the inside of the camp to see these massacred bodies and to get an idea of the living conditions.[240] We had been joined by Howard Cowan of the *Associated*

Press.[241] The General then did a very brave thing: he chose two armed guards and accompanied us and the Belgians inside on a tour of the camp. We found plenty of stacks of bodies all right but the quick come before the dead. The pitiful stacks of bodies—and we were told that hundreds had been thrown into the river when the Nazis got hurried last night—were like all those we had seen.

The barracks surround a great bare open exercise ground about the acreage of five big football fields side by side although it is difficult to estimate exactly. Here again these veteran enemies of Nazism had already begun to act like the intellectuals so many are. They had formed a giant ring of hands around this open space and were doing their best to keep everyone back in or near their barracks. Outside this great ring milled the thousands of thin men still cheering with their hoarse weak throats. Trying vainly to keep up with the general we went into one barracks after another. They are about the size which the American army builds to house 72 men or less. Each of these rooms was jammed and the Belgians and French whom we could understand said that each barracks held at least 1,000 men. In one of them I will swear there were at least one thousand and possibly 1,500 but so many were sick and possibly dying of starvation and beatings that they merely lay or leaned or sat shoulder to shoulder too weak to do more than grin glassily. It was here that we even found some Hindus.

Remember that all this time the cheering went on and we were being forcibly mobbed by hundreds of men strong as only the half insane can be, kissed and kissed again by men who stank like the inferno, obviously sick toward death of all kinds of illnesses and pounded and wrenched and tugged and generally mauled. One giant Russian held me for at least 30 seconds while he kissed all over the U.S. (United States) insignia on my coat and the General's party began to vanish far ahead surrounded by hundreds of screaming men. They shouted in all languages but sometimes in American phrases, such as one little Pole who ran beside us until he dropped flat shouting desperately: "Hello boys! Hello boys!"

The tour lasted twenty minutes some of the longest worst minutes in anyone's life but in that time we had seen the final horror of Dachau: what it is for sick and dying and tortured men whose only hope is a quick death and who know that the one thing they could not expect from the Nazis was a quick death—what it is for such men to have to live like rats jammed together. One can only imagine what an especial torture this must have been to men of culture breeding taste education and refinement to watch themselves necessarily growing more beastly every day and to find themselves at last caring nothing for their lives. For all day these men told us that most of the time they only wanted death quick beautiful merciful death and the coming of the Americans was to many of them only a hope that could only be absurd.

As we got out of the camp the Germans began to shell Dachau with 88s and 105s. This was the last German touch to the day. They knew of course exactly where to zero in on the camp; perhaps they guessed that the prisoners must be held there until they can be fed and treated and watered and bathed and transported. General Linden had brought up two more companies to preserve order for the prisoners were still leaking happily out of the camp bound for anywhere. Incidentally, let me add F.Y.I. that a number of Russians I've talked to through German-speaking doughs do not—repeat, not—want to go back to Russia—they fear the Russians will somehow not understand their working in Germany. All the Russians seem to want to go directly to the United States. Oh, they're terrific people these Russians, the toughest jolliest[242] hard drinking hard fighting fearless characters you can imagine. They have an intense virility which is so blazing it makes the men of other nations often seem pallid characters.

The shelling after everything else literally scared the living daylights out of us. We were all long since horribly sick of Dachau. I had seen too many dead men for even my Swedish stomach but the live ones were even worse because so many of them were obviously mentally scarred for life by what they have endured. We were now told that there was another barbed-wire enclosure not far away where the Nazis kept all the hopelessly insane prisoners for what uses I can only imagine. But here I failed in my job as a reporter: I had had enough. I have two alibis: one was the shelling and the other was the need to get somewhere to write a story that might reach *Time & Life* editors in time for use. The shelling was a creeping barrage and it finally got close enough that the doughs ducked into cellars and so did we although there again facing the agonies of the question whether or not the cellar housed live Nazis with burp guns. The barrages were coming at three-minute intervals we decided so we made a run for it after each barrage. But we got hopelessly lost. This was sheer hell because there were no landmarks to guide us but the interminable stretching barracks that all look the same. Had they been cleared? There was no one to say. But they looked suspiciously quiet and there were no doughs around. Suddenly during one of our runs we were joined by two half-drunken Czechs both carrying loaded automatic German rifles. This was a very bad time. One of the Czechs said grinning happily "SS?" You see they don't know what American uniforms are like. Here I acted very quickly falling on his neck and roaring *"Comrade Amerikaner!"* Ridder and Cowan got very close to the other one and so did the two doughs from the 42nd.[243] But this was no good. Just then about twenty feet from us came running a bare-handed SS lieutenant, running for his life from barrack to barrack. We were all in the way of the two doughs from the 42nd until he had ducked behind the next house. Then along came two hard-running GIs with automatic rifles and expertly with that beautiful natural ease at taking cover which they know they began working around the house. We shouted to the Czechs "SS!" and pointed around the house. For a second this was bad as they raised their guns drunkenly but then they charged off after the German. At that moment there came the quick flooding burp of one of the American rifles and we ran as hard as we could in the other direction. Beyond the next barrack we met two Poles with an Albanian. The Albanian's face was all blood; he had one newly broken tooth and his eyes were already puffing closed. He shouted to us and when we came up he said that he too had been a prisoner for five years and that he spoke five languages and for God's sakes help! But the two Poles spoke English and one said that this Albanian had helped the Nazis beat up the prisoners and that they could swear to it. You must understand that correspondents are usually mistaken for officers. We could not decide the merits of this and were stuck plainly and flatly stuck while they waited for our decision. But just then the crash of the German shells got resoundingly close and we all took off again at a desperate run and finally came in sight of that long railroad train filled with bodies only this time we were on the other side of it. From here we could see that the bodies had been spilled out here in two great heaps. We kept on running but still carefully for mines and watching for booby wires and got back to the jeeps at the Kessel house. From within it came the sound of drunken singing echoing hugely in the great empty vat rooms. We got in the jeeps and took off to drive back through the roadblocks in the dark. It was now 8:30 in the evening.

Today (April 30th) incidentally is my birthday. Dave Scherman went on down tonight late and will get the pictures.[244]

Albest Endit Sidney Olson

SIDNEY OLSON CABLE 48
FROM GERMANY TO DAVID HULBURD
SENT APRIL 30, 1945; REC'D APRIL 30, 1945

For Battlefronts and attention Hersey: Two adds and corrections:

I am told by the second wave of correspondents to reach Dachau that I was naive in thinking that the *Brausebad* or shower rooms were designed to give the prisoners a bath. This actually is a gas chamber, they assert, with hermetically sealed doors and inlets for gas only, not for water. They say that the bewildered victims, puzzled by this sudden Nazi kindness in giving them a bath, were issued soap and a towel and told to step inside where they were then gassed. The soap and towel was [*sic*] then retrieved and issued the next victim. This is what they tell me; I went through what seemed to be the shower room too hurriedly on my way to the ovens. Another point I saw but omitted: many victims after death were tagged on the foot. The tag meant that these were suitable for dissection, usually to obtain gold from the teeth.

Another point: I learned later last night that while Cowan, Ridder and I were ducking in with the infantry that Marguerite Higgins, the smart and pretty young blonde correspondent of the *New York Herald Tribune* and Peter Furst of the *Stars and Stripes* were actually the first to reach the central enclosure of Dachau prison. Furst in a jeep had put Miss Higgins in a weapons carrier and the two barreled up to the main entrance of the enclosure with an armored column and General Linden, whom I mentioned before and who is short, stocky, from Minneapolis, and looks like a retired businessman but is very tough. The Nazis here hung out a white flag from the camp gates and an SS emissary and a German posing as a Swiss Red Cross man tried to surrender to Miss Higgins, who was hiding behind a wall.[245] General Linden accepted. With the SS man and the Red Crosser riding on their jeep La Higgins and Peter Furst then drove directly into the enclosure where the prisoners were so happy they even kissed the SSer. This explained the waves of cheers that we heard as we were ducking from barracks to barracks, dodging all the SSers who had not been told of the surrender.[246] Higgins and Furst left soon after. In traveling about Furst acts as a kind of WAC (repeat, WAC) to La Higgins, who has been blitzing many tired old daily paper correspondents along the front with a steady trail of scoops. She has advantages over most of the veterans in that she came very late to the wars and doesn't yet quite know about being killed and all that, and she is quite pretty so the dogfaces scramble about furiously for the pleasure of escorting her into danger. I also hear she writes quite well but wouldn't know, as I don't see her stuff. Perhaps she is worth a press story. Furst used to be Hollywood man for *PM* (repeat, PM) which is nearly sufficient characterization except that he is really brave. We call him the poor man's Louis Lochner if you know what I mean, although *Time* was too rough on old Lou, who is a nosey old fussbudget but hardly more phoney than scores of correspondents not yet taken up in *Time*. Lochner also really does know the Germans and Germany but does not quite realize what has happened.

[1945] [Diary]

April 30 The ride home on my birthday—Z's letter
May 1 Munich May Day—snow & underground

6. VICTORY IN EUROPE

SIDNEY OLSON CABLE[247]
FROM GERMANY TO DAVID HULBURD
SENT MAY 2, 1945; REC'D MAY 2, 1945

Dear Dave:

I've had it again. I have asked permission to transfer to the Paris office for two weeks beginning May 5 or 6. I hope to see Grover there. I have advised Wertenbaker. I came a shade too close at Dachau and Munich. Meanwhile I am making one more overnight trip this time in an effort to drive to Innsbruck and catch all the big shots such as Stalin's son, Schuschnigg, Niemoeller, etc., at a place I know.[248] If possible I will try to drive on to the Brenner Pass and make a junction with the Fifth Army.[249] That will be my last piece of copy with the Seventh Army, I hope.

[1945] [DIARY]
    May 2–3 Innsbruck
    May ? Innsbruck – Dillingen

SIDNEY OLSON CABLE No. 49[250]
FROM 7TH ARMY PRESS CAMP, GERMANY
MAY 3, 1945

Germany Today:

Perhaps a good way to describe Germany today is by a series of snapshots. Lauda is a little town on the Tauber River in southern Germany.[251] Each of its three tiny stone bridges over the Tauber is barely wide enough for cart traffic and big American trucks could barely squeeze past the ancient statues of Christ on the main bridge, a bridge constructed in the year 1378. The little town slumbers in the sun in a cloud of apple blossoms and smells richly of cow manure. A middle-aged German woman did my laundry in one of the little houses that cluster together behind masses of lilacs. She did a great mass of laundry for me three times, and each time charged me what she obviously regarded as the maximum: three marks, which equals thirty cents. She did it beautifully too. The last time I went there when she knew we were moving out of town, she gathered her young daughter and her grandson close behind her and nerved herself to ask the big question that had obviously preyed on her mind for some weeks: "When are you Americans going to send us all to Siberia?"

We drove into Inchach some thirty miles south of the Danube just as the last snipers were being cleared from the far end of town by troops of the 42nd Division.[252] At our end a captain of Military Police was telling his men: "We will set up the Information Booth on this corner." As we drove down the street we met about fifteen Belgians who had not been liberated more than thirty minutes. All of them were carrying boxes of shoes.

A little farther a small riot was going on in and around the town's main shoe store. We crowded our way in to find the whole store had been stripped almost completely of its stock while the frantic Germans ran around wailing and wringing their hands. The Russians had begun to get angry as the stock ran out and had carried away food dishes and even the proprietor's violin. The proprietor, a middle-sized, balding German about forty was especially frantic, and was outraged that the Americans would permit such things. We asked him if he had not heard that the German army itself had done such things in France, Belgium, Greece, etc., etc. He drew himself up proudly and said: "Sir! The German army would never stoop to such things!" We asked him mildly how he knew and he said, "I was a soldier myself." Still mildly we asked to see his *soldbuch*, the little service record book all German soldiers must carry. This was most interesting: it showed that he had been discharged from the army that very morning, Sunday, April 29th. He had gone to his commanding officer, told him that he was in his own home town and that the war was over and that he wanted to go back into the shoe business. This seemed sound to his CO, who discharged him honorably. He had then changed clothes and played his violin for the first time in several years, getting ready for Monday's shoe trade. We escorted him outside to the lone GI who had arrived to guard the place, and the GI took him off to the prisoner of war cage. As we left, three liberated Frenchman drove up in a car they had captured a few minutes before and tried to make their way through the jam of jabbering Russian women. They had lots of money: they said they wanted to buy shoes. We told them that they'd had it; that the store was closed for repairs, and ["they"—written in pencil] drove off after kissing a few selected Russians.

In Dachau on the tremendous day of its liberation some Poles had cornered eight German flak regiment soldiers in a concrete court.[253] They had shot the Germans carefully in the stomachs and let them die slowly. They told us that it made them very happy when the Germans begged to be dispatched quickly. None of these flak regiment soldiers, as far as we could learn, had ever been stationed in Dachau where only the SS was permitted, never any members of the Wehrmacht. From time to time they went in among the dead Germans, inspecting them very carefully for signs of life.

The last two weeks of April and the first days of May have been very cold in Bavaria, with occasional snow and sleet storms driven by high winds. Down the superb autobahn, Hitler's superhighway that the United States can match only by its little stretch of the Pennsylvania turnpike, marched a column of German soldiers several miles long, plodding steadily into the striving sleet.[254] These were the defenders of

Munich. Each company was guarded only by two doughs and one American jeep moved slowly at the head and one at the tail of the column. The Germans had that disheveled look that all soldiers get the moment they become prisoners, weaponless, often hatless, unbuttoned, and beltless. Despite their obvious fatigue most of them seemed happy. Many were smiling, many waved at our jeep as it passed. Some were women, but these were the equivalent of our WACs. Many of these prisoners had been clerks in the equivalent of our SHAEF until a few days ago and had never fired a gun in anger. Most of them looked as if they didn't have a care in the world now that their greatest care—the fear of death—had been removed. They slogged off into the sleet. They looked as if they would gladly have sung a song if it had been permitted.

In Munich an officer in charge of counter intelligence referred to his latest secret sheet of information. His unit had moved in only a few hours before. He riffled over the pages to the latest report on the condition of Hitler's famed brown house. The sheet said: apparently intact. We rushed over to the spot that was so sacred to the Nazis; it was only a few blocks away. All that was left were parts of three walls and a fine pile of rubble from which some radio correspondents were making broadcasts, surrounded by embarrassed GIs.

Munich is beautiful. Many central parts of the city near the railroad yards are bombed out utterly and most of the Nazi shrines are pretty well beaten up. The people of Munich tell you: "Isn't it terrible? All our beautiful city gone!" When we told them that Munich was very, very lucky; that almost all other great German cities but Heidelberg were mere masses of bricks and twisted steel they wept, exclaiming: "Worse than Munich! Impossible!" Yet Munich by the standard of Frankfurt, Cologne, Wurzburg and Mainz is almost intact. We told the citizens grimly: "You are better off than almost all Germans. You have two things they do not: electric light and running water."

One German told us: "The blackest day in all German history was last July 20th. On that day the attempt on Hitler's life failed. Until then we had not felt the war very much, but after that came the terrible bombers. Almost all the real damage to Germany has been done in those last eight months. [closing quotation mark is missing]

Munich is gay, almost Parisian. Here the people welcomed the Americans as liberators; and they really meant it. Again and again and again the Germans said: "We have waited so long for you to come" or "You have taken so long to come!" Somewhat piffed [*sic*] off, the Americans usually answer: "Well, we had a long way to come."

In Munich the tankers carried lilacs on their tanks. In Munich the women are very numerous, very accessible, and often very attractive. In Munich it is astonishing to find how many women come up to you with little notes, saying in effect: "Please take good care of *Fraulein* Anna Blank. She was very good to me and helped me in my escape and is a friend to all Americans. Signed by an American prisoner of war." In Munich the famed Munich beer is very poor. But the warehouse cellars are so fall [*sic*] of champagne that the soldiers and the *liberés* are still hauling it out days later. The liberated prisoners of several nationalities have an excellent system in handling the throngs who crowd into these cellars and come out many minutes later lugging bags and boxes full of liquor of all kinds. Usually they open a small office at the head of the stairs and then take charge of the single file that is returning with staggering loads. Soldiers and Russians, French, Poles, etc. are permitted to carry out their loot without hindrance, but all German civilians are firmly relieved of their loads. In this way much labor is saved as it is a long haul out of those underground caves.

Several (?) [*sic*] Six days before Munich was taken two American prisoners escaped to the 42nd Division. They told us that the camp commandant, a Nazi named Captain (Hauptmann) Mulheim spoke good American slang and was a nice guy.[255] They said he made a speech to them several times in almost exactly these words: "Now lots of you guys are going to try to escape. Lots of you are going to make it. I just want to impress on you one thing: when you escape, make it good and keep on going. Stay in the woods and travel by night and go toward the Rhine. We will probably catch you all right. But what I mean is this: that kind of escape is honest and I won't be hard on guys that really are trying. But for God's sake don't just go into Munich and shack up with those Munich whores. They'll just turn you in after a while. I'll be rough on any guys we catch who've been shacked up with those girls." The escapees said he was as good as his word. They also said that cigarettes were the real money of the camp at Munich. They swore that for one cigarette you could get a bar of soap, for twenty cigarettes you could get a woman, for fifty cigarettes you could get plenty of liquor and for two thousand cigarettes you could meet a man in Munich who would conduct you safely all the way to the Swiss border. They insisted this was true and gave the name of one American Airforce officer who had a standing offer: he would give five hundred dollars for five hundred cigarettes, which was all he needed to complete the necessary two thousand for his escape. The PWs got their cigarettes from their Red Cross packages twice a week.

The mystery of where the SS has gone to is being cleared up steadily. They went into civilian clothes and are seeping back into the little German towns. Yesterday eight of them were caught in Dillingen, a pleasant little town just on the Danube when some blue-turbaned Hindu ex-prisoners recognized the men who used to hit them with rifle butts in their prison camp. The screening of all German civilians by the Military Government is very slow necessarily, as it is an enormous job for a small outfit and Germany is a big place in which to hide. Meanwhile, it's a very odd feeling to walk through streets in which are many husky, tanned, brutal-looking Germans in civilian clothes who stand about rather stiffly or bicycle past you with averted faces.

The conflict now seething within American soldiers between their hatred of Germans and Germany and Nazism and their natural Christian upbringing and kindness and susceptibility to beautiful children and attractive women and poor old ladies, is one of [the] great stories of today. The same doughs who went through Dachau's incredible horrors were the very next day being kissed and wreathed in flowers by the German women of Munich. Some doughs say they hate all the Germans, and they obviously do, and yet others ["who" written in pencil] have been through just as much bitter fighting and obvious trickery will tell you that they only hate the Nazis and they like many Germans. I heard one say: "I even want to shoot all the pregnant women because I know that what's in their bellies will someday be shooting at my children." His buddy was giving a little German girl (?) while he was speaking.

In Munich there were many underground movements, and only a few of them knew of the existence of any others. Correspondents have already talked to five such groups, and Military Government officials say there are several others. Each group has its lists of Nazis still in town, and knows where guns and ammunition have been hidden. Members of one group we talked to were setting out that night to kill a Nazi bigwig whose hiding place they knew. They told us to come back tomorrow and they would prove that they had done it. They had regularly murdered Nazis for about eight months. They never held a meeting of more than ten people at one time. They told us that Americans will never realize how powerful the Gestapo were. In Munich there is the plaque on the wall where in 1923 the first Nazi *putsch* was bloodily defeated.[256] This was of all places the spot most holy to the Nazis, and here each year Hitler and Company placed wreaths in great pageantry. Every German man, woman and child who passed this spot, no matter how many times a day, was supposed to throw out his arm and roar a good loud *Heil.* Two armed guards were always on duty, night and day, to see that this was done. Failure, even through absent-mindedness, meant Dachau. Munchners faithfully *heiled* and muttered a curse as soon as they were past, according to them. But two months ago, after the bombings, the guards were withdrawn and since then they swear that not a single Munchner ever *heiled* the plaque.

Few Germans can ever in the ruined great cities which are so close to plagues of typhus, and where the Germans get thinner every day unless they move to their friends in the country, can yet realize the place of Germany at the bottom of the list of civilized nations. They learn with shock and shame of the American non-fraternization policy. Many of them simply cannot understand it. They thought they were fighting in an honorable war. When parents realize that they lost all their sons in a cause unspeakably dirty they are filled with a despair that will mark the rest of their lives. Of course they should have realized it years ago when they were *heiling* the *Fuehrer*. But they lived two lives, they say, one of exaltation at his great political promises of the wonderful new Germany to come, and one of terror that the Gestapo might knock on their door that night. But the overall, inescapable fact is that they are so solidly, thoroughly indoctrinated with so much of the Nazi ideology that the facts merely bounce off their numbed skulls. It is clear that Josef Paul Goebbels is one of the masterminds of this century for he clearly and completely did the job he set out to do. The fear of Russia is ineradicably strong in these people. I know personally that many lock their doors each evening and pray at least an hour that they will not be visited by the hordes of Russians pouring over the roads and through the towns piled heavily with loot.

(NOTE: I suggest that you excerpt some paragraphs from my unused Nuremberg piece as much I have seen since is a repetition of what is there written, particularly of condition of German cities, and word pictures of the long trek homeward of the thousands of displaced persons.)[257]

Aberdeen Morning News
"Somewhere in Germany" [May 2 or 3, 1945][258]
by Walter Ridder

American troops entered Innsbruck late one night. I was in my customary place near the head of the column with the intention of grabbing the first bed and having a good night's sleep as a reward for my strenuous exertions during the day. However, I got side-tracked with a patrol which pushed on beyond Innsbruck, and when I returned to the city, there was no room for me in any of the army inns. I found Sidney Olsen [sic] of Time and Life magazines and Cpl. Howard Byrne of the Stars and Stripes in the same unpleasant predicament.

Heartlessly, the army told us if we wanted beds, we would have to fend for ourselves. I might add that "fending for yourself" at 2:30 in the morning in a recently captured city is a highly unpleasant and nerve-wracking business. Who knows but that some sniper might also be keeping late hours?

We finally located a large hotel and an old Austrian janitor dubiously admitted us through the door. We asked for rooms. "It distresses me beyond comprehension, gentlemen, but it so happens that right at this moment every room in the hotel is taken . . . won't you please come again sometime?"

By whom were the rooms possessed? Americans? "Oh, no, by some highly-born gentlemen from Germany." Well, then, it distresses us beyond comprehension but we are very tired and it is, as the Herr Janitor will undoubtedly understand, imperative for us to have some rest in a comfortable bed, and would he therefore be so kind as to kick five of the highly-born gentlemen from Germany out of their beds right now at this moment?

"Ach, so, under these conditions, perhaps it might be possible to find sufficient rooms for the five American gentlemen." Whereupon, the janitor suddenly found he had, after all, several vacant rooms in the hotel, and we were soon in bed, leaving a call for 800.

Came the dawn. One of our group strolled into the dining room for breakfast and found to his and to their surprise, 28 fully-armed

Reichswehr officers placidly enjoying their ersatz coffee and rolls. Our man ran upstairs to my room to report he had seen the whites of their eyes. He came to me, I suppose . . . because I was the only one who could speak German. . . .

I handed the problem over to Cpl. Byrne, a member in good standing of the U.S. army. He retained me as interpreter. He ordered the officers to be disarmed and the senior officer to be sent to my room.

So glad were the Germans to surrender that I didn't have a chance to get out of bed before a *Reichswehr* lieutenant colonel presented himself. Propping myself on a pillow and smoothing out the wrinkled blankets, I translated Byrne's surrender terms: all the officers were to leave their weapons in the dining room and were to retire to their rooms to await further orders. The officer accepted the ultimatum. . . .

We celebrated the crushing of this fanatical resistance with a breakfast of rolls, coffee, cheese, butter, champagne, wine and cognac, in company with three slave-labor girls, two Dutch, one Russian, whom our brave deed of derring-do had liberated.

[1945] [DIARY]

May 5 Dillingen Sarrebourg
May 6 Sarrebourg Paris—Ce Soir—no dinner
May 7[259]

MAY 5, 1945[260]

Sidney Olson
Time & *Life*
21 Rue de Berri
Paris

Would you be unhappy if I suggested you should return home soon for interesting new job here? Stop.[261] Grover will tell you about it in London within a week but I need to know how you feel about coming home. Stop. My feeling in part is that you have had great experience and done fine job but that original globe trotting idea does not make as much sense as formerly. Stop. All best,

Harry Luce

RCA
May 7, 1945[262]

Personal[263]—Henry R. Luce, Time Inc. New York
From Sidney Olson, *Time-Life* Correspondent, Paris

Points in order:
I would be soaringly happy if you'd let me come back and scrub floors. Agree thoroughly original globetrotting plan should be scrapped. I realize I'm completely beaten up emotionally at moment; I only have enough sense left to know I've had enough. I had driven car captured from Gestapo in Innsbruck, Austria, for 40 hours wondering all the way how best to break the news to you that I wanted to come home. I drove directly to *Time* office and the first thing I saw was your cable. I'd like two weeks in Paris to collect my senses and baggage and if possible brief breather on my father-in-law's Utah ranch where Zembra and children are. Whatever the job is it's okay as I'd gladly be understudy in *Time*'s Education Department. One last word: God has been very good to me for the last five months. All the best,

Sidney Olson

.

MAY 7, 1945[264]

Sidney Olson
Time & *Life*
21 Rue de Berri
Paris

Good. Stop. Take two weeks in Paris and visit Utah. Stop. Too diffi-cult to outline new job by cable and don't try to guess. Stop. Grover will tell you all about it as soon as he lands. Stop. If you don't like it there's more where it came from but hoping you'll think it's a honey. Stop. All best as ever,

Harry Luce

Sidney Olson Cable Unnumbered[265]
to David Hulburd, Paris
Sent May 7, 1945; Rec'd May 7, 1945

Attention Hulburd:

Many thanks for your kindest message number 41. By "I've had it again" I merely meant I was once more utterly beaten up emotionally and physically and couldn't take any more death, destruction and danger. I arrived last night from Innsbruck after a long drive through the Austrian Alps, Harz and Vosges Mountains in a seven-passenger town car of best German make which a Gestapo Colonel was kind enough to surrender to me and General McAuliffe, the man who said nuts at Bastogne, was kind enough to let me keep.[266] I am giving the car to Busch who will give it to Wert for Paris office use as the office is far under the allotted SHAEF quota. This is probably my most substantial contribution to the News Bureau on the trip. I believe I am pretty well set for the Devers piece as I worked with most of his important divisions.[267] I saw the final surrender of the last group actually fighting American armies. This was at Innsbruck. Please advise whether I should save this material for the Devers piece, in which I think it would best fit, or whether to shoot it on now as research. Also explain "final closeup to be written in New York." Do you mean by me, darling? If you do, I love you and will give you a most useful souvenir which I've lugged around some time. If not should I write research or should I try to write it as a piece. Albest.

MAY 10, 1945
Darl, Mother and Dad, Cliff and Stan:

Darl,

I'm sending you the top copy of this letter, the first carbon to the Folks, and the second to Cliff. One of you please send a copy on to good old Stan, because once more I've lost his address, along with six shirts and some Nazi daggers.

As I cabled you, I'm coming back home. I arrived in Paris at 5 p.m. Sunday night, May 6, driving a seven-passenger town car which I personally captured from a Gestapo colonel at Innsbruck, Austria. There was nothing brave about it; it was just once again the old beautiful Olson luck and the help of the God who has watched over me for five months night and day. General McAuliffe, the man who told the Germans "Nuts" when they asked him to surrender at the Bastogne pocket, had told me at dinner the night before in a little Alpine town that I could have a car if I could get one. Next day Colonel Harding of the 410th regiment told me to go to the big garage and pick one out.[268] I drove over and looked at them; all kinds, little Fiats, big Mercedes-Benz, Daimlers, Opels, everything. But most of them had no ignition keys, or had bum tires, or the motors sounded bad, although some of them were pretty sporty. I didn't see quite what I wanted. Just then up drove this Gestapo car, with the big blue, ghostly blue at night, spotlight that the Gestapo used. He was driving in to town to surrender. The little crowd of Austrians hissed him as he stepped out. He handed the keys to me, I stepped in and drove off while the people cheered. It's a marvelous car, the best the Germans make, an Auto-Union W, that goes 120 kilometers an hour (65 mph) without even touching the gas pedal. It's the same make as their racing cars; wish I could take it home. I took it to division HQ where I gave a man a beautiful little Mauser pistol and the order from General McAuliffe for the paint job, and so had the necessary big white stars painted on it. Then I took off through the Alps in the sleet storm, arrived at Dillingen on the Danube at 11 p.m., left next morning via Ulm and Gunzburg for Kehl and about 7 p.m. that night, after going through the Harz mountains, I crossed the Rhine at Strasbourg. I was so emotionally beaten up by this time, after days and nights and weeks of terrific experiences, that I almost cried with happiness at getting out of Germany. I yelled *"La belle France!"* at *le police militaire* and buzzed on. That night I slept with a Negro rear outfit near Sarrebourg and drove all next day to Paris. All the way the people in the little French towns had been lining up for the parades they expected to hold any minute, and all the soldiers anxiously asked me if there were any news of the peace. I drove directly to the *Time-Life* office where Wertenbaker was just leaving to go to the meeting in Rheims where the peace was signed (he didn't get in). His secretary handed me a message from Luce which had just come in from New York for me. It said about as follows: "Would you be unhappy if I asked you to return New York for interesting new job? Grover will see you soon and tell you details but I need to know how you feel about returning." He then said some stuff about what kind of a job I'd been doing and added that the original globetrotting idea for me probably wasn't such a good idea any longer what with the end of this war etc. I almost cheered my head off, as that's what I wanted above everything. With Wert's secretary I had a bottle of champagne and then went off to the hotel for a bath and dinner and sleep. I have been sleeping most of the time since, except for an occasional look at the most beautiful city in the world, as they've turned the lights on and the fountains on and put the flags out and millions of Parisians—it's Thursday morning now—are still marching up and down the great wide streets singing and cheering and drinking. I love the French, almost every man woman and child of them.

I cabled Luce okay and cabled you, Darl, and did some work on a lot of queries that had piled up for me. But mainly I've been resting and collecting my senses. So many things happened, hour after hour, day after day, in those last terrific weeks in Germany, that it will be a long time before I can quite steady down. I still jump up in my sleep at night sometimes. But actually I feel fine, with a terrific appetite. Yesterday I had what I believe is my first salad since I left, with it I had some pate de foie gras, a steak, about five vegetables and a bottle of *Clos du Vougeot* 1938.

Yesterday I got another wire from Luce saying "New job too difficult to describe by cable; Grover will give you details; don't try to guess what it is; if you don't like it there's more where it came from but hope you'll think it's a honey." Now my interest is whetted very keen. I had told Luce I wanted Paris breather of two weeks in which to collect my senses and baggage and then wanted to go to northern Utah ranch for breather with Zembra and children and he okayed both of these.

I will leave here anywhere from the 19th to the 23rd depending on transportation. I hope to fly as a boat would chew up another week or ten days, but that depends on my luck again. One reason I'm staying on in Paris a bit is to rest, another is to do a little shopping, a third is to see Paris, a fourth is the practical one: everyone and his brother is trying to get home now and the chances are dim. In two weeks things should be coordinated.

Darl, I just don't know what the hell you're going to do about a place for us to live. Obviously the thing to do is to cancel the lease quickest if you can. Otherwise we'll have to stand up somewhere, or live in a hotel, or rent another house in Larchmont, or I don't know what. I know that it will all be very difficult for you; from here I just cannot tell what's best to do. But you'd better act quickly, and if necessary, don't hesitate to use the long distance telephone to Tom Sutton, because we'll need to act quickly.[269] Roughly I expect to arrive in New York by June 1 at latest unless I get screwed on the boat deal. I want to take off almost immediately for Utah, flying again if possible; stay with Zomb at the Hotel Utah,[270] see Dad and Mother, go to Bear river and go fishing with Paul and see old Irontit the cow, and then take my little family back to New York. Wish like everything I could get to California to see you, Cliff, and maybe it can be done—I'd give anything to take Darl all alone without any kids around on a quick fourth honeymoon out there, and maybe we can work it. But that's up to Darl, and whatever plans you make, dear, because whatever you decide I'll love to do, and it's hard to tell from here what's best. I certainly think you ought to have some kind of vacation, though, after holding down the fort so long. Besides, I'd love to get you all alone for myself for just once, much as I love Whitney and John and everyone else. But anyway, you make the plans, and I'll subscribe. Don't worry about dough—this is one time we should freely spend a little, to celebrate the war's end and everyone being safe, etc. (knock on wood).

Well, I love you all and will write you separately soon as possible. I've been too tired to write sooner. Love all. Sid

To: Mr. Larsen
From: Mr. Billings

MAY 10, 1945

Editorial Report [excerpt]

Time and *Life* have been clicking by at such a rate that it is hard to report on their activities—except to repeat the well-known fact that they both have done a superb job of news coverage from Roosevelt's death to V-E day. . . .

The magazines got through magnificently, sure—but at the cost of considerable nervous wear and tear internally. Specific wants: another senior editor on *Time*; one or two crack writers for *Life*; an art director and an assistant for *Fortune*. *Time* has six editing senior editors on the masthead—but only three are 100% reliable (Alexander, Osborne, Tasker). Olson is heading home from his travels with his future (probably not *Time*) still unsettled;[271] Chambers' health is a large question mark; Kay is not pulling his weight as a back-of-book editor and may quit eventually. John Walker has been doing senior editor work in Battlefronts but his department is now being telescoped to the Pacific war and there are doubts about his capacity as an all-around senior editor. Hillis Mills has been helping out as an editor—but he doesn't rate permanent promotion yet. Hence, the idea is to try to find a man of senior editor calibre (and price) on the outside.

[1945] [DIARY]

May 8 VE night—Maison d'A[272] (Lunch—Busch)

May 9 Lunch Siebert—Club 45 Col Tully

May 10 Lunch C. Rodgers[273]

May 11 Wrote dispatches

May 12 Sat Col. Tully Club 45—Seine boat—villa

Sidney Olson Cable 53[274]
From Paris to David Hulburd
Sent May 12, 1945; Rec'd May 12, 1945

Six days after Ed Kennedy got the great scoop through, the debate still rages at the Hotel Scribe until the earliest hours of the morning. The great majority of reporters here believe that Kennedy's scoop was a piece of foul play which blackened the name of the entire American press on the grounds that he broke his word of honor and thus gave the incompetent SHAEF-sters an opportunity to strengthen censorship in the future.[275] This great majority of course includes all of the boys who were beaten on the story, and touches of comedy are especially apparent in the fact that such Hearst-lings as Jimmy Kilgallen and Bill Corum are among the loudest denouncers of Kennedy. The facts are that Kennedy made a mental reservation when in the airplane Reims-bound. General Allen, SHAEF press chief, merely stated that the usual rules would prevail.

Afterwards when Kennedy resolved he would bust censorship, he tried to see Allen to tell him that he was going to get the story through. Allen sent out word that he was too busy to see Kennedy, who then informed an aide that he was going to get it through; whereat the aide merely laughed and told Ed to go ahead and try as it was impossible.

Kennedy then sought out the chief of the SHAEF field press censorship group, Colonel Merrick and told him the same thing directly. Having served formal notice, Kennedy went ahead getting it through. At [the] AP staff meeting, Kennedy, who is an off-the-cob guy, very earnest and sincere, told staffers: "Now I want you all to swear that you'll never tell anyone how I got the story through, no matter what pressure they bring to bear, even under torture." One staffer remarked in anguish: "Gee Ed. I might break under torture." What *Time* should keep in mind is that over the years, censors and SHAEF-sters have grown so certain of their power, that they have almost no memory of the ancient practice of freedom of the press. These bureaucrats, solidly wedged in, suddenly through the Kennedy scoop, quickly followed by the exploits of Seymour Freidin of the *New York Herald Tribune* and others in somehow getting through army red tape and into Berlin the SHAEF-sters see their power slipping.

Actually Kennedy's scoop was a pretty good sacrifice on the old altar of press freedom, and I beg you to read with jaundiced eye editorials from such papers as the *New York Times* and many others denouncing its immorality long after all such newspapers had profited circulation-wise by using the Kennedy story. This *post facto* morality seems a little sickening as well as being a series of apologies for such guys as Ray Daniell who were scooped cold. Perhaps Kennedy's action was immoral. I leave judgment to you in the light of the foregoing facts. Kennedy well knew that the Associated Press is managerially yellow-streaked and that he might even lose his job after AP chiefs had heard from highly moral subscribers who had already printed the story, but were later furious that their own special correspondents had been beaten.

A great thing to keep in mind is that over here you find a whole younger generation of correspondents who never worked for a free uncensored press and did not grow up in the tough, police-reporting, scoop atmosphere of American journalism. Many sure are horrified at even attempting to do something the American Army might disapprove of; they are so used to eating army food, wearing army clothes, smoking army cigarettes, and when at armies (camps) in merely rewriting hand-outs of stories dug up and actually covered only by division and corps press relations officers. There are very many of these and they know nothing of the idea even of freedom of the press; they are a kind of army camp-follower whose readjustment to civilian life will be so difficult that some of them mentally hope that the war will last indefinitely.

Another important matter which most deeply concerns Time Inc. and the future is what kind of coverage, what kind of censorship we will have in postwar Europe, especially out of Germany.[276] If it is to continue under the same auspices in the keystone period of Germany's and Europe's reconstruction, you will just not be getting the truth out of Europe. Perhaps there is a *Life* editorial here written from [a] better New York perspective, but I mainly want to pass on the warning that if Time Inc. wants the truth out of Germany and Europe in the months and years to come, there must be enormous readjustment of present censorship standards, ideals and procedures. Otherwise, all you'll get will be short features on American occupation armies, sports carnivals in Nuremberg Stadium and army hand-outs via British and Russian censorship in key areas. I do not want to make Kennedy and Freidin *et al.* out as heroes but the struggle is much bigger than they are and to me is a bigger one even than the American Army, inconceivable as that may seem to SHAEF-sters.[277]

[1945] [DIARY]

May 13 Sunday—Bois—Cafe—bed early

May 14 worked hotel room[278]

May 15

May 16 Dinner Busch Davenport Maison d'A—Club 45 (Letter from Z.)

May 17 Dinner—Les—Claridges—home early

Supreme Headquarters   RESTRICTED
Allied Expeditionary Force
Main APO 757

JUNE 1, 1945

AG 201-AGP-Olson, Sidney (Civ)
Subject: Letter Order No. 5

To: Mr. Sidney Olson, U.S. War Correspondent, SHAEF Reg. No. 940
    You are authorized to proceed on or about 3 June 1945 from Paris, France to the United States.
    Travel will be performed by military, naval or commercial aircraft, army or naval transport, commercial steamship, belligerent vessel or aircraft and/or rail. A baggage allowance of sixty-five (65) pounds is authorized while traveling by air.
    Information concerning War Department, army or personal activities of a military nature within this theater will not be discussed in private or public and will not be disclosed by means of newspapers, magazines, books, lectures or radio, or any other method, without prior clearance through the War Department Bureau of Public Relations or the appropriate Public Relations Officer of army installations.
    By direction of the Supreme Commander,
    M.K. Goddard
    Major, AGD, Ass't Adjutant General

Distribution: 10-Mr. Olson, 1-PR Division, 1-ETOUSA, 1-TAC, Wash D.C., 1-ATC, 1-AG Personnel, 1-AG Records

[1945] [DIARY]

June 4 Left Paris 11pm __ [?] airport—8p. to 11p. to airport—the sorrow at leaving beautiful Paris—Eagerness to get home

June 5 11am Left Azores (twice)—flt socked in—

Arr June 5 midnight at Gander—motored abt Gander[279]

June 6 morning—deep lakes—flew to Stevensvl[280]—flew to New York—arr evening—customs—caught 11:25 to L'mont—Phyllis and Bill—Borscht—sleeping pill—Paris hat. next day office—money change—binoculars—caught train—arr S.C. [Salt Lake City]

June 10—Sick.

District girdling for the *Post*, Washington, D.C., 1936.

Sid and Zembra, Washington, D.C., ca. 1936.

Covering the Jefferson Island story, Chesapeake Bay, 1937. Left to right: Bob Kintner, unknown, Majority Leader Joseph T. Robinson, Nate Robinson, Sidney Olson.

Reporters Get President's Message, State Department, September 27, 1938. This was the scene in the State Department in Washington, D.C., the night of September 27, 1938. Newsmen were summoned to get President Roosevelt's message to Adolf Hitler, his second appeal for peace in Europe. Michael McDermott, chief of the Division of Information, seated, is surrounded by reporters taking notes as he reads the president's message. (Olson, in glasses, stands between man in light suit and man with cigarette.)

Sidney A. Olson, New York, ca. 1943–1944.

Olson's list of supplies, 1944.

Certificate of Identity, War Department, 1944.

PROCUREMENT AUTHORITY: The travel herein authorized is directed as necessary for the accomplishment of an emergency war mission. Travel expenses are to be borne by the Time Magazine. If transportation by water is provided on an Army transport no fare will be assessed. Payment for subsistence will be made by the individual.

Regulations governing the procurement of military clothing and equipment in the United States are published in Section I, Circular 399, WD, 1944. Mr. Olson is in Group I.

The Commanding General, appropriate port of embarkation, will issue a Certificate of Identification, WD, AGO Form No. 65-8 to Mr. Olson.

Mr. Olson may be contacted through Major James S. Ruby, Bureau of Public Relations, War Department, Washington, D. C., telephone REpublic 6700, extension 2749.

Olson's Travel Orders (detail), 1944.

Windsor, England, 1944.
PHOTOGRAPHER UNKNOWN; COURTESY PRIVATE COLLECTION.

In a pub, Marlowe, England, 1944.
PHOTOGRAPHER UNKNOWN; COURTESY PRIVATE COLLECTION.

With Col. Joseph Moller, 390th Bomb Group, England, 1945.
PHOTOGRAPHER UNKNOWN; COURTESY PRIVATE COLLECTION.

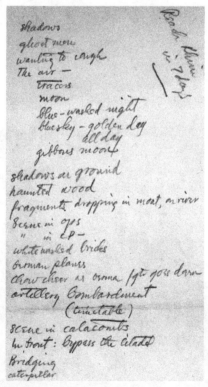

Olson's Field Notes, February 23, 1945.
AUTHOR'S PHOTO.

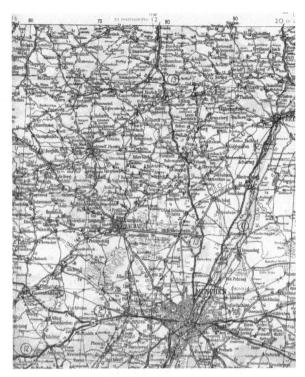

Map of Germany, 1945.
AUTHOR'S PHOTO.

With Clare Boothe Luce, Heidelberg, 1945.
PHOTOGRAPHER UNKNOWN; COURTESY PRIVATE COLLECTION.

Nuremberg, 1945: "There are no cities left."

Page from Olson's Diary, April 1945.

An officer of the 42nd Infantry (Rainbow) Division carries to a jeep and medical aid the only man found alive out of hundreds locked and starved to death in freight cars on a siding outside the Dachau prison camp, April 29, 1945. (Olson stands in center background wearing glasses.)

jd
#2 List
Lailey - 4

SIDNEY OLSON CABLE 47

From Germany to David Hulburd - April 30, 1945; rec'd April 30, 1945

FOR BATTLEFRONTS:

I have been in Dachau today from the time the first American troops entered until the place was cleared. I will tell you about it chronologically with no attempt to embellish so that you may judge for yourselves. Perhaps the United States is satiated with horrors after the other prison camps; certainly there is a limit to how much horror the mind can absorb. But when all the other names of prison camps are forgotten the name of Dachau will still be infamous. It was the first great concentration camp that Rudolf Hess set up for Adolf Hitler and its mere name was a whispered word of terror through all Germany from the earliest days of Nazi control of Germany. It was not only the (omission?) largest of all/German opponents of Nazism were sent. Here came the Social Democrats and then later the intellectuals, the journalists, the professors of all nations that fell into Hitler's hands. And here were concentrated the flower of Nazi sadists, the beasts'

Olson's Dachau dispatch (detail, page 1).

With Whitney and John in Utah, June 1945.
PHOTOGRAPHER UNKNOWN; COURTESY PRIVATE COLLECTION.

With Luce and colleagues, ca. 1946–1950.
PHOTOGRAPHER UNKNOWN; COURTESY PRIVATE COLLECTION.

CHAPTER III

Postwar

By July, Olson was back in New York, staying at the Dorset Hotel. Although he had returned to Time Inc. as a battle-hardened war correspondent, his reentry was impeded by the constant jockeying for power. On July 5, he wrote in his diary that he "went to dinner with Luce at Racquet Club, to discuss my future." On July 9, he made an unrelated but nevertheless intriguing note that he had just spent two hours talking to "Lt. Murray of Army Intelligence."

He was being pushed over to *Fortune*, which he viewed as a troubled publication but one that Luce hoped could be improved: "while I go to *Fortune* as a Senior Editor, I will actually be a writer. I will write two or three stories, to discover how *Fortune* works. Then we will make *new plans*. My objective, actually, is 6 months of comparative peace and quiet—hours 9:30 to 5p., Sats & Suns off, while I cultivate my soul, contemplate my navel, and decide what I can do with myself *really*."[1]

The next day, he added a short entry that contained an uncharacteristic hint of apathy: "Bastille Day. In celebration I stayed in bed most of the day reading. Bathed and went out for cheap dinner at 8 p.m. Back at 10 p.m. Tomorrow to Port Chester for Luce weekend. They wanted me for both days, but I like to be alone." Eight weeks earlier, he had sprinted through Dachau; was he now showing (understandable) signs of trauma? Unless one was hospitalized with "shell shock" or "battle fatigue," the psychological wounds of war went largely unaddressed.

He wrote to Zembra, who was still in Utah with the children, and explained the situation to her, running through his options at Time

Inc. He sounded resigned. The machinations of reentering the working world must have seemed tiresome after proving his worth time and again. On August 14, 1945, Olson updated his personnel file. Beneath his brand-new title of "senior editor, *Fortune*," he typed up a few paragraphs detailing his accomplishments at *Time* thus far. An administrator attached this to his job application from 1939, which includes three rather extraordinary references: "Eugene Meyer, Publisher, Crescent Place, Washington, D.C.; Steven T. Early, Secretary to the President, The White House; Senator Robert M. LaFollette, Senate Office Building."[2]

Far too soon, Olson was on the move again. On August 17, he wrote that he was in Houston "on the cotton story, and am there on V-J Day."[3] While traveling, he filled several pages of a notebook with plans for a novel about World War II: "The Book I intend to write needs a working title. 'Blood' is the first that occurs to me, and by that term I would include its use denoting breeding. But such a title might repel would-be readers, and although I hope to repel them, first they must be readers. And I am determined this book shall sell."[4] Evidently, he was beginning to process the enormity of what he had witnessed overseas. Some of his colleagues had already written about their experiences; it would be a natural next step for any correspondent.

He intended for the book to be a work of fiction. "By 'I' in this notebook, I will not always, or even often, mean myself, as it will be largely imaginary, although based more or less on my experiences." The book's focus, he wrote, was that "there should be so many battle scenes, one after another, that the reader can get that cumulative horrifying feeling of fear, fear, fear and dead, dead, dead men." In quiet moments over the next five years, Olson built several outlines based on his war experiences, layering in details as he recalled them.

Although intended to be fictional, these outlines do reflect Olson's movements during the war. The lists contain "catch" words meant to trigger his memory. Similar, sometimes even identical, observations can be found in his dispatches and letters from the front. For example, one outline contains the following description: "Little battle near s'Hertogenbosch, Holland, with the Canadians. Rubber-tired hack to bridge, explanation of boat commando-failures. Landscape. Weather. Battle at night in sleet. Morning after battle. Sniping. Dash in the day. Standing in the German's body." The same information can be found in his February 5, 1945, dispatch about Kapelsche Veer and in his letter to Zembra of the same date.

On March 24, 1947, he wrote in his diary, "The novel occupies my thoughts night and day now. I keep thinking of doing it as a play instead—but I think automatically in movie terms, of shots, scenes, expressions, etc." On May 12, 1947, he wrote, "I have acquired a real and very deep and excited confidence in my novel. I was always (since Apr. 1945) determined to write and finish it, even if it was only for my own satisfaction. Now I firmly believe it is going to be a very good novel. Oh, to finish it by fall! All I need is a little free time, regularly—and I'll make the time."

But work was always calling. His articles for *Fortune* and *Life*—long pieces on business, politics, and entertainment—required extensive research and travel. He was always planning the next story and working his contacts. After months of preliminary planning, followed by weeks spent in Hollywood, Olson's article "The Great Throat: Bing Crosby—First in Films, First on the Air, and First on the Phonographs of His Countrymen," was published in *Fortune* in January 1947.[5] "Getting to Crosby took sharp work," Olson recounted in one of *Time's* interoffice newsletters. "[We] . . . concentrated on the little clique of his half-dozen cronies, a set of solid, regular but somewhat beat-up guys, including prop-men, worn-out song-and-dance men, and general utility characters. These are Bing's best friends because they are the only people he knows who don't want something from him."[6]

His next big piece, "The Republicans," was political; it was published in *Fortune's* April 1947 issue.[7] On May 27, he received a letter from the head of Paramount, who wrote, "Glad to know that you are pleased with the cooperation given you." His article, "Paramount: Oscar for Profits," was published in *Fortune* the following month.[8]

On November 23, 1947, the daughter of Olson's former boss, Eugene Meyer, promoted his latest piece in her *Washington Post* column: "Sidney Olson, now in Washington for *Life*, contributes a lengthy analysis of the movie hearings."[9] She was referring to the hearings being conducted by the House Un-American Activities Committee; the controversial proceedings were designed to expose and discredit Hollywood writers and actors with suspected ties to Communism. Olson's article, "The Movie Hearings," appeared in the November 24, 1947, issue of *Life*.[10]

Olson continued at a relentless pace throughout 1948. In April, *Life* published two of his articles, one called "The MacArthur Gamble," followed by "The Democratic Plan to Draft Eisenhower: The Party Schemers Think They Know How to Get Rid of Truman 'with Honor.'"[11]

In August 1948, Olson flew to Germany to cover the Berlin Airlift for *Life*. In letters to his family, he reeled off the names of all the generals he had interviewed, including General LeMay, who,

> put me on the last plane of the morning air block for the Berlin airlift; so I flew in a rickety old DC-3 loaded with three tons of flour sacks up over the Russian zone and past all the Russian fighter planes, pretty tense, and into Tempelhof airfield at Berlin, where the Esthonian DPs, who hate Stalin, started unloading the plane even before I had my parachute off and could get out. Was met and motored through the Russian sector to the Press club, which had run out of whiskey and was serving only vodka, had lunch, and saw General Clay in the late afternoon, and by great luck managed to catch the last plane of the night block to Wiesbaden (the planes fly to Frankfurt all night but not to Wiesbaden) and there were a long series of explosions in the night in the Russian zone, which we couldn't figure out, but reported anyway (it wasn't flack or artillery) and finally in the dark sat down at Wiesbaden and had dinner at 11 p.m.

On his return to the United States, Olson sent Luce his notes from an interview with General Clay in which the latter disclosed that he lacked almost any guidance from the American government while performing the herculean task of feeding the German people who were starving to death while walking a fine line between the Russians and Allied Europe. All of it, Olson warned Luce, is "off-the-record."[12]

By 1948, Olson had taken to calling his novel *The Search*. He had the first scene worked out on paper—the battle at Kapelsche Veer—but he kept altering it, crossing out lines, adding details, and shuffling the page order. Stapled together, the pages read like a recurring nightmare:

> A flare fell and he pushed his whole body flat in the icy water. The flare flickered and went out suddenly. Now he was really soaked; with his whole heart he silently sang a long fierce song of purest sacrilege, blaspheming and cursing in a long purging rave of rage that was almost ecstasy; raving and cursing and saying every dirty word he knew; then, picking out the most satisfying word he said it over and over fifty times, giving it every inflection he could invent. Then his anger flickered out like a flare, and he was merely alone and wet. The flashes were all on his left. He began to crawl forward again, forward and left. The flashes were mostly German, he guessed; the Cargylls were holding fire in order to get close and chuck grenades; the flashes were give-aways—they told where the holes were. He kept crawling, not eagerly, not fast. No prizes are given, you know, said his mind. *A dead correspondent only gets a paragraph on page 18, you know,* said his mind.[13]

Olson was pulled in so many directions that it is likely that he simply could not find the time to complete his novel. But it also seems plausible that he found it disturbing to revisit his wartime experiences. Perhaps he lacked the will to finish. His refusal to attend a string of postwar ceremonies for war correspondents could be interpreted as another sign of his ambivalence.

At Time Inc., postwar sales and advertising were beginning to decline, but television presented new possibilities for growth. Olson—who had written the news for live radio in the early 1930s—saw an opportunity here. He anchored a number of televised interviews in June and July during the Republican and Democratic conventions, both of which were held in Philadelphia. In several black-and-white photos, he is seated with various political figures; handwritten captions on the reverse side include phrases like "First televised convention" and "1948 Dem convention."

On the evening of November 2, 1948, the presidential election was broadcast live on television for the first time in history. Only those cities connected to the coaxial cable would have been able to receive the broadcast. The audience was limited: not everyone owned a television set yet. The event was televised at *Life*-NBC's "campaign headquarters" in New York City and ran all night long, continuing into the early hours of November 3. Olson sat between announcers John Cameron Swayze and Ben Grauer; the three men chatted live in an unrehearsed way, with awkward silences and occasional bursts of reporting. After reporting the final tally, they read aloud from New York Governor Thomas Dewey's telegram conceding the election to President Harry S. Truman.[14]

Although he was productive both at work and at home, Olson was not entirely happy, as his diary entry from January 17, 1949, reflects: "The number of matters on which I keep silent in conversation—an ever-growing number—should serve as a pretty fair index to the general cramping of my life. This is true now . . . of my business life, in which I was once much too free with my opinions, views and casual comments, and in which I now make known almost no opinions of any shade about any subject unless the subject is popular and practically neutral and I am safe in joining in light mockery."

Olson still toiled endlessly to satisfy Luce. The pressures had not diminished in the postwar era—only the enemies had changed: now the twin threats of a nuclear arms race and the spread of Communism dominated the agenda.

Olson felt pressure from his detractors, too. Some at Time Inc. had long disapproved of his close ties to Luce and also disliked his conservative politics.[15] On February 16, 1950, he submitted a *Fortune* "short" on a Danish shipowner named Hans Isbrandtsen. At the top of his typed draft, Olson wrote in red pencil, "My last piece for *Fortune*—never printed." And just below he added in pencil, "Del Paine and others regarded it as 'too rightist.' It is simply about freedom."

That same day, Olson was called into John Billings's office and fired. Billings recorded the encounter in his own diary:

> I gave Luce a memo recommending that I fire Sid Olson, for his own future good. Luce agreed. The Personnel Advisory Committee came up with a discharge figure—about $30,000 including annuity and trusts. I took this to Larsen and got his O.K. Then I called Olson in and told

him "this is it"—that he was at a dead end, that he had no future here, that he should get out to further his own career. He was crestfallen and hurt—but agreed to what I said. . . . Luce was greatly relieved that it was successfully over—and he did not have to do it himself. What a coward he is on such matters![16]

As always, Olson's true nature—confident, determined, and adaptable—came to the fore. A day later, Billings wrote, "Olson came in to announce that Paramount had offered him a $500 per wk. job as a writer and he was going to Hollywood. . . . This is the bright side of my discharge of him. I knew he'd get better work—but not so quickly as this."[17] Olson typed up a farewell letter to Luce:

> I leave a pretty fair-sized legacy of ideas and work here, beginning with the reconstruction of the entire scope and content of the National Affairs section; the first outline and real establishment of a Washington Bureau suitable to the prestige of Time Inc.; the entire re-making of the News Bureau correspondent system, which led me into my bloodiest battles, but which even now is managed along the lines I laid down and by the standards I set up, more than even you could know. And I include my 1948 pioneering of television for *Life*, for which somehow I was done neatly out of credit—and I do not say this bitterly at all, but in the sense of claiming credit for top-level planning which I actually did. I do not intend to rehearse the long series of scoops and stories done in NA or USAW or Business, because this was journalism due to the salary paid me.[18]

Luce replied the same day, promising to sit down with Olson in the near future. *Time* had been a complicated place to work for all of its writers and editors; many had already broken away from the influential magazine empire. Although Luce was a towering presence in mid-century America, the work environment he fostered was exceedingly difficult, a veritable hornet's nest. Nevertheless, the two men remained friends and continued to correspond until Luce's death in 1967.

Fortune
350 Fifth Avenue New York
JULY 16, 1945

Darl-dear:

I guess you can tell from the letterhead where I am.[19] Yup, yup, yup. The sole reason I haven't written earlier is that I didn't want to worry you with the negotiations and dickerings which went on steadily until last Friday, July 13, when I finally agreed to go on *Fortune*. By a peculiar coincidence, that's the exact anniversary of the day I came to *Time*, July 13,1939. Then I spent the weekend with Harry and Clare at Greenwich, and reported off the train for work this morning.

This is just a fast newsletter written right after lunch on my first day, Monday. I shook hands all morning and haven't anything to do this afternoon. I had lots of time and opportunities to write you sooner, but I didn't want to go through all the finaiglings *[sic]* on paper until something was settled. I go to *Fortune* as a Senior Editor, but actually for six months I will be a writer of articles for the magazine. At the end of that time Del Paine, Harry and I will make up our minds over again as to whether, when I've learned the *Fortune* ropes, I will be a *Fortune* editor of some stature or not. I don't really care, personally. I've got what I mainly and honestly wanted: hours 10 a.m. to 5:30 p.m., five days a week—with Saturdays and Sundays off.[20] That ought to please you. Certainly it pleases me. Anyway, for at least six months we will be living as completely normal a life as anyone could. This should be a terrific novelty for us, since it will be the *first time* in our married lives that we've ever had a chance to live like other people. I hope you like it.

I couldn't go back on *Time*. Matthews just wouldn't stand for it, and I wasn't, as you know, eager to go back and work under that clunk, since I neither respect nor trust him.[21] *Life* wanted me, and hasn't given up yet, and may renew their bid after the six months are up. They are turning over the whole News bureau to C. D. Jackson, a fine change, and he would like to have me as a character in that setup. That may still develop, and it could if I had wanted to be really stubborn about not going to *Fortune*. Again, after six months we'll see. Third, I can have South America if I want. This has some attractions, of course. But mainly it would mean that the four of us moved to Buenos Aires for at least five years, intending to make S.A. our permanent home. It could be quite a career. But I passed that, at least until I talk to you. And for the moment I'm tired of travelling. Now—any questions?

I've been having a good time. . . . I had lunch with Winnie and Otto Fuerbringer—on me—and with Hillis, and with Joe Purtell, and with Tasker, so far. I spent my first weekend at Greenwich alone with Harry for two days, just swimming and talking. I took ten dollars off him in gin rummy. Then I laid around another whole week while the debate swirled on around my head, and then it was settled Friday and as I said I just spent this second weekend out there, only this time with HRL's son Peter, Margaret Case, and about twenty other people.[22] Maggie Case taught me a hot new version of gin rummy which she and Theresa Helburn, the Theater Guild's chief, thought up, a wild thing called Oklahoma. On that I lost $1.40 to Harry and $3.57 to Clare. The food at the Luce's is so out of this world that I can hardly bear to think of it.

I'm living, as I wired you, at the Dorset Hotel, 30 W. 54, where I expect millions of booted mail from you—and I mean it. It's at the back of the Museum of Modern Art, Sculpture Garden side of the street, across from those modernistic new apartments. Very quiet, very very nice, and I have a juicy suite. No hotel in town literally would let me have a room for more than five days; only two had suites, so I took this suite. I paid in advance for it: $500 for two months. That's all the bad news, however. Big big living room and big double-bedroom and swell baths and closets and perfect laundry service, etc.

I guess that right now I love you more than I ever have in my life. The kind of thing I just never can say to you when I'm saying goodbye—and all our lives I've been saying goodbye to you, it seems—is that you were even more wonderful to come home to than I had dreamed, and you know how I can dream. But I always choke up so, like a big baby, and can't say anything to you except "Be a good girl—and write me." Then you never write me, and that's that.

But I want to get this off, so I'll save the love for another letter right after this one. But darling, to me you're everything that's lovely and perfect and good and beautiful in this world . . . I'm proud of you, happy with you, and worship you.

Please don't get caught in the train traffic jam out there; go down and see about tickets now, even if the rules say five days. What I hear is that people go down now and make reservations secretly, which the clerk pulls out of the drawer on the date five days before the train goes. At Larchmont, where I got some clothes, the house still looks fine and the garden shaggier than ever. I suggest you write Andrea whatshisname and say that they simply must cut the lawn oftener, clip the hedges and do a little weeding. The rose garden looks foul, although the roses are simply enormous this year. Take your biggest Salt Lake rose and double it and you can imagine what our roses were like—not so many but simply huge. Don't buy any boots and shoes out there—wait till you get here. I worship you darling. Please please write me—often. Surprise me. Love to all and wish me luck.

Your slave, S.

APRIL 4, 1947 [NOVEL NOTES]

Chapter I. "First Try"[23]

This was his first battle. This was the first time he was really up there. He squatted in the Dutch mud watching the flashes. The only things he could see were the flashes and a few yards forward to his right the dim white shapes of two snowsuit soldiers, not moving, not firing, both lying in the mud. The sleet drove hard in the night; sometimes when a big flash came he could see the shape of the storm, the sleet driving in a steady slant.

There was not much noise. No barrage had been laid on for the surprise attack. The loudest noise was the thump of his blood in his neck and chest most of the time drowned suddenly without warning in that spitting cough of *schmeissers*[24] aa-aa-aa-aa-aa-aa-aa-ing and then the pumping whoom of the tanks pounding right into the holes at short range. The Cargylls seldom snapped their rifles, just crawling on and on in the mud through the sleet near the tanks but not too near waiting to get [in] to grenade range of the holes, and the Germans held back their machine guns, so telltale in the night.[25]

I am not really scared yet, he thought, because I am not lying down in the mud, I'm still squatting trying to keep mud off my coat and face. But there was mud on the long khaki muffler around his neck; the mud was in a wet freeze, and when he moved the mud crust on the muffler sawed his neck and frozen drops of mud slid down his collar and along the hot skin of his sweating back.

Well, I'm up here, he thought. Now let's go back quick to a nice warm place and drink some cognac and write a piece about how it is up there with our brave boys, I mean our brave Allies and drink some more cognac and go to bed and wake up tomorrow when the batman brings in the mug of hot brown sugary tea. Only these guys will still be here in the mud.

But nobody would blame me. Everybody back there would respect me for having been damnfool enough to be up here, really up here, at all. But they don't count. And the guys up here think I'm nuts anyway and if I went back now not one of them would think I'm yellow but only smart and they would simply envy me and then forget me except once in a

305

while they would mention to each other that a correspondent was really up here once with them.

The tank forward on his left began cracking desperately with a machine gun answered by a heavy German machine gun, falsetto and baritone dueling and then duetting and then three German grenades splashed on the tank and it began to burn and all along the line for three hundred yards German machine guns began splattering at the tank as it lit up burning bigger and bigger. The turret opened slowly but no one came out. Still no one came out. The tank was burning in one long explosion of burning and still no one came out and as the whole stretch of mud and grass lit up the white snow suits were running slowly through the sleet toward the darkness, in any direction toward darkness but mainly up the little slope toward the holes, now revealed black in the light and in sword-flashes of tracers by the machine-guns and the Cargylls were very close to the holes now and grenades were splattering in.

He was on his face in the mud now not moving not breathing acting dead in the stretching fringes of light from the burning tank fifty yards away. The two snow suits on his right were gone. He lay with his face down but one eye to the light and thought goddamn this - - - -ing muffler I hereby vow to burn this muffler this - - - -ing - - - -ing muffler it must hold a ton of sleet and mud. Nothing burns like a tank, he thought. Even airplanes don't burn like a tank. Airplanes burn fine, though; but it's a different lighter cleaner fire; tanks burn the way a refinery oil tank burns with a wide billowing pillar of smoke up which the flames rush in long greasy shuddering thrusts. Still no one had come out. The tank's right tread was off and hung in a curl. Machine gun bullets began to crack off in a heavy burst that puzzled him; he had never heard a machine gun like that; and then he realized that the tank's ammunition was exploding. He got up and ran to his right and forward a little in a diagonal as hard as he could slosh in the mud and fell suddenly headlong in a mud hole three feet deep, filled with water. He was so shocked he had no breath to swear; he stayed kneeling devotionally in the puddle, his chin resting on the other bank.

Very funny, he thought. Will you kindly stop clowning in the midst of an Allied offensive? Will you please not go around falling in - - - -ing mud holes screwing up the whole strategy and lousing up the Four Freedoms?

He crawled out of the hole and kept crawling to the right. His hand came on a combat boot. "Sorry," he whispered but even as he whispered it he knew the whisper could not be heard. He crawled forward. The Cargyll's snowsuit was all knocked out in front; his viscera hung out in ropes and hunks as he lay on his side. His face said nothing; it was a quiet, sweet boyish face, looking about seventeen; the brown hair curling damply under the helmet, under a parka hood of white denim. He was freshly dead. He looks like the kid who used to deliver the newspapers to our house, he thought. He lay there almost face to face with the dead boy, looking at him calmly. He looked at him for quite a while. The bursts were getting farther and farther off to his left, far beyond the burning tank. In the dim light he looked at the boy. A sweet kid. No girls for you, kid. No postwar for you, kid. Just a fine big short burst in your guts, kid and the lights out. I'm better off than you are, kid, even if I die screaming of cancer fifty years from now. Because I can go back right now and get nice and drunk on post-liberation cognac and go to sleep and wake up and have another chance tomorrow to do something. No more chances for you, kid; you're fresh out of chances.

He turned over in the mud and dug a handkerchief out of his hip-pocket, grunting as he tugged up the trench-coat, and wiped the wet sleet off the boy's face and then pulled the parka hood forward to keep the rain off the fresh young mouth.

He looked around and stood up slowly. The sleet was slackening into a cold rain; he started to shiver and then saw a tank a little distance to his right, it was puffing and mumbling indecisively. He didn't move; he knew the tankers were wondering whether to risk a dash past the burning tank on the narrow muddy slope; whether the Germans would paste them and whether the tank could make it past without slithering down the slope into the burning tank. In that state of mind they'll take a snapshot at anything, he thought, and he stood still in the wet dark, fearing they might take him for a German since he was not in a snow suit.

307

Headquarters First Army
Office of the Commanding General
Governors Island, New York 4, N.Y.

7 May 1947
Mr. Sidney Olson
21 Pryer Lane
Larchmont, New York

Dear Mr. Olson,

The War Department has requested me to forward to you the inclosed certificate of appreciation for your services as a War Correspondent during the recent conflict.

I regret that you were unable to attend the presentation ceremony held here at Governors Island on April 9th to receive this award.[26]

We of the Army are grateful to you for your part in the magnificent accomplishment of reporting throughout the war. Your day-by-day account of events as they occurred will be the basis of the history books of tomorrow.

May I also add my personal appreciation to that expressed by the Secretary of War in the inclosed certificate. With kindest regards, I am

Very sincerely yours,
Courtney H. Hodges
General, U.S. Army

FEBRUARY 17, 1950

Dear Harry,

A few notes as part of my legacy to Time Inc.:[27]

1. No matter what representations are made to you over the next several years, please beware of Defense Secretary Louis Johnson. You are surrounded by powerful advocates of Johnson, who manage to alibi him successfully, as his friends. I have naturally hesitated to mention this before, but I feel free to now.

I believe, from my interviews with such men as General LeMay, General Norstad, General Huebner, General Fredericks, General Clay—and you will remember that I was perhaps the only defender Clay had in Time Inc. during the first two months of the airlift, as a result of my Berlin interview with him—and from Admiral Forrest Sherman:

That the general defense-and-attack mechanism of the United Sates will gradually be revealed to be as inadequate, outdated and feeble as that of Britain in 1938, when Chamberlain was forced to bargain for time in which to prepare. I do not accuse Johnson, who is at least a patriot; I merely say it is his responsibility, and that he should be judged according to his discharge of that responsibility. I believe that penetrating reporting, done freely and without intervention by friends of Johnson, will show this.

The whole problem is long-term, of course, but terms however long have a habit of ending sometime. My warning in the first paragraph above is to protect you: someday when all comes out in the wash I would think it safer for *Life* and *Time* not to have in their files a long record of pre-Johnson editorials and stories. In short, reserve judgement.

For even if these and other generals and admirals are wrong, and if I am wrong, there is still no harm in suspending praise from Johnson unless he so unequivocally earns it that you cannot restrain yourself.

2. Stevenson, publisher of the London *Daily Herald*, the Labor paper, is here on a visit. He told me the other night that the betting is now 3-to-1 on a Labor victory; that there is no probability whatever of a return of Churchill. There it is, although I hope he is wrong.

3. The *Herald Tribune*'s Costello interview today is by my chief Costello source, Leslie Midgley. I saw the original list of questions submitted to Costello last September, perhaps August, and the chief difference is very amusing: in this list there are neither questions nor answers pertaining to O'Dwyer.[28] One example: when Dick Clark, publisher of the *New York Daily News* has traffic trouble with his newspaper trucks he calls Costello, not City Hall. And *Time*'s own Bonaggio research answers the questions about Costello in Kansas City.

4. An important journalistic service can be done the U.S. simply by reporting and photographing the truth, and reiterating it: that the Democratic Party is the party of the rich. The new rich, of course; the poor old rich, that little band, are fading fast away. Consider merely the minks, the jewels, the money on display at Democratic banquets; consider the list of fat cat contributors to the Democratic party. What a shift from the time Al Smith spoke to the Liberty League dinner in Washington in 1936! The oilmen and all the other new barons are Democrats, naturally; and the great monopolists of labor are in no instance possible to classify as poor.

We should—we in the past tense—emphasize this both as a service to the Republic and the Republicans.

5. *Time*'s failure to review Marshall Andrews' book, *Disaster Through Air Power*, is notable. Perhaps the book should have been denounced, and its thesis shredded; I don't know as I haven't read the book. But simply to ignore the book is not right.

6. According to the Cyclists, a very severe depression, as severe as that of 1932, is imminent.

I have seen the Cyclist chart. It shows the market acting exactly as it has for the past six weeks (it was published in January, but the break the other day shows on it as predicted), zigzagging for another month and then shooting sharply up in the spring, halting on a brief summer plateau, then shooting very sharply up again, with a terrific downbreak to come in August. The August break is supposed to be like that in 1929. Depression is supposed to follow, and continue through 1951 and 1952.

All I know about economic history is that each past depression has come from a different source. In each case everyone went around nailing boards over the ratholes and checking the storm-windows—and despite all precautions the depression came about from a wholly new source.

I don't vouch for this prophecy. Certainly, for random examples, my friends at both American Can and Johns-Manville, both strategic business reflectors, dismiss all this as nonsense. AmCan is about 7% over last year's enormous business already this year.

But it might be worth a *Time* story or *Life* chart. Depressions interest everybody.

These items are all I have on the hook at the moment.

Now, Harry, on the main matter; I have some thoughts which I would be little too shy to say directly. And I might phrase them less exactly, or mumble them too indistinctly, in direct conversation.

The first of these is to express to you my profound gratitude for all you have done for me. I say this as sincerely as I know how.

In all things, large and small, for what is now almost eleven years, you have conducted yourself to me generously, fairly, or more than fairly. And I have learned a very great deal.

In leaving Time Inc. I ask you only to remember that in all the years in which my various foes—and what a collection I have had! (If it is true you measure success by the weight and power of your enemies then I certainly can lay claim to an enormous success here)—in all those years of trial, when these foes were plunging their knives into me, I want you to remember that on no single occasion did I ever use an interview with you to pay them back; that I never once derogated the ability or motives of any editor or officer here.

Even in the days of the Cabal, even when we were most intimate, I never used such influence with you as I was supposed to have to make the meagerest hint against the men whose complaints of me must have at times overflowed your desk. I tried always to keep to the issue, which was always to me the form of the week's journalism and not the form of the masthead. In sum, I leave with a clear conscience, in that I tried to conduct myself as a Christian gentleman—without claims to scholarship.

I leave a pretty fair-sized legacy of ideas and work here, beginning with the reconstruction of the entire scope and content of the National Affairs section; the first outline and real establishment of a Washington

Bureau suitable to the prestige of Time Inc.; the entire re-making of the News Bureau correspondent system, which led me into my bloodiest battles, but which even now is managed along the lines I laid down and by the standards I set up, more than even you could know. And I include my 1948 pioneering of television for *Life*, for which somehow I was done neatly out of credit—and I do not say this bitterly at all, but in the sense of claiming credit for top-level planning which I actually did. I do not intend to rehearse the long series of scoops and stories done in NA or USAW or Business, because this was journalism due to the salary paid me. But one point does give me a kind of sardonic pleasure, which I cannot refrain from expressing: before I went to *Fortune*, no *Fortune* story had been reprinted in the *Reader's Digest* for almost ten years, whatever the reasons. I had five or six in a row, and since I left, almost no *Fortune* stories have been reprinted there.

This is enough, and perhaps more than enough. I have very fine memories of you, Harry, of almost innumerable thoughtfulnesses on your part, and also of Time Inc. For Zembra herself could testify that it is alien to my nature to harbor enmities; even in my home I have never spoken against my ill-wishers here, not so much out of a great stock of charity as out of simple realism that what is done is done and only the next shot counts. In sum, I will not now or ever write a novel about Time Inc.; I came in good faith and I worked here in good faith, and I still have it.[29]

There is a novel I do intend to write, and for which I should now have the requisite clarity—once I began to tell you about it but shied off when I found you were really interested. It should take me 90 days, perhaps 100; I used to think I would sometime nerve myself to ask you to be my patron to the extent of continuing my salary while I wrote it on leave from *Time*. But that, too, is over.

I have no immediate plans beyond the book. I must first adjust myself to another world. I'll know better in a week or two.

Thanks for everything. My best regards to Clare.

Good luck and blessings.

Sincerely,
Sidney Olson

Henry Luce
9 Rockefeller Plaza
New York NY 20

FEBRUARY 17, 1950

Dear Sid:—

This is just a radar signal. Message received. Deeply appreciated.

In other words, I have a good deal to say about my feelings for you and about you—and indeed about all the things we have talked about for years. But I shall not try to say it now. I hope we can make a date for Monday afternoon or evening when I get back from seeing my boy in Cleveland.

Just one point, now. I think everyone concerned believes me when I say that to my knowledge you have never made an unfriendly move toward anyone.

Looking forward to continuing the conversation for many years to come,.

Sincerely yours,
Harry

CHAPTER IV

A New Beginning

FINALLY, OLSON WAS FREE TO WRITE, TO *REALLY* WRITE—SOMETHING he had yearned to do since his college days. While preparing an in-depth *Fortune* article about Paramount Pictures in 1947, Olson had gotten to know Henry Ginsberg, the vice president of studio production.[1] Ginsberg offered him a three-month contract at $500 a week to start, with the option to renew.[2] Olson kissed his wife and children good-bye and drove across the country, arriving at his rented bungalow on March 18 after stopping to pick up his Paramount Pictures "Scenario Department" ID card.

"Wonderful feeling," he wrote Zembra on March 22, 1950, "not having to report anything: all I have to do is just invent, and they will film anything I can think of—within reasonable cost bounds. Enormous feeling of power, almost too naked. Wow! Just have to shake my lifetime reporting habits, and get that Time Inc. out of my system."

He completed two original scripts and signed a contract for each: "The War in Westchester, or, The Battle of the Sexes" and "The Traitor."[3] Based on a letter he wrote to a colleague in 1970, his "Traitor" script may have formed the basis for a controversial anti-communist film by Leo McCarey: "I wrote movies for Paramount in 1950, none of them notable, but also an original which, of all things in the days of the Unfriendly Ten, was an anti-communist movie. The treatment was killed, but Leo McCarey later re-wrote it as *My Son John*."[4]

Olson's letters from this period were sprinkled with the names of interesting Hollywood people and places. He met Lauren Bacall, lunched with Hedda Hopper, attended parties and movie screenings, and went to nightclubs.[5] To his great delight, he was invited to attend the twenty-second Academy Awards. He continued to correspond with Luce but kept it light, never asking for favors and even offering article ideas. Unfortunately, there are no extant letters from his final two months at Paramount. By the time his six-month contract had expired, he was back in New York.

Jimmy Sarno, a close friend at Paramount, kept in touch with regular letters: "I am happy to hear that for the present at least you have solved the unemployment problem through Newsom & Co."[6] Olson had landed at Earl Newsom's public relations firm, where he was hard at work distilling volumes of research into a mission statement for the Ford Foundation, which was in formation.[7] Unwilling to let his connection to Luce wither, Olson mailed him the finished document. Luce responded, "It seems to me to be an almost perfect rendition of the prevailing conventional thought-patterns of the U.S. at midcentury. This is to be understood both as a compliment and a criticism." He concluded encouragingly, "What I mean by way of criticism I will try to express to you at our next bull session."[8]

There is no evidence that Olson wished to return to journalism; apparently, his break with *Time* marked a seismic shift in his career. He was moving in to a new phase. With Newsom's support, Olson next applied to Ford's two advertising agencies in Manhattan: J. Walter Thompson and Kenyon & Eckhardt. On May 9, 1951, he wrote in his diary, "Accepted Kenyon & Eckhardt offer," and on May 14, he reported for work as a member of the copy staff.[9]

He excelled at advertising from the start. In October, K&E's president, Bill Lewis, congratulated him: "I would like to commend you to the skies for the fine job you did in a hurry on the first 'American Road' advertisement."[10] Another colleague accused him of having, "among other gifts, a golden typewriter."[11] Olson was grateful to have found creative work that interested him and paid well; the punishing atmosphere he had grown to hate at Time Inc. was now a thing of the past.

Things were rewarding at home, too. In June 1952, Zembra gave birth to their third child, Stephen. In one of his Ford advertisements from this period,[12] Olson conveyed a spirit of tenderness and concern that would have resonated with war-weary parents. The ad's image, "The Walk to Paradise Garden,"[13] was taken by W. Eugene Smith, a photographer who had been based in the Pacific during World War II. It depicted two small children emerging from the woods into a clearing. "Those small happy innocents," the text read, "stumbling toward the sunlight and shadow of the world their fathers made, must someday carry the whole fearful load of our times."

On October 25, 1952, Luce wrote to him, "Just a radar signal through the chasms of New York. I haven't heard from you since September 18th. Are you okay and how's the Opus?"[14] Olson was writing a book about Henry Ford and had been given exclusive access to Ford's vast collection of personal papers.[15] He was also busy cowriting the script for the *Ford 50th Anniversary Show*, a live television broadcast which aired on CBS and NBC on June 15, 1953. He worked closely with Henry Ford II and producer Leland Hayward; the show was choreographed by Jerome Robbins and included major stars like Ethel Merman, Frank Sinatra, Marian Anderson, and Edward R. Murrow. *Variety's* television critic described it as "Television's dream show, far and away the most costly, elaborate and star-studded production in video annals."[16]

In March 1954, Olson was made a vice president at Kenyon & Eckhardt. Two years later, he joined J. Walter Thompson Company, where he continued to work on Ford accounts (Ford Cars and Ford International) as well as Pan American World Airways, Scott Paper, and Eastman Kodak.[17]

In 1957, 12 years after World War II had ended, Olson finally fulfilled his dream of traveling the globe. He embarked on a lengthy trip through Asia and the Middle East, scouting locations for J. Walter Thompson's "Proved and Approved Around the World" ad campaign for Ford.[18]

In 1958, he began commuting to Dearborn, Michigan, to work on Ford's Fairlane Committee. The Ford Division's general manager, Lee Iacocca, required its members to meet in total secrecy either inside an airless room nicknamed "The Tomb"[19] at the Ford Division or at the Fairlane Motel. Their collaborations resulted in the Ford Falcon

(1959)[20] and the Ford Mustang (1964). As they were wrapping up, Iacocca assembled a small group of creatives to work on an exciting new project that would eventually gain fame as the Ford Mustang.[21] According to Iacocca, Olson was a brilliant writer who was once a speech writer for F.D.R. and, among other things, coined the phrase 'The Arsenal of Democracy.'"[22]

Olson's days were jam-packed. His diary pages are filled with hastily scrawled ideas, meeting notes, and the names of key players in business and advertising. Bursts of ad copy—slogans and taglines—sprinkle the pages. He corresponded infrequently with Luce, but the two men appear to have enjoyed occasional in-person meetings. After Luce's death in 1967, Olson slipped a small handwritten note from Clare Booth Luce into his files: "Dear Sid, Thank you for your letter that said, in so few words, so much about Harry. . . . You were one of the ones whose special quality brought out a side of Harry that was a delight."[23]

In 1973, he retired from J. Walter Thompson. Sid and Zembra moved from Larchmont to Darien, Connecticut, with their son Stephen. Sid continued to serve as a consultant on a number of public relation projects, among them the civic center in Worcester, Massachusetts. He also pursued his lifelong interests in reading, painting, drawing, and taking photographs. In the 1980s, he began to suffer from Parkinson's disease. Zembra and Sid endured the tragic loss of their son Stephen, who was diagnosed with a brain tumor and died shortly after his fortieth birthday. Their grief was compounded by growing health difficulties, but they were resolute—a characteristic they had always shared—and they tried to enjoy each day together. They had been married for nearly fifty-eight years when Sid died at the age of eighty-six on January 9, 1995.

Olson's career spanned decades. He rode the crest of a wave: the rollicking evolution of American media, moving from radio broadcasts to newspaper journalism, then on to popular magazines, the movie industry, public relations, and early television. From 1934 to 1950, he reported the news, witnessing many exciting and some historic moments, while delving into the intricacies of the nation's social, political, economic, and judicial policies. From 1951 to 1973, he influenced America's golden age of advertising. Many of the people whom he met, covered, and worked alongside made history. Now Olson's World War II dispatches may be added to the canon of war reporting and will serve as his special legacy.

Appendix

RESTRICTED
HEADQUARTERS
U.S. FORCES, EUROPEAN THEATER

GO 315   26 Nov 1945

European-African-Middle Eastern Campaign Ribbon I
European-African-Middle Eastern Campaign Ribbon (Posthumous) II

I—EUROPEAN-AFRICAN-MIDDLE EASTERN CAMPAIGN RIBBON.

1. Under the provisions of War Department Cable WARX 29101, 30 January 1945, the European-African-Middle Eastern campaign ribbon is awarded, for outstanding and conspicuous service with the armed forces under difficult and hazardous combat conditions, to these American War Correspondents:

Marjorie B. Avory
David M. Anderson
Lou Azrael
F. F. Banker
E. W. Beattie Jr.
Jack Belden
John A. Bell
Victor Bernstein
John A. Bockhorst

Aaron Bohrod
Therese Bonney
Harold Boyle
Holbrook Bradley
Bertram Brandt
Hugh J. Broderick
W. Wright Bryan
John Bryson
E. C. Buddy

Winston Burdett
Noel F. Busch
Edgar M. Calmer
John M. Carlisle
Cecil Carnes
Iris N. Carpenter
Lee Carson
Robert J. Casey
James F. Cassidy

Morley F. Cassidy
Lewis Cass
W. W. Chaplin
Herbert Clark
Frank A. Conniff
Horace Cort
Ruth Cowan
Catherine Coyne
Kenneth P. Crawford
Robert A. Cromie
Christopher Cunningham
E. A. Currivan
E. C. Daniel, Jr.
Russell W. Davenort
Floyd Davis
Gladys Davis
Price Day
J. A. Dearing
Rene A. Despouey
Kenneth L. Dixon
Howell. E. Dodd, Jr.
William Douglas
William R. Downs
Joseph F. Driscoll
Clifford Epstein
Vincent Flaherty
John Ted Florea
Edward T. Folliard
Stanley Frank
Lou Frankel
J. Gordon Fraser
Paul Gallico
Gordon Gammack
Lewis Gannett
Roland C. Gask
Betty Gaskill
Henry T. Gorrell
Sol S. Gottlieb
Herbert B. Graffis
Frederick Graham
Thomas B. Granden
Bruce Grant
Donald Grant
Gordon Grant

Hamilton Greene
Roger D. Greene
Daniel J. Grossi
Harry Harris
Lewis Hawkins
William Randolph
Hearst Jr.
W. C. Heinz
Martha Gellhorn
Hemingway
Ernest M. Hemingway
Thomas Henry
George F. Hicks
Carlyle Holt
Ann Hunter
Henry Jameson
W. W. Johnson
Richard H. Johnston
V. O. Jones
Warren H. Kennet
George Kent
Percy Knauth
H. R. Knickerbocker
Seymour M. Korman
Jess Krueger
Austen R. Lake
Will Lang
Clark Lee
Max Lerner
Boyd Lewis
Jack H. Lieb
A. J. Liebling
Andrew Lopez
Roelif A. Loveland
Walter R. McCallum
Lee McCardell
John F. MacVane
Ted Malone
Robert Massell
Foster May
George Meier
Robert L. Meyer
Frank F. Miles
R. C. Miller

William J. Miller
Sherman Montrose
R. E. L. Moore
John G. Morris
Ed Muller
J. E. Murray
Larry Newman
Albert H. Newman
John M. O'Connoll
Sidney A. Olson
Eleanor C. Packard
Nathaniel R. Packard
Jack D. Parker
Ivan H. Peterman
H. A. Peters
V. M. Pinkley
Herbert H. Plambeck
K. R. Porter
Thomas A. Priestley
Helena H. S. Pringle
William Reusswig
Robert W. Richards
Charles H. Robbins
Byron H. Rollins
Edmund A. Russell
Frank Scherschel
Hugh J. Schuck
Eric Sevareid
Willard F. Shadel
David E. Scherman
Lionel S. B. Shapiro
James Vincent Sheean
Joseph G. Sheahan
John D. Shelley
Duke Shoop
Harold Siegman
Arthur G. Silk
William Slocum
W. C. Small
Howard K. Smith
Martin Sommers
Theodore A. Stanford
Richard L. Stokes
William Strand

Willian H. Stringer
Elizabeth Ann Stringer
Neil Sullivan
John H. Thompson
Dixie Tighe
Sonia Tomara
Richard W. Tragaskis
Vincent Tubbs
Alexander H. Uhl
Robert V. Vermilliaon

William Wade
Mark S. Watson
Joseph Robert Wear
J. H. Wellard
Oscar E. Werner
George Wheeler
W. S. White
Don F. Whitehead
Howard Whitman
Peter Whitney

Thoburn H. Wiant
John R. Wilhelm
Ira Wolfert
S. J. Woolf
Tom Yarbrough
Lawrence W. Youngman
Harry Zinder
Hugh Baillie

2. Under the provisions of War Department Cable WARX 29101, 30 January 1945, the European–African–Middle Eastern campaign ribbon is awarded, for outstanding and conspicuous service with the armed forces under difficult and hazardous combat conditions, to these American War Correspondents:

William C. Allen
J. Edward Angly
Charles Arnot
E. D. Ball
Judy Barden
Lowell Bennett
Damaree Bess
Bjorn Bjornson
William F. Boni
Margaret Bourke-White
Mallory Browne
Robert Capa
Peter J. Carroll
Charles W. Chamberlian
Rhona Churchill
Donald G. Coe
C. C. Collingwood
Clinton Conger
H. S. Cowan
W. L. Cronkite, Jr.
Tatiana Daniel
Raymond Daniell
David Darrah
Francois Delalande

John Dored
Rudolph Dunbar
Robert Eunson
Joe Evans
Janet Flanner
Jack M. Fleischer
Hal Foust
W. F. Frye, Jr.
J. W. Gallagher
Gordon Gaskill
Abraham I. Goldberg
Joseph Grigg
Buckley S. Griffin
Henry L. Griffin
Sydney Grusen
Charles Haacker
E. L. Haaker
Rosette Hargrove
Ernest Hauser
Marguerite Higgins
Gladwin A. Hill
Russell J. Hill
Richard C. Hottelet
William J. Humphreys

V. D. Hurd
Pierre J. Huss
W. Allan Jackson
Max A. Jordan
Leon L. Kay
Helen Kirkpatrick
Robert T. Landry
Maurice Lecardeur
J. Edgerton Lee
Louis P. Lochner
John P. Maccormac
James Macdonald
Gault Macgowan
John B. Mcdermott
Fred M. Mackenzie
Donald Mckenzie
Richard D. Mcmillan
B. J. Mcquaid
Arthur E. Mann
Paul Martelliere
John M. Mecklin
Francois G. G. Mejat
Raymond. A. M. Mejat
Ralph Michaelis

Allan Michie	Edward V. Roberts	John U. Terrell
Drew Middleton	George Rodger	Edward B. Toles
Lee Miller	Larry Rue	Thomas J. Twitty
Pugh Moore	H. T. Russell	Rita Vandivert
Ralph Morse	Joel G. Sayre	William Vandivert
Malcolm Muir, Jr.	Danna A. Schmidt	Henry G. Wales
Edward R. Murrow	Sigrid L. Schultz	William Walton
Robert S. Musel	Charles C. Shaw	Marcel H. Wallenstein
Yves Henri Naintre	A. H. Singleton	Charles C. Wertenbaker
Ned E. Nordness	Alton D. Smalley	Philip W. Whitcomb
John D. O'Reilly	Kingsbury Smith	John Emlyn Williams
Geoffrey Parsons	Frederic Sonders	Joseph F. Willicombe
Cecil A. C. Phillips	Ronald M. Stead	Robert G. Wilson
Roy Porter	Alan J. Steinkopf	Thomas H. Wolf
Wilmot Ragsdale	Ollie Stewart	Edward S. Worth
Frederick J. Ramage	Monica Stirling	
Walter T. Ridder	William H. Stoneman	

II—EUROPEAN–AFRICAN–MIDDLE EASTERN CAMPAIGN RIBBON (POSTHUMOUS).

Under the provisions of War Department Cable WARX 29101, 30 January 1945, the European–African–Middle Eastern campaign ribbon is awarded, posthumously, for outstanding and conspicuous service with the armed forces under difficult and hazardous combat conditions, to these American War Correspondents:

Harold Denny	Harold Kulick	Ernie Pyle
John F. Frankish	David Lardner	T. S. Treanor
George Bede Irvin	Gaston Madrue	

By Command of General Patton:
Official: W. B. Smith
Lieutenant General, USA, Chief of Staff

[signed] R. B. Lovett
Brigadier General, USA, Adjutant General

TIMELINE

April 30, 1908	Born in Salt Lake City, Utah.
1925–1928	University of Utah.
1928–1933	Stevens & Wallis, Salt Lake City.
1933–1934	*Deseret News*, Salt Lake City.
1934–1939	*Washington Post*, Washington, D.C.
January 1937	Marries Zembra Holmgren. Attends Franklin Delano Roosevelt's inauguration.
October 1937	Birth of daughter Whitney.
July 1939	Begins working at Time Inc., New York.
1940	Opens Time Inc. office, Washington, D.C.
September 1941	Moves to 21 Pryer Lane house, Larchmont, New York.
December 7, 1941	Attack on Pearl Harbor.
December 8, 1941	United States declares war on Germany.
January 1942	Visits manufacturing plants in Michigan.
March 1942	Made senior editor, "National Affairs, Army and Navy," *Time* magazine.
July 1942	Birth of son John.
July 1943	Senior editor, "U.S. at War," "Business and Finance," "Press," *Time* magazine.
December 1944	Issued War Department travel orders for "the accomplishment of an emergency war mission" and a Selective Service permit, Class 2A, to collect material for Time Inc. in the European Theater of Operations; cosigns agreement with War Department's Bureau of Public Relations to accompany "U.S. Army Forces Overseas" as a correspondent representing Time Inc.; issued a Noncombatants Certificate of Identity as a war correspondent.
December 17(?), 1944	Boards the *Queen Elizabeth* bound for Scotland.
December 22–23, 1944	Disembarks at Gourock, takes a train to Glasgow, then takes an overnight train to London; checks in at the Dorchester Hotel.

December 28–29, 1944	SHAEF Accreditation authorized by Public Relations section of the U.S. Army, U.K. headquarters, European Theater of Operations.
January 1945	Visits the U.S. Eighth Air Force base; meets with Lord Beaverbrook at Arlington House, London; visits Royal Air Force base.
January 18, 1945	Attends Churchill's House of Commons address on the "War Situation and Foreign Policy."
January 21, 1945	Departs London.
January 22, 1945	To Paris via Newhaven and Dieppe; stays with Charles Wertenbaker of *Time*'s Paris office.
ca. January 24, 1945	Flight to Brussels.
January 27, 1945	Heinsberg, Germany.
January 28, 1945	In Eindhoven, Sittard, and Nijmegen, Holland.
ca. January 28–31, 1945	Interviews Amsterdam's harbor master as well as General Harry Crerar, commander of the First Canadian Army. Lunch with Canadian Major General Chris Vokes, Fourth Armored Division. Caught in action during the battle at Kapelsche Veer, Holland.
February 4, 1945	Travels along the British-Canadian front from Ghent, Belgium, to Breskens, Holland, including Eindhoven, Germany, and Nijmegen, Holland. According to his reading list, he is in Maastricht on February 3, 4, 12, 13, 17, and 20.
February 5, 1945	With the Ninth Army.
February 8, 1945	In a Dutch convent in an unnamed town near the German border at the headquarters of Major General Alvin Gillem of the 13th Corps of the Ninth Army. Generals Eisenhower, Simpson, and Bradley gather in "war room" with divisional generals.
February 9, 1945	Crossing of the Roer River is postponed when a network of German dams is compromised.
February 10, 1945	With the Ninth Army at an unnamed press camp in Holland. Crosses the Siegfried Line twice a day. Interviews General William H. Simpson.
February 21, 1945	Generals Simpson, Bradley, and Hodges and Field Marshal Montgomery meet in Holland to plan the Roer River crossing.
February 24, 1945	Crosses the Roer River at Jülich, Germany.
February 26, 1945	Erkelenz is taken; onward to the Rhine by March 4.
March 2, 1945	Arrives in Neuss, facing the Rhine and Düsseldorf. Into München-Gladbach with the 29th Division. Stays in Goebbels' castle, Schloss Rheydt.

March 3, 1945	The First Army crosses the Erft River, heading for Cologne. Interviews residents and troops in München-Gladbach. Hopes to leave the Ninth Army after several days.
March 5, 1945	Writes home that he is sick of the front and wires Luce for permission to move ahead with his planned itinerary. The First Army moves into the suburbs of Cologne.
March 6, 1945	Jeeps through Cologne with General Maurice Rose and the Third Armored Division. Observes tank battle at Cathedral Square and inspects cathedral.
ca. March 10, 1945	Brussels.
March 11–25, 1945	Paris.
March 25, 1945	Arrives at the 12th Army headquarters.
March 27, 1945	Namur, Belgium.
March 28, 1945	At the 12th Army Group press camp, Oberstein, Germany.
March 29, 1945	Suggests Hitler as the next *Time* cover. Interviews General George Patton.
March 30, 1945	Jeeps to Mainz. Interviews Major Clarence G. Martens of the military government in Mainz as well as liberated prisoners originally from Stalingrad. Crosses the Main River. To 12th Corps headquarters. To Frankfurt. Dinner with General Manton S. Eddy.
March 31, 1945	Jeeps to Lauterbach, Bernshausen, to join the 90th Division.
April 1, 1945	Jeeps through Ravolzhausen to Hanau and across the Main River to Offenbach.
April 2, 1945	Jeeps to airstrip.
April 3, 1945	Jeeps through Trier and Luxembourg. Plays gin rummy with photographer Robert Capa and Charles Wertenbaker.
April 4–5, 1945	Luxembourg briefing.
April 7–8, 1945	Flight to Kaiserslauten, Landstuhl, and Heidelberg.
April 8–9, 1945	Jeeps to Tauberbischoffheim, Lauda. At the Seventh Army press camp. Asks Luce again for permission to continue to the Balkans.
April 10, 1945	To Geldersheim to watch the bombing of Schweinfurt.
April 11, 1945	To Schweinfurt and Würzburg.
April 12, 1945	Tours Schweinfurt's VKF and Kugelfischer factories. President Roosevelt's death.
April 13, 1945	To the 10th Army to get reactions to the president's death.
April 14–15, 1945	To Heidelberg. Dinner with Generals Devers and Harrison, Prince Ali Khan, journalist Henry J. Taylor, Clare Boothe Luce, and Henry Cabot Lodge. Interviews Johannes Hoops, president of the University of Heidelberg.
April 15, 1945	Lauda.
April 16, 1945	Heidelberg.
April 17–18, 1945	Buchenbühl.

April 19, 1945	With the 45th Division in Nuremberg. At Nuremberg's stadium.
April 20, 1945	Day off in Lauda. On this day, Nuremberg is finally taken.
April 21, 1945	Returns to Nuremberg. In Schwabach and Katzwang.
April 22, 1945	To Nuremberg, then returns to Lauda.
April 23, 1945	Lauda. Writes "Notes for Nuremberg" piece.
April 23–25, 1945	Lauda. Works on the Nuremberg piece for *Life* magazine.
April 26, 1945	Dillingen. At the Seventh Army Press Camp.
April 27, 1945	Augsburg.
April 29, 1945	Dachau.
April 30, 1945	Cables 47 and 48 are sent to New York.
May 1, 1945	Munich.
May 2–3, 1945	Innsbruck with the Seventh Army. Dinner with General McAuliffe of the 103rd Division. Cables Luce asking for time off in Paris. Requisitions a Gestapo car with Colonel Henry J. Harding's (410th Regiment) approval.
May 5, 1945	Drives through Dillingen, Ulm, Günzburg, and Kehl and crosses the Rhine, then on to Strasbourg and Sarrebourg.
May 6, 1945	Arrives in Paris.
May 7, 1945	Signing of the German surrender takes place at Reims. *Time's* May 7 cover features Hitler's portrait with a large "X."
May 8, 1945	In Paris for V-E Day.
May 12, 1945	Files dispatch about Ed Kennedy Germany's surrender.
May 12–22, 1945	Paris.
June 4, 1945	Departs Paris.
June 5–6, 1945	Flight to the Azores, then Newfoundland; arrives in New York City, then Larchmont.
June 7, 1945	Boards train to Salt Lake City.
June 10, 1945	Salt Lake City.
July 1945	Begins work at *Fortune* magazine, New York.
July 20, 1945	Interviewed on WJZ by Van Voorhis.
July 26, 1945	Potsdam Declaration is issued, requiring Japan's unconditional surrender.
August 6, 1945	"Little Boy" atomic bomb dropped on Hiroshima.
August 9, 1945	"Fat Man" atomic bomb dropped on Nagasaki.
August 15, 1945	V-J Day.
August 1948	In Germany to cover the Marshall Plan and the Berlin Airlift. Interviews Generals Tunner, Huebner, Lemay, and Clay. Accompanies an airlift to Berlin.
November 2, 1948	Olson, John Cameron Swayze, and Ben Grauer announce the results of the Truman–Dewey presidential election on a live television broadcast.
February 1950	Leaves Time Inc.
March 1950	Begins a six-month stint at Paramount Pictures, Hollywood.

September–October 1950	Ford Foundation project for E. Newsom & Company, New York.
1950–1953	Research for his book *Young Henry Ford: A Picture History of the First Forty Years* (completed in 1953, published in 1963).
May 1951	Accepts position at Kenyon & Eckhardt, New York.
June 1952	Birth of son Stephen.
June 1953	Cowrites television script for *50th Anniversary of the Ford Motor Company*.
1956	Accepts position at J. Walter Thompson Company, New York.
1973	Retires and moves to Darien, Connecticut.
January 9, 1995	Dies at age 86.

NOTES

PREFACE

1. April 1957.

2. Allen Grover, memo to "*Miss Magazine*, Cc. Mr. Gottfried," October 1, 1952, Time Inc., MS3009-RG3, New-York Historical Society.

CHAPTER I

1. Sidney Olson, Dispatch to David Hulburd, January 31, 1942. A portion of his dispatch was used (without byline) in "Detroit: A New Era Begins," *Time*, February 9, 1942, 18.

2. "Third Term Will Win, Says *Time* Staff Man," *Deseret News*, July 3, 1939.

3. "Made a Senior Editor of *Time*," *Washington Post*, March 12, 1942.

4. Sidney Olson transcript, Office of the Registrar, University of Utah, 2019.

5. "By 1932, over 12 million Americans—nearly one-quarter of the workforce—were unemployed." William E. Leuchtenburg, "Franklin Delano Roosevelt: Life before the Presidency," Miller Center, University of Virginia, https://www.millercenter.org/president/fdroosevelt/life-before-the-presidency (accessed January 10, 2024).

6. "Spurs Announce Frosh Pledges," *Utah Daily Chronicle*, March 13, 1928; "Teachers Named for Box Elder," *Salt Lake Telegram*, April 16, 1929.

7. Olson Diary, November 1932.

8. "University of Utah News Bureau," *Beaver County News*, February 5, 1926.

9. "KSL Radio: On-Air Highlights," *Deseret News*, May 3, 2002.

10. Olson Diary, February 1933.

11. "A Tragedy of the Storm in the Mountains of Utah," Rotogravure Picture section, *New York Times*, March 4, 1934.

12. Sidney Olson, Letter to Robert Hawes of J. Walter Thompson, April 24, 1951.

13. Olson, Letter to Hawes, April 24, 1951; see also Olson Diary, January 1957.

14. Joseph Cannon, Letter to Sidney Olson, August 1934.

15. Sidney Olson, Letter to Zembra Holmgren, August 10, 1934.

16. Olson Diary, March 1935.

17. Sidney Olson, Letter to Zembra Holmgren, December 12, 1934.

18. Advertisement, *Washington Post*, April 2, 1935: "Sidney Olson, who weaves scattered news threads into a complete historical tapestry, has to read 50 newspaper files, 20 magazines, 10 or 11 books and a *Sears-Roebuck* mail order catalog each week to know what's going on and why."

19. Olson Diary, February 1935.

20. "Mr. Meyer took care that his key reporters and editors cultivated the right contacts, and in the interest of better general information on international affairs he organized a series of off-the-record seminars for a select group of *Post* writers. . . . These meetings were smokers held at Mr. Meyer's home in Washington." "Rise of the *Washington Post*," *Fortune*, December 1944, 135. It is likely that Olson contributed to this article.

21. Sidney Olson, "A Year of Violent Struggle at Home and Turmoil Abroad," *Washington Post*, December 29, 1935.

22. Olson Diary, February 1936.

23. The event was at the Willard Hotel. "Newspapermen Have President at Annual Fete," *Washington Post*, March 8, 1936.

24. B. H. Winfield, "Franklin D. Roosevelt's Efforts to Influence the News during His First Term Press Conferences," *Presidential Studies Quarterly* 11, no. 2 (Spring 1981): 191.

25. Zembra Holmgren, Letter to her parents, May 15, 1936.

26. "On to Cleveland . . . with *The Post*," *Washington Post*, June 4, 1936.

27. "And Now, to Philadelphia . . . with *The Post*," *Washington Post*, June 19, 1936.

28. "Record Political Audience Hears President," *Washington Post*, June 27, 1936.

29. "Trip of the President, Oct. 27–29, 1936" itinerary with list of "Newspaper men, Picture men, Broadcasting, and Telegraph representatives."

30. Harry C. Butcher, *My Three Years with Eisenhower* (New York: Simon & Schuster, 1946).

31. "Wedding Rite in East Holds Interest Here," *Salt Lake Telegram*, January 19, 1937.

32. "'The Boss' Has Matured during Four Years in White House," *Washington Post*, January 20, 1937.

33. Olson Diary, December 1937.

34. *Who's Who in America 1944–1945*, vol. 23 (Chicago: A. N. Marquis Company, 1944), 1599.

35. Olson's current boss Eugene Meyer was seated at the head table with FDR and other dignitaries. Seating chart, the Gridiron Club of Washington, D.C., Spring Dinner, April 9, 1938.

36. Sidney Olson, Letter to Zembra, May 10, 1939.

37. Alexander F. "Casey" Jones, *Washington Post* managing editor, 1935–1947.

38. A ProQuest search conducted at the New York Public Library in 2020 revealed Olson's remarkable output and legacy at the *Washington Post*.

39. In 1939, "the company's revenues rose to a new record $29,311,057. . . . Rewards at Time Inc. continued to increase, not only for the key employees but for the rank and file, maintaining a scale of benefits unsurpassed in the publishing business." Robert T. Elson, *Time Inc.: The Intimate History of a Publishing Enterprise, Vol. 1, 1923–1941* (New York: Atheneum, 1968), 402.

40. This building's address was later changed to 1 Rockefeller Plaza.

41. "Third Term Will Win, Says *Time* Staff Man—Returns to Salt Lake on Visit," *Deseret News*, July 3, 1939.

42. Billings Diary, June 4, 1940, John Shaw Billings Papers, South Caroliniana Library, University of South Carolina. Billings functioned "very efficiently as Luce's deputy," according to Robert Elson, "a role he understood, intervening as little as possible, using his authority with the managing editors with great restraint, on occasion fulfilling the role of mediator between them and the editor-in-chief." Robert Elson, *The World of Time Inc.*, vol. 2 (New York: Atheneum, 1973), 84.

43. Newspaper clipping (unknown publication), ca. July 12, 1940.

44. Doris Kearns Goodwin, *No Ordinary Time—Franklin & Eleanor Roosevelt: The Home Front in World War II* (New York: Touchstone/Simon & Schuster, 1994), 193.

45. Olson, Letter to Hawes, April 24, 1951.

46. Robert E. Sherwood, *Roosevelt and Hopkins: An Intimate History* (New York: Harper & Brothers, 1948), 226.

47. Ed Lockett, McCloy Memorandum on Production to David Hulburd, September 20, 1941.

48. Olson's colleague at *Time*, Hersey published "Hiroshima" in *The New Yorker* in August 1946.

49. "Made a Senior Editor of *Time*," *Washington Post*, March 12, 1942.

50. Manfred Gottfried, Memorandum to writers and researchers, August 6, 1942; Henry Luce, Memorandum to Editors, August 24, 1942.

51. Olson Diary, January 1957; Phone conversation with Larchmont, New York, assessor's office, 2019.

52. "A Letter from the Publisher," *Time*, July 12, 1943, 19.

53. Lord John Maynard Keynes was a British economist, financier, and journalist whose theories substantively changed the economic policies of governments.

54. Beardsley Ruml was an American statistician and economist. Willi Schlamm would go on to cover the war for *Time*; he later urged William F. Buckley Jr. to found the *National Review*.

55. W. W. Johnson, Memorandum to Grover, Matthews, Alexander, et al., May 6, 1944, Time Inc., MS 3009-RG 14, New-York Historical Society.

56. Henry Luce, Memo to Editors, August 21, 1944, Henry R. Luce Papers, MS 3014, New-York Historical Society.

57. David Hulburd, Cable to Walter Graebner, December 13, 1943, Time Inc., MS 3009-RG 14, New-York Historical Society.

58. Sidney Olson, Letter to George Frazier, April 19, 1950.

59. Forrest C. Pogue, *United States Army in World War II: European Theater of Operations, The Supreme Command* (Washington, DC: Office of the Chief of Military History, Department of the Army, 1954), 88–89.

60. "Censors were guided by a press censorship bible, a 200-page mimeographed document containing the censorship policy of British, Canadian, and U.S. forces in the European theater. This was supplemented by daily directives, known as Press Relations Censorship Guidances and Press Censors' Guidances, which listed items to be stopped or passed by the censors; by the Secret List, issued monthly by the War Office, containing

the security classification of Allied equipment; by 'Trend of Copy,' a summary of the type of newspaper copy which had been passed or stopped by the censors; and by pertinent Ministry of Information statements." Pogue, *United States Army in World War II*, 90.

61. Inspector of H.M. Immigration Office, Ibex House, December 29, 1944.

62. On April 17, 1944, Olson received a permit from the Selective Service allowing him to travel to England for 90 days as an editor representing Time Inc. He did not go. By the time he sailed for Scotland in December 1944, his status had been changed from I-A to II-A ("deferred in support of national health, safety, or interest"). The duration of this trip was lengthened to six months, and his terrain was expanded to "European Theater of Operations."

63. W. W. Johnson, Memorandum to Grover, Matthews, Alexander, et al., May 6, 1944, Time Inc., MS 3009-RG 14, New-York Historical Society.

64. Although Olson's letter is undated, his comments relate to events in the weeks leading up to Election Day 1944. Sidney Olson, Letter to Henry Luce, ca. September–October 1944, Time Inc., MS 3009-RG 2, New-York Historical Society.

65. Thomas Dewey ran for president in 1944 and lost to FDR, who then began his fourth term.

66. A section of *Time* called "U.S. at War."

67. T. S. Matthews of Time Inc.

68. Twenty years later, Luce would authorize Elson to write a two-volume history of Time Inc.; ironically, Olson's role and contributions received minimal attention (see Elson, *The World of Time Inc.*, vol. 2, 93–94).

69. Felix Belair of Time Inc.

70. A draft of the telegram was passed to Olson by "A.G." (presumably Allen Grover).

CHAPTER II

1. Sidney Olson, Letter to Henry Luce, December 27, 1944, Time Inc. Bio Files, MS 3009-RG 2, New-York Historical Society.

2. Sidney Olson, Letter to Henry Luce, January 17, 1944, Time Inc. Bio Files, MS 3009-RG 2, New-York Historical Society.

3. Olson's SHAEF travel ticket and embarkation card: "London-Paris Service via Newhaven and Dieppe . . . for AEF personnel."

4. "Facility Visit—Mr. Olsen," January 27, 1945.

5. For example, on April 10, 1945, he wrote in his notes, "Filed 2,000 on Schweinfurt bombing, #42."

6. D-Day took place on June 6, 1944. Charles Wertenbaker, Memorandum to Hulburd et al., June 16, 1944, Time Inc., MS 3009-RG 14, New-York Historical Society.

7. Ronald Weber, *Dateline—Liberated Paris: The Hotel Scribe and the Invasion of the Press* (Lanham, MD: Rowman & Littlefield, 2019), 104.

8. Andy Rooney, *My War* (New York: PublicAffairs, 1995), 202.

9. Sidney Olson, Novel Notes, December 27, 1946.

10. Weber, *Dateline—Liberated Paris*, 103–5. See also Julia Kennedy, ed., *Ed Kennedy's War: V-E Day, Censorship, and the Associated Press* (Baton Rouge: Louisiana State University Press, 2012), 142.

11. Charles Wertenbaker, *The Death of Kings* (New York: Random House, 1954), 297–98.

12. Robert T. Elson, *Time Inc.: The Intimate History of a Publishing Enterprise, Vol. 2, 1923–1941* (New York: Atheneum, 1968), 205.

13. My thanks to historian Sam Kassow for recommending Abzug's moving book to me.

14. Paul Fussell, *Wartime: Understanding and Behavior in the Second World War* (New York: Oxford University Press, 1989), 164.

15. Olivia B. Waxman, "Long-Forgotten Cables Reveal What *Time*'s Correspondent Saw at the Liberation of Dachau," *Time*, April 21, 2020, https://www.time.com/5812523/liberation-of-dachau-time-reporter.

16. Corbett mentions Ridder also. Sam Dann, ed., *Dachau 29 April, 1945: The Rainbow Liberation Memoirs* (Lubbock: Texas Tech University Press, 1998), 46.

17. Dann, *Dachau 29 April, 1945*, 19.

18. Marguerite Higgins, "33,000 Dachau Captives Freed by 7th Army," *New York Herald Tribune*, May 1, 1945; Howard Cowan, "Dachau Prison Camp Taken, 32,000 Set Free by Yanks," Associated Press, May 1, 1945.

19. "Saturday" would have been May 5. Vincent Tubbs, "War in Europe Over in Any Language," *Baltimore Afro-American*, May 19, 1945.

20. Weber, *Dateline—Liberated Paris*, 158. See also Kennedy, *Ed Kennedy's War.*

21. Weber, *Dateline—Liberated Paris*, 164.

22. Fragments of Olson's dispatch were used in a pool-reported article, "The Army's Guests," *Time*, May 21, 1945, 56–58.

23. *Time* correspondent Mary Welsh wrote to her parents, "I expect to be leaving here about March 21, and will have to go home by boat. Journalists are no longer allowed to fly home, unless they are prepared to say their trip will be of vital importance to the war effort." Letter to Thomas Welsh, March 20, 1945, Mary Welsh Hemingway Papers, Yale Collection of American Literature, Beinecke Rare Book & Manuscript Library, Yale University.

24. *Salt Lake Telegram*, "*Time* Editor Visits Native Salt Lake," June 20, 1945.

25. Historian Alan Brinkley wrote that "Luce apparently had no knowledge of the successful outcome of the Manhattan Project and very likely had known nothing of the project at all." *The Publisher* (New York: Vintage Books, 2010), 315.

26. Welch was with "G-2, XV Corps." Following Japan's surrender, Victory over Japan, or V-J Day, was celebrated on August 14, 1945.

27. The "secret weapon" to which Olson refers was presumably the atomic bomb, dropped on Hiroshima and Nagasaki on August 6 and August 9, respectively. That Olson wrote he was outside Dachau on "May 1st" is also interesting. It has been established that he was at Dachau on April 29; we do not know exactly where Olson was on April 30. He toured Munich on May 1. It is certainly possible that he returned to Dachau a second time; some of the other correspondents mentioned making a return trip.

28. This ribbon has not been found.

29. Spelled "Wear" hereafter.

30. Bonney, an American-born photojournalist, was already well known for her coverage of the war by the time Olson met her.

31. French painter in Fauvist style.

32. Written in the early morning hours of December 24 (not December 23); the next entry is December 24.

33. Greenock, Scotland, port of Gourock.

34. Ben Lomond, or Beacon Mountain, is located in the Scottish Highlands and must have been visible from Gourock.

35. Altschul was with the Civil Aeronautics Board in 1941 as a senior analyst; during World War II, he served in the U.S. Air Force, participating in the strategic bombing survey of Germany.

36. On the inside cover of his diary, Olson wrote, "Lt. Commander Russell S. Stratton, Rm 3541 Navy Dept, Washington, D.C.," followed by the notation "in London, % Lt. Commdr Rains, ComNavEu." *Com NavEu* stood for "Commander, U.S. Naval Forces in Europe."

37. Bill Johnson of *Time*'s London office.

38. Wilmott Ragsdale of *Time*'s London office.

39. Dennis Scanlan of *Time*'s London office. Lord Beaverbrook owned the *Evening Standard*.

40. V-mail was written on special stationery, photographed, put on microfilm, and then shipped to the United States, where it was printed and mailed to the recipients. Only three of Zembra's letters (all V-mail) survive and are not included in this book.

41. The aforementioned Russell S. Stratton.

42. The baby was named Noel, according to his January 3 letter, not included here. Schrafft's was a popular restaurant in Manhattan.

43. Their closest Larchmont friend, Phyllis McGinley Hayden, was a poet and author; she won a Pulitzer Prize in 1961.

44. Harry: Henry Luce. Sidney Olson, Letter to Henry Luce, December 27, 1944, Time Inc. Bio Files, MS 3009-RG 2, New-York Historical Society.

45. UNRRA: United Nations Relief and Rehabilitation Administration.

46. OWI: Office of War Information.

47. Churchill used the term "a new dark age" in his "Finest Hour" speech, June 18, 1940.

48. Iddon was a reporter for London's *Daily Mail* in Washington, D.C.

49. Lord Beaverbrook (Canadian-born Max Aitken) owned the British newspapers *Daily Mail* and *Evening Standard*; Winston Churchill had appointed him minister of aircraft production.

50. PM: prime minister.

51. "Jack Manthorp has a full-time job here just helping our editors get quickly to where they need to go overseas . . . getting anywhere except to England is almost impossible unless the correspondent is officially accredited to the Army or Navy. That means weeks being looked up by the F.B.I., G2, or Naval Intelligence, and then getting cabled permission from the U.S. Area Commander. (For that matter, there is absolutely no way of getting through to most war zones except on Army or Navy ships or planes.) Before a

correspondent can even apply for a passport he must get permission from his local draft board to leave the country—and after the passport comes through the visa rush begins." "Letter from the Publisher," *Time*, August 30, 1943.

52. Olson and Bill Johnson (representing *Time* of "2 Dean Street") cosigned an accreditation agreement with SHAEF's Public Relations Division on December 29, 1944.

53. Because Olson's Cable 2384 (Houghton Library, Harvard University) is almost entirely about Dean Inge and his views on the fate of country houses, we have chosen to omit it.

54. U.S. military post exchanges, or PXs, provided enlisted men with necessary goods while overseas.

55. Margaret "Margot" Lapsley Post was the widow of *New York Times* correspondent Bob Post, who was killed while covering a B-24 bombing mission over Germany in 1943. Eric Ambler was an influential English novelist; by the end of World War II, he was a lieutenant-colonel and assistant director of the army film unit. Grahame was an English actress.

56. Wormser was a foreign service officer who joined the Free French movement in London.

57. V-2 rockets were launched at London by the Germans from mobile units, taking just five minutes from launch to landing, beginning in September 1944. Each rocket carried 900 kilograms (one ton) of explosives. The V-2 replaced the V-1, which was known as a "buzz bomb" or "doodlebug."

58. "Bbr": bomb (or bombardment) group

59. Kahle was a Communist who fled Nazi Germany and fought with the 11th International Brigade during the Spanish Civil War. He was interned for a time as an enemy alien, then recruited anti-Nazi refugees for the Free German Brigade.

60. Colonel Joseph A. Moller, commander, 390th Bomb Group, was very likely based at Station 153, Framlingham (Parham).

61. Olson's comments about bombing drew the attention of censors: part of point #2 was neatly cut out of the letter owned by the New-York Historical Society; in the carbon copy sent to Zembra (same date), *all* of point #2 was removed.

62. Geoffrey Crowther, "Noble Negatives," *The Economist*, December 30, 1944.

63. "Pantomimes," *Life*, January 29, 1945, 37–40.

64. The Eighth Air Force carried out strategic bombing operations in Europe during World War II.

65. Edward Stettinius was named U.S. secretary of state by President Roosevelt in 1944.

66. RAF Wing Commander Walter Gibb, 239 Squadron, 100 Group, probably located at RAF West Raynham, which was equipped with de Havilland Mosquitos.

67. This is a reference to the RAF's base in Iraq; see Olson, Letter to Henry Luce, January 17, 1945.

68. Sidney Olson, Cable to David Hulburd, January 13, 1945, Time Inc. Bio Files, MS 3009-RG 2, New-York Historical Society.

69. Air Transport Command (ATC) airlifted key personnel, mail, and cargoes to European and Mediterranean theaters of war.

70. Either a typographical error or Luce was using a bit of editorial humor.

71. The note clipped to Olson's letter reflects the editorial interest in Olson's reports, which were mined for publishable information.

72. Sidney Olson, Letter to Henry Luce, January 17, 1945, Time Inc. Bio Files, MS 3009-RG 2, New-York Historical Society.

73. Walter Lippmann (1889–1974) was an influential political columnist.

74. Lord Beaverbrook.

75. Olson had known Willkie professionally and wrote most of Willkie's obituary "With All My Heart," *Time*, October 16, 1944 (per Olson Diary, November 1945).

76. Roosevelt's speechwriters.

77. Lewis was correspondent for the *Times* of London based in Washington, D.C.

78. Bevan was a prominent member of the British Labour Party.

79. Vandenberg's image was used on the April 30, 1945, cover.

80. A tidal power project in Eastport, Maine.

81. Possibly a reference to Raimund Pretzel, aka Sebastian Haffner, of the London *Observer* but more likely Raimund von Hofmannsthal, who was part of Luce's inner circle and well-connected within European society.

82. Sidney Olson, Cable 2539 to David Hulburd, Dispatches from *Time* Correspondents: First Series, Roy Larsen Papers, Houghton Library, Harvard University.

83. Press pass no. 86, Members Gallery, House of Commons, stamped January 18, 1945.

84. John G. Winant was U.S. ambassador to Britain from 1941 to 1946.

85. One of Churchill's confidants, Anthony Eden served many roles in Britain during World War II, including Leader of the House of Commons.

86. Clement Attlee, leader of the Labour Party, succeeded Churchill as prime minister in July 1945.

87. Canadian sector.

88. The food embargo that had been instituted by the Germans as a counteroffensive was lifted in early November 1944; however, severe shortages continued, leading the Dutch to call the resulting famine a "Hunger Winter."

89. B-17s, or Flying Fortresses, flying from England to Germany on bombing raids.

90. Booby traps.

91. Olson's offer to submit a piece about Holland was apparently declined by his editors, who preferred to use Noel Busch's piece on Queen Wilhelmina of the Netherlands.

92. General Harry Crerar of the Canadian First Army.

93. Vokes of the Fourth Canadian Armored.

94. Tommies was the nickname for British troops.

95. Sidney Olson, Cable to David Hulburd, February 5, 1945, Dispatches from *Time* Correspondents: First Series, Roy Larsen Papers, Houghton Library, Harvard University.

96. German Field Marshal Gerd von Rundstedt.

97. The Meuse River, also called the Maas, flows through the Netherlands, Belgium, and France.

98. Kapelsche Veer was finally retaken by the Canadian Fourth Armored in a difficult battle, January 26–31, 1945. This was Olson's first experience in battle.

99. "The Watch on the Maas had involved few operations on such a scale. It had how-ever meant unremitting vigilance, constant patrolling (including many incursions across the river into enemy country) and frequent raids: all under the most wretched conditions of ground and weather." C. P. Stacey, *The Canadian Army, 1939–1945: An Official Histor-ical Summary* (Ottawa: King's Printer, 1948), chap. 14, 245–46.

100. Sidney Olson, Cable to David Hulburd, February 7, 1945, Dispatches from *Time* Correspondents: First Series, Roy Larsen Papers, Houghton Library, Harvard University.

101. Olson was forced to hold on to his dispatch for reasons of censorship: the Germans had released the water from a network of seven dams, causing the Roer River to flood its banks, thereby preventing the U.S. Ninth Army from making their planned crossing on February 10. Once the river was finally crossed on February 23, Olson updated his dateline and added the final sentence, then cabled it to New York on February 28.

102. Sidney Olson, Cable to David Hulburd, February 10, 1945, Dispatches from *Time* Correspondents: First Series, Roy Larsen Papers, Houghton Library, Harvard University.

103. The Siegfried Line was a defensive line composed of concrete "dragon's teeth," pillboxes, and bunkers built by the Germans along their western border beginning in the 1930s.

104. Portions of Olson's unnumbered cable dated February 7 were used (no byline) in "Western Front: Right and Ripe," *Time*, February 19, 1945, 25–27.

105. Bracken ran London's *Financial Times* and was a Churchill supporter and minister in the British Conservative cabinet.

106. Ava Alice Muriel Astor, ex-wife of Luce's friend Raimund Von Hofmannsthal.

107. In fact, Welsh was from the American Midwest; in the years leading up to the war, she wrote for London's *Daily Express*. In 1944, she began seeing Hemingway and became his fourth wife in 1946. Gellhorn was a correspondent for *Collier's* and was Hemingway's third wife.

108. Robert Capa was already famous for his photos of the Spanish Civil War. Lael was the wife of Charles Wertenbaker.

109. *Time* and *Life* correspondent William Chickering was killed in January 1945 while covering the war in the South Pacific.

110. Lerner wrote for the left-leaning daily newspaper *PM*, founded in 1940 by former Time Inc. executive Ralph Ingersoll.

111. Per a V-mail from Zembra dated February 15, 1945.

112. Elisabeth de Miribel typed up General de Gaulle's historic Appeal of June 18, 1940, a BBC Radio broadcast that inspired the French Resistance. She provided Olson with a letter of introduction and a press pass to attend de Gaulle's press conference on January 25, 1945.

113. Sidney Olson, Cable 20 to David Hulburd, February 12, 1945, Dispatches from *Time* Correspondents: First Series, Roy Larsen Papers, Houghton Library, Harvard University.

114. The correct spelling is Kapelsche Veer.

115. As stated earlier, Olson was thwarted by the postponement of the river crossing.

116. Sidney Olson, Cable 21 to David Hulburd, February 17, 1945, Dispatches from *Time* Correspondents: First Series, Roy Larsen Papers, Houghton Library, Harvard University.

117. Sidney Olson, Cable 22 to David Hulburd, February 17, 1945, Dispatches from *Time* Correspondents: First Series, Roy Larsen Papers, Houghton Library, Harvard University.

118. Probably the German Messerschmitt Me 262.

119. Olson was mentioned, and a few of these lines were paraphrased in "A Letter from the Publisher," *Time*, March 12, 1945.

120. American infantrymen.

121. Fighter aircraft.

122. reccy: reconnaissance.

123. ack-ack: antiaircraft gunfire.

124. German antiaircraft and anti-tank artillery.

125. Betsy: type of rifle.

126. Mae West: life vest.

127. When transmitting a cable, a dispatch would have been read aloud, which is why punctuation like "seriatum" would need to be spelled out. "Press Wireless, Inc. handles a large portion of its press communications service by means of voice communication; again with equipment, antennas, and personnel simultaneously furnishing worldwide radiotelegraph service." Department of State, *Memorandum of the Post War International Information Program of the United States* (Washington, DC: U.S. Government Printing Office, 1945), 30.

128. Loosely translated: "life flies with the hours."

129. Sidney Olson, Cable 27 to Time Inc., February 28, 1945, Time Inc. Bio Files, MS 3009-RG 2, New-York Historical Society.

130. Portions of Cable 27 were incorporated (without byline) into "The Allies Drive for the Rhine," *Life*, March 12, 1945, 25–29.

131. Koming: indicates to the editor that this information is forthcoming.

132. The ancient Roman town was called Iuliacum.

133. *Wehrmacht*: Nazi Germany's armed forces.

134. Portions of Cable 28 were published in "A Thing of Beauty" (with byline), *Time*, March 12, 1945, 31.

135. *Gestapo*: secret police.

136. Henry Luce, Telegram to Sidney Olson, March 2, 1945, Time Inc. Bio Files, MS 3009-RG 2, New-York Historical Society.

137. Olson mistakenly assigned "29" to two different cables (on March 3 and March 6), so the numerals I and II have been added.

138. Sidney Olson, Cable to David Hulburd, March 4, 1945, Time Inc. Bio Files, MS 3009-RG 2, New-York Historical Society.

139. *March of Time* was a monthly newsreel produced by Time Inc.

140. Beaton was an eminent English photographer of the day; landscapes by the surrealist painter Salvador Dali resemble war-torn landscapes.

141. Born in Austria, Schlamm was already an established journalist before emigrating to America in 1938; he joined Time Inc. in 1941.

142. Historic castle just outside of München- Gladbach, seized by Goebbels until the Americans arrived in March 1945.

143. Olson helped Midgley launch his career at the *Deseret News*; in 1945, Midgley worked for the *New York Herald Tribune* in Paris.

144. Olson's colleague at the *Washington Post*.

145. Sidney Olson, Cable 29 [II] to David Hulburd, March 6, 1945, Dispatches from *Time* Correspondents: First Series, Roy Larsen Papers, Houghton Library, Harvard University.

146. A number of photographers captured the tour on camera. See New York World-Telegram & Sun Collection at the Library of Congress; see also British Pathé.

147. Portions of this dispatch were used (with bylines) in "Mission Accomplished," *Time*, March 19, 1945, 33, and in "Underground Cologne," *Life*, March 19, 1945, 28.

148. German hand, or "stick," grenade.

149. *Stars & Stripes* journalist Andy Rooney appears to have reached the scene just before Olson. He wrote in his memoir, "I ran toward the tank, lifted and dragged the third man to the ground . . . there was nothing but a ragged pant leg, wet with blood where his leg had been. There were no medics near us." Rooney, *My War*, 250; see also Adam Makos, *Spearhead: An American Tank Gunner, His Enemy, and a Collision of Lives in World War II* (New York: Ballantine Books, 2019), 202–3, and Thomas Brading, "Hero of Cologne," U.S. Army, Army News Service, September 19, 2019.

150. *Waffen SS* was the combat portion of the German paramilitary, or *Schutzstaffel*.

151. The *Burgomeister* was the mayor or chief magistrate of a German city or town.

152. The Lancaster was another Paris hotel occupied by American and British correspondents.

153. *Herald Tribune* correspondent Homer Bigart.

154. Thibault de Champrosay, Parisian author and editor.

155. American Military Government.

156. According to Les Midgley, Olson threw a party for the *Herald Tribune*'s international office in Paris. Leslie Midgley, *How Many Words Do You Want? An Insider's Stories of Print and Television Journalism* (New York: Birch Lane Press, 1988), 62.

157. Olson saved his entry card from the Maison des Alliés.

158. Sidney Olson, Cable to David Hulburd, March 14, 1945, Time Inc. Bio Files, MS 3009-RG 2, New-York Historical Society.

159. Henry Luce, "The Day of Wrath," *Life*, December 22, 1941.

160. Les Midgley wrote in his memoir, "More and more correspondents in uniform kept arriving in Paris en route to take a look at the ruins in Germany. Among them was the mentor of my youth, Sidney Olson, now a principal writer for *Life*. The *Time-Life* contingent lived high on the hog, not in the Scribe with the ordinary working press. The Ritz was more to their taste. Even fancier than the Ritz was the Lancaster, a small hotel on the Rue de Berri just down the block from the *Herald*. Charlie Wertenbaker was the senior *Time* man and he lived in this elegant little hostelry . . . Charlie had a suite,

complete with grand piano, which had formerly been occupied by Marlene Dietrich." Midgley, *How Many Words Do You Want?*, 62.

161. Correct spelling: René Arturo Despouey.

162. In Olson's Cable 28 (March 2), Hall is mentioned in relation to the U.S. role overseeing the surrendered town of München-Gladbach.

163. Quirk was Patton's public relations officer (PRO), responsible for arranging Olson's interview of the general. Many of the names in Olson diary were correspondents—for a definitive list, see Appendix: November 26, 1945, List of Correspondents.

164. We are grateful to Ron Weber, Professor Emeritus of American History at the University of Notre Dame and author of *Dateline—Liberated Paris*, for sharing Quirk's letter. James Quirk, Letter to his wife, March 29, 1945, James T. Quirk Papers, Box 1: WWII, 1942–1946, Harry S. Truman Presidential Library.

165. Sidney Olson, Letter to David Hulburd, March 29, 1945, Time Inc. Bio Files, MS 3009-RG 2, New-York Historical Society.

166. *Time* placed Hitler on the cover of the May 7, 1945, issue, painting a large "X" on his face.

167. This and several other lines from Cable 34 were used in "A Letter from the Publisher," *Time*, April 9, 1945, 17.

168. The residents of Lidice (in former Czechoslovakia) were massacred by the Germans in 1942; the residents of Oradour-sur-Glane in France were massacred in June 1944; the concentration camp Maidanek, outside of Lublin, Poland, was discovered by Russian soldiers in July 1944.

169. Elements of this piece were folded into the cover story "Third Army's Patton: The Star Half-Back," *Time*, April 9, 1945; although Olson was not given a byline, he was credited in "The Press: Getting the Story," *Time*, April 16, 1945, 75.

170. In August 1943, in two separate incidents, General Patton slapped hospitalized soldiers, angered by their claims of battle fatigue; Eisenhower forced him to publicly apologize.

171. "The Press," *Time*, April 16, 1945, 73. Olson describes his trip to see Patton in late March; the original dispatch has not been located.

172. PRO Captain Merle Potter of XII Corps on General Manton Eddy's staff.

173. Months later in New York City, Olson "talked for 2 hours with Lt. Murray of Army Intelligence," per his July 9 diary entry.

174. General Manton Eddy led XII Corps, part of Patton's Third Army, until April 1945.

175. A March cable about war atrocities by Olson has not been located.

176. Beginning with this line, Olson's dispatch was published (with a byline) as "Searching for the Heart," *Time*, April 9, 1945, 30–33.

177. Creighton Abrams and his 37th Tank Battalion worked in tandem with Harold Cohen and his 10th Armored Infantry Battalion.

178. On April 5, Olson added *The Haunted House*, by Hilaire Belloc, to his booklist: "borrowed in chateau in Luxembourg."

179. Cable 36 was sent one day *after* Cable 38.

180. A summary of the results was published in "The Soldiers Think of Home," *Time*, April 16, 1945, 24.

181. Rose was killed on March 30, 1945.

182. TAC: Tactical Air Command.

183. Vincent Tubbs of the Baltimore *Afro-American* was the first African American journalist to cover the war in the Pacific, arriving in 1943.

184. Some of Cable 41 was used (with byline) in "Chaos and Comforts," *Time*, April 16, 1945, 38.

185. This is one of Olson's rare references to the persecution of Jews; it is disappointing, to say the least, that Olson's editors chose to omit this paragraph from the aforementioned *Time* article "Chaos and Comforts."

186. Sidney Olson, Cable "a" to David Hulburd, April 9, 1945, Time Inc. Bio Files, MS 3009-RG 2, New-York Historical Society.

187. In 1944, Pyle won a Pulitzer Prize for his war reporting; he was killed on Ie Shima on April 18, 1945.

188. Hersey's first book, *Men on Bataan* (New York: Alfred A. Knopf), was published in 1942.

189. Clare Boothe Luce toured the European battlefront as part of a congressional delegation (she was serving her second term as a Connecticut representative).

190. Sidney Olson, Cable "b" to David Hulburd, April 9, 1945, Time Inc. Bio Files, MS 3009-RG 2, New-York Historical Society.

191. Many believed that Hitler would retreat to his fortified chalet in the town of Berchtesgaden in Bavaria.

192. *Festung*: fortress or stronghold.

193. Already suggested by Olson on March 29.

194. Reference to the fourth part of Richard Wagner's famed music cycle *Der Ring des Nibelungen* and, by definition (according to *Merriam-Webster*), the collapse of a society or regime via catastrophic violence or disorder.

195. In Cable 42, medics discuss "Red," an injured soldier with a deep wound to his ankle.

196. Olson is referring to strategic bombing raids conducted by the Eighth Air Force in 1943, which targeted the ball-bearings plants in Schweinfurt.

197. Focke-Wulf: German airplane manufacturer.

198. VKF: Vereinigte Kugellager Fabrik. The full name of the second factory was Fischers Aktien-Gesellschaft (FAG) Kugelfischer.

199. "Prex": President Roosevelt died on April 12, 1945.

200. Swedish ball-bearings manufacturer SKF (Svenska Kullager Fabriken). Batt was an American mechanical engineer who became president of SKF; in 1943, he was made vice president of the U.S. War Production Board.

201. Otto Schaefer was the younger son of the founder of Kugelfischer and ran the firm with his brother Georg. The company—an important component of Hitler's war machine—continued to prosper after the war.

202. Based on his 1942 trip to Michigan to observe the auto industry's conversion, Olson felt confident enough to affirm that Schweinfurt's output had been compromised.

203. He is referring to the reactions to the news of the president's death.

204. Peckham oversaw *Time*'s foreign news research; she was the first woman at Time Inc. to be named a senior editor.

205. Correspondent Herb Plambeck described the situation as he advanced with Olson into Nuremberg: "Fanatical resistance the following day held up our troops . . . in house to house fighting, our boys got down to the wall surrounding the old city, now a Nazi fortress. Olsen [*sic*] and I went only as far as was considered safe. En route we saw the huge stadium, the unfinished Nazi party hall, the march field, and the huge arena. . . . Finally, we reached our destination, a regimental command post." Herb Plambeck, WWII Broadcast Scripts from Front: 21 April 1945, Box 34, WHO Radio Collection, Archives of Iowa Broadcasting, Wartburg College.

206. In his dispatches, Olson changed this spelling to "Buchenbühl." It is located a few miles north of Nuremberg's center.

207. German assassins.

208. In 1960, the article was republished in *Great Reading from Life: A Treasury of the Best Stories and Articles Chosen by the Editors* (New York: Harper & Brothers, 1960).

209. Omitted from Cable 46 but included in Olson's April 23 notes was a description of the April 21 flag-raising ceremony presided over by Major General John W. "Iron Mike" O'Daniel, Major General Robert T. Frederick, General Wade H. Haislip, and General Alexander Patch: "Lined up for the ceremony, blinking into the dust, battalions from the 3rd, the 45th, representations from the 42nd, the combat engineers, the tanks, the tds, the generals—ODaniell, Fredericks, Haizlip, Patch. The Red Cross girls. The flag raising. The wall that fell with a great crash of dust and bricks as Patch spoke, and the steady leaking-down of bricks always. The bang in the wind of roof-sheets against walls. 'The Star Spangled Banner.'"

210. In his notes, Olson wrote, "Karl Holz and Will Liebel in the tunnel."

211. In his notes, Olson alluded to the disappearance of this priceless trove: "The *Reichskleinodien*, Vienna and back and gone." It was eventually located by the Monuments Men; see Rihoko Ueno, "Recovering Gold and Regalia: A Monuments Man Investigates," *Archives of American Art*, https://www.aaa.si.edu/blog/2014/04/recovering-gold-and-regalia-monuments-man-investigates (April 11, 2014).

212. The "morgue" was Time Inc.'s research archive in New York.

213. Robert Capa's iconic photo of the "Victorious Yank" was used on the cover of the May 14, 1945, issue of *Life*. It depicts an American soldier standing in front of the huge swastika above the center of the main grandstand, which was blown up shortly thereafter. Olson disapproved of the explosion, writing in his December 1946 novel notes, "Nuremberg. the great swastika. exploding it thought up by rear correspondents for safe story aftermath, symbolic. What price news?" Footage of the explosion can be viewed online: United News Company, accession no. 1992.529.1, United States Holocaust Memorial Museum.

214. The city was taken between April 16 and 20.

215. Correct spelling: *Männleinlaufen*.

216. City councilmen Fries and Schmeissner led Walter Horn of the U.S. "Monuments Men" to the Imperial Regalia." Ueno, "Recovering Gold and Regalia."

217. Henning's official account can be found in Dann, *Dachau 29 April, 1945*, 15.

218. Dann, *Dachau 29 April, 1945*, 83. For Hazard's first photo of the survivor, see Dann, *Dachau 29 April, 1945*, 76.

219. Decades later, the misplaced print was stamped "The *LIFE* Magazine Collection, 2005" and eventually wound up in the collection of the International Center for Photography, New York. Hazard has explained that "most of the negatives of these *Reveille* scenes were made available to the press pool (a regular depository for official army photographers) and are lost as far as I know. . . . I processed the negatives and made several contact prints and/or enlargements for press pool use. The prints or negatives were made available to the wire services on demand." William Hazard, Letter to Art Lee, October 10, 1994, Rainbow Division Veterans Archives, Box 16, Folder 1, Records, Archives, and Special Collections, University of Nebraska–Lincoln Libraries.

220. Suellen McDaniel, e-mail to author, August 11, 2023.

221. Hugh C. Daly, *42nd "Rainbow" Infantry Division: A Combat History of World War II* (Baton Rouge, LA: Army & Navy Publishing Company, 1946), 104. See also https://archive.org/details/42ndRainbowInfantryDivisionACombatHistoryOfWorldWarIi/mode/1up.

222. "He just kind of gazed down the river and said 'I don't really like to talk about that.'" Waxman, "Long-Forgotten Cables Reveal What *Time*'s Correspondent Saw at the Liberation of Dachau," *Time*, April 21, 2020, https://www.time.com/5812523/liberation-of-dachau-time-reporter.

223. Olson forgot to include the date at the top of "RCA" Cable 47, but he mentioned three times in the text that "tomorrow" would be April 30. The second version states the cable was "rec'd April 30, 1945."

224. As a journalist, Olson was accustomed to gathering facts and recording them quickly in a typed account. Within hours, he sent this report to military censors hoping for the earliest-possible publication.

225. It is now known that Auschwitz-Birkenau was the largest concentration camp in the Third Reich. See "Auschwitz Birkenau German Nazi Concentration and Extermination Camp (1940–1945)," UNESCO World Heritage Convention, https://whc.unesco.org/en/list/31/#:~:text=Auschwitz%20Birkenau%20was%20the%20largest,combined%20extermination%20with%20forced%20labour.

226. "I for item": I Company.

227. Downard was part of the 42nd "Rainbow" Division.

228. Lieutenant Colonel Felix Sparks led the 157th Regiment; the 45th is known as the Thunderbird Division.

229. In Germany, a concentration camp was called *konzentrationslager* or "KZ" for short.

230. In the second version of the cable, this word is "couves" (a typographical error).

231. Suellen R. McDaniel, editor of *Rainbow Reveille* and *Rainbow Trail History Newsletters*, Rainbow Division Veterans Foundation, has meticulously researched which soldiers were involved in this sequence of events.

232. *Rainbow Reveille* photographer Sergeant William "Hap" Hazard caught this moment with his camera; Olson (wearing glasses) stands in the background.

233. The word "others" has a line struck through it in pencil, and the word "dead" is written above it.

234. Ridder of the *St. Paul Pioneer Press-Dispatch* (one of the Ridder family's newspapers).

235. The literal translation is "shower room." Olson amended his reference to bathing in Cable 48.

236. Brackets are penciled around the word "Fifteenth," and the word has been crossed out.

237. The name is misspelled; Olson misread the spelling on the sheet of paper that Nerin Gun handed to him on that day. It includes Gun's professional details. After the war, Gun published a memoir called *The Day of the Americans* (New York: Fleet Publishing Corp., 1966).

238. Probably the International Prisoners Committee.

239. In the first few hours of Dachau's liberation, the main gate was tightly controlled while pockets of fighting continued inside the compound. During that time, two incidents occurred: Dachau guards were executed by a handful of U.S. soldiers (see also Olson, Cable 49), and, shortly thereafter, General Henning Linden of the 42nd "Rainbow" Division got into an altercation when Lieutenant Colonel Felix Sparks of the 45th "Thunderbird" Division refused to cede control of the camp. By nightfall, soldiers, medics, supplies, and more journalists began to stream through the camp's gates and continued to arrive for days and weeks to come.

240. Linden mentions Olson by name in his *Report on Surrender of Dachau*, which was submitted on May 2, 1945, to Major General Harry J. Collins, HQ, 42nd Infantry Division: "I then took three reporters—Mr. Olson of *Time-Life*, Miss Higgins of the New York *Herald Tribune*, and Mr. Cowan of the Associated Press, with myself, four of my guards, the aide [Lieutenant William Cowling], and representatives of the Prisoners Committee on a brief tour of the camp." Dann, *Dachau 29 April, 1945*, 15.

241. Olson's account echoes Cowan's in a number of ways, and Cowan mentions Olson by name in his own article: "Inside as well as outside were gas chambers, with crematory ovens adjoining. Sid Olsen *[sic]*, of *Time* magazine; Walter Riddler *[sic]*, of the St. Paul *Dispatch*, and I followed a fresh trail of blood into one brick building with a huge smokestack." Howard Cowan, "Dachau Prison Camp Taken, 32,000 Set Free by Yanks," Associated Press, May 1, 1945.

242. "Jolliest" was changed to "wooliest" in the second version.

243. According to Scott Corbett, "At one point a couple of correspondents and I came to a large open area, possibly the Eikeplatz, when three burly liberated Czech inmates who had been given arms stuck their rifles into our bellies, probably because we all had the green patches on our lapels worn by correspondents. I think we all yelled, 'We're Americans!' in the same split-second. Fortunately, they got the idea." Scott Corbett, Letter to Art Lee, January 1995, Box 16, Rainbow Division Veterans Association, Records, Archives, and Special Collections, University of Nebraska–Lincoln Libraries.

244. *Life* photographer Scherman is perhaps best known for his portrait of photojournalist Lee Miller as she bathed in Hitler's bathtub. Scherman traveled to Dachau with Miller, whose photos have become symbols of the horrors of the Holocaust. Antony

Penrose, (ed.), *Lee Miller's War: Beyond D-Day* (London: Thames & Hudson, 2005), 12. See also Lee Miller, "Believe It: Lee Miller Cables from Germany," *Vogue*, June 1, 1945, 103–5.

245. SS Lieutenant Wickert surrendered the camp; Victor Maurer was a representative of the International Red Cross.

246. While Olson could hear distant cheering, perhaps triggered by Higgins's arrival, Higgins reported that she could hear fighting from somewhere within the camp: "While a United States 45th Infantry Division patrol was still fighting a way down through S.S. barracks to the north, our jeep and two others from the 42nd Infantry drove into the camp inclosure through the southern entrance." Marguerite Higgins,"33,000 Dachau Captives Freed by the 7th Army," *Herald Tribune*, April 29, 1945 (delayed).

247. Sidney Olson, Cable to David Hulburd, May 2, 1945, Time Inc. Bio Files, MS 3009-RG 2, New-York Historical Society.

248. Kurt Schuschnigg was the exiled chancellor of Austria. Martin Niemoeller was a German theologian and Lutheran pastor who, though politically conservative and nationalistic, broke with Hitler early on.

249. Some political prisoners were force marched by their Nazi captors to Niederdorf in the Italian Tyrol; after a tense standoff, they were freed by the U.S. Fifth Army on May 5, 1945.

250. Parts of Cable 49 were included in Olson's aforementioned article, "Defeated Land," *Life*, May 14, 1945.

251. Lauda is located more than two hours northwest of Dachau.

252. In his *Life* article, "Inchach" was changed to the correct spelling of "Aichach," a town 35 minutes northwest of Dachau. Olson is describing the events of Sunday morning, April 29, *before* he arrived at Dachau.

253. Here Olson described the events of the afternoon on April 29. It has been well documented that several American soldiers from the 157th Infantry Regiment were responsible for executing up to 18 German guards in an area called the coal yard. Interestingly, Olson wrote that "Poles" had done the shooting. Did he have all the facts, did he mask some of the facts, or did some prisoners carry out additional executions in this location?

254. Here Olson described being in Munich on May 1.

255. *Hauptsturmfuhrer*: rank equivalent to that of a captain in the Nazi paramilitary.

256. The Munich, or Beer Hall, *Putsch* was a failed coup attempt by Hitler and others to seize power in Munich. Hitler was accused of treason and spent five years in Landsberg Prison, not far from Dachau, where he wrote *Mein Kampf*.

257. Not only did Olson's editors follow his suggestion regarding his piece about Nuremberg, but they also took his advice by publishing "Displaced Persons: The Millions of People the Nazis Uprooted Start Their Great Trek" and "DP's Return: A Frenchman Goes Home," *Life*, May 14, 1945.

258. The events described by Ridder must have taken place May 2 or 3, the only nights Olson was in Innsbruck. Ridder, it may be recalled, accompanied Olson through parts of Dachau. Walter Ridder, "Somewhere in Germany," *Aberdeen Morning News*, May 23, 1945.

259. On May 7, 1945, Germany signed an unconditional surrender at Reims. V-E Day was declared on May 8. Also on May 7, Olson's Dachau article was published in *Time*.

260. Henry Luce, Cable to Sidney Olson, May 5, 1945, Time Inc. Bio Files, MS 3009-RG 2, New-York Historical Society.

261. Luce's telegram was waiting for Olson when he arrived Paris the evening of May 6.

262. Sidney Olson, Cable to Henry Luce, May 7, 1945, Time Inc. Bio Files, MS 3009-RG 2, New-York Historical Society.

263. After reading Olson's cable, Luce wrote "CBL" in pencil at the top, directing the memo to his wife Clare Boothe Luce. Boothe Luce had seen the horrors inside Buchenwald on April 21.

264. Henry Luce, Cable to Sidney Olson, May 7, 1945, Time Inc. Bio Files, MS 3009-RG 2, New-York Historical Society.

265. Sidney Olson, Cable to David Hulburd, May 7, 1945, Time Inc. Bio Files, MS 3009-RG 2, New-York Historical Society.

266. General Anthony C. McAuliffe, 103rd Infantry Division.

267. General Jacob L. Devers, Sixth Army Group. A cable about Devers has not been located.

268. Colonel Henry J. P. Harding, 410th Infantry Division.

269. Larchmont realtor.

270. Nickname for Zembra.

271. We know from Olson's diaries and letters to Zembra that he disliked working for T. S. Matthews at *Time*, so Billings may have expected Olson to migrate to *Life* or *Fortune* on his return. John S. Billings, Memo to Larsen, May 10, 1945, Time Inc. Subject Files, MS 3009-RG 1, New-York Historical Society.

272. Olson saved his Maison des Alliés entry pass as well as his membership card from Club 45.

273. Probably Cicely Rodger, who worked in the *Time-Life* offices in Paris and was married to George Rodger, British war correspondent for *Life*.

274. A few lines from Cable 53 were used in "The Army's Guests," *Time*, May 21, 1945, 56–58.

275. SHAEF assigned a select number of reporters, including Kennedy, to cover Germany's unconditional surrender at Reims. They were told to suppress this news until the Russians could arrange a similar surrender in Berlin. Kennedy broke the story early, believing it was the right thing to do. Many journalists felt they had been unfairly "scooped," and most were furious about the absurdity—and danger—of delaying the announcement. See also Kennedy, *Ed Kennedy's War*.

276. In 1948, Olson returned to Germany to cover the Berlin Airlift, where he was would have been, presumably, subject to military censorship once again.

277. In Paris, Kennedy's detractors among the press signed a petition decrying his actions; Olson did not sign it. "Writers Charge AP with Deliberate Double-Cross," *The Capital Times*, May 8, 1945.

278. On May 14, *Life* published "Defeated Land."

279. RCAF Station, Newfoundland, Canada.

280. Stephenville Air Base, Newfoundland, Canada.

CHAPTER III

1. Olson Diary, July 13, 1945.
2. Sidney Olson, Time Inc. Bio Files, MS 3009-RG 2, New-York Historical Society.
3. Japan's surrender was announced in the United States on August 15, 1945. Olson was writing an article about Anderson, Clayton & Company, the world's largest trader of cotton: "Will Clayton's Cotton," *Fortune*, November 1945.
4. Sidney Olson, Novel Notes, August 17, 1945.
5. Sidney Olson, "The Great Throat—First in Films, First on the Air, and First on the Phonographs of His Countrymen," *Fortune*, January 1947, 128–35, 144, 146, 148, 150, 153–54, 156, 158, 160.
6. *FYI* newsletter, Time Inc., undated (ca. April 1947).
7. "The Republicans: The Honeymoon Is Over. The G.O.P. Is Hard at Work, in a State of Tension—For It Cannot Win in 1948 with a Sawdust Candidate," *Fortune*, April 1947, 77–85, 213–15, 217–18, 220, 223–24, 226, 228.
8. Barney Balaban, Letter to Sidney Olson, May 27, 1947; "Paramount: Oscar for Profits," *Fortune*, June 1947.
9. Katharine Graham, "The Magazine Rack," *Washington Post*, November 23, 1947. Graham led the *Post* from 1963 to 1991.
10. Sidney Olson, "The Movie Hearings," *Life*, November 24, 1947, 137–48.
11. Sidney Olson, "The MacArthur Gamble," *Life*, April 5, 1948, 55; Sidney Olson, "The Democratic Plan to Draft Eisenhower," *Life*, April 12, 1948, 48–50.
12. Sidney Olson, Letter to Henry Luce, September 20, 1948, Henry R. Luce Papers, MS 3014, New-York Historical Society. Series V. Subject Files: Clay, Lucius D.
13. Sidney Olson, Novel Notes, January 5, 1948.
14. The footage is available on YouTube.
15. Robert T. Elson, *The World of Time Inc.: The Intimate History of a Publishing Enterprise, Vol. 2, 1941–1960* (New York: Atheneum, 1973), 93–94.
16. John Billings, Composition Notebook, February 16, 1950, 230–31, John Shaw Billings Papers, South Caroliniana Library, University of South Carolina.
17. Billings Notebook, February 17, 1950, 232–34.
18. Sidney A. Olson, Letter to Henry Luce, February 17, 1950, Time Inc. Bio Files, MS 3009-RG 2, New-York Historical Society.
19. *Fortune's* Editorial Offices, 350 Fifth Avenue, New York (the Empire State Building).
20. Like all senior editors, Olson had been obliged to work Wednesday through Sunday, sacrificing weekends with his family.
21. A few days earlier, on July 10, 1945, he remarked in his diary, that he had "lunched with Del at Oak Room of Plaza; he not keen to have me on *Fortune* quite apparently; the old Matthews-Grover-Hulburd-Divver axis still at work agin me. . . . My morale began to drag, but Harry called me up . . . and told me to keep my chin up."
22. Case was a contributing editor at *Vogue*.

23. Between 1945 and 1950, Olson made numerous attempts to describe his frightening experience at Kapelsche Veer.

24. *Schmeisser:* German submachine gun.

25. Cargylls: division of Canadian soldiers.

26. Olson declined to attend several ceremonies where he would have received a theater ribbon and a "certificate of appreciation for your patriotic service as a news correspondent with our Armed Forces in an overseas theater of combat." The first was held on November 23, 1946, at the Statler Hotel in Washington, D.C., and the second was held on March 4, 1947, at the Waldorf Astoria in New York City. Because he failed to appear, General Hodges invited him to an informal meeting on April 9, 1947, at Governors Island. Olson again declined. General Hodge finally wrote him this personal letter of thanks.

27. Olson had just been fired by John Billings, with Luce's approval. Sidney Olson, Letter to Henry Luce, September 17, 1945, Time Inc. Bio Files, MS 3009-RG 2, New-York Historical Society.

28. William O'Dwyer, mayor, New York City, 1946–1950.

29. Olson wanted to reassure Luce that he would not be among the ex-*Time* men to publish a "tell-all."

CHAPTER IV

1. "Paramount: Oscar for Profits," *Fortune*, June 1947, 90–95, 208–21.

2. Frank Cleaver, Letter to Sidney Olson, February 28, 1950.

3. The signed contracts (both dated June 29, 1950) and one screenplay (June 28, 1950) were found among Olson's papers; the screenplay for *The Traitor* has not been located.

4. Sidney Olson, Letter to "Dan" (probably Dan Seymour of J. Walter Thompson), June 3, 1970, 2.

5. "Sidney Olson, one of Henry Luce's important writers on *Fortune*, is now at Paramount doing an original story for the screen." Hedda Hopper, *Daily News*, March 26, 1950.

6. Jimmy Sarno, Letter to Sidney Olson, September 13, 1950.

7. After receiving bequests from Henry Ford and his son Edsel in the late 1940s, the foundation had grown into the largest private endowment in the world. *Report of the Study for the Ford Foundation on Policy and Program* (Detroit: Ford Foundation, 1950).

8. Henry Luce, Letter to Sidney Olson, September 22, 1950.

9. "Personnel News," *New York Herald Tribune*, May 31, 1951.

10. William B. Lewis, Letter to Sidney Olson, October 9, 1951.

11. Edwin Cox, in William D. Patterson, ed., *America: Miracle at Work: The Best Public Interest Advertising of 1952 Based on the First Saturday Annual Review Awards* (Englewood Cliffs, NJ: Prentice Hall, 1953), 41.

12. Ford Motor Company, "Their Future Is at Our Fingertips," in *The American Road—XI* (Kenyon & Eckhardt, 1952).

13. The photo, taken in 1946, was part of the "Family of Man" exhibition, curated by Edward Steichen, at the Museum of Modern Art in 1955.

14. Henry Luce, Letter to Sidney Olson, October 20, 1952.

15. Alfred Friendly, "Ford Was Not Simply a Writer," *Washington Post*, May 17, 1953. The book was not published until 1963.

16. "Ford's Half-Century TV Cavalcade: A 500G, 2-Web Star-Studded Jubilee," *Variety*, June 17, 1953.

17. *J. Walter Thompson Company News* 11, no. 24 (June 11, 1956).

18. Sidney A. Olson Papers, 1957, J. Walter Thompson Company Archives, David M. Rubenstein Rare Book & Manuscript Library, Duke University.

19. Sidney Olson, interview by Colin Dawkins (transcript 1), July 19, 1979, 24–25.

20. The Ford Falcon was introduced in April 1959. Sidney Olson, interview by Colin Dawkins (transcript 1), July 19, 1979, 24–25.

21. The Ford Mustang was introduced at the New York World's Fair in 1964.

22. Lee Iacocca with William Novak, *Iacocca: An Autobiography* (New York: Random House, 1986), 63.

23. Clare Boothe Luce, Letter to Sidney Olson, 1967.

Works Cited

Abzug, Robert H. *Inside the Vicious Heart*. New York: Oxford University Press, 1985.

Brinkley, Alan. *The Publisher*. New York: Vintage Books, 2010.

Butcher, Harry C. *My Three Years with Eisenhower*. New York: Simon & Schuster, 1946.

Cochran Kennedy, Julia, ed. *Ed Kennedy's War: V-E Day, Censorship, & the Associated Press*. Baton Rouge: Louisiana State University Press, 2012.

Daly, Hugh C. *42nd "Rainbow" Infantry Division: A Combat History of World War II*. Baton Rouge, LA: Army & Navy Publishing Company, 1946.

Dann, Sam, ed. *Dachau 29 April, 1945: The Rainbow Liberation Memoirs*. Lubbock: Texas Tech University Press, 1998.

Department of State. *Memorandum of the Post War International Information Program of the United States*. Washington, DC: U.S. Government Printing Office, 1945.

Elson, Robert T. *Time Inc.: The Intimate History of a Publishing Enterprise*. Vol. 1, *1923–1941*. New York: Atheneum, 1968.

———. *The World of Time Inc.: The Intimate History of a Publishing Enterprise*. Vol. 2, *1941–1960*. New York: Atheneum, 1973.

Fussell, Paul. *Wartime: Understanding and Behavior in the Second World War*. New York: Oxford University Press, 1989.

Goodwin, Doris Kearns. *No Ordinary Time: Franklin & Eleanor Roosevelt: The Home Front in World War II*. New York: Touchstone/Simon & Schuster, 1994.

Gun, Nerin E. *The Day of the Americans*. New York: Fleet Publishing Corp., 1966.

Hersey, John. *Men on Bataan*. New York: Alfred A. Knopf, 1942.

Iacocca, Lee, with William Novak. *Iacocca: An Autobiography*. New York: Random House, 1986.

Kennedy, Julia, ed. *Ed Kennedy's War: V-E Day, Censorship, & the Associated Press*. Baton Rouge: Louisiana State University Press, 2012.

Launius, Roger D. "World War II in Utah." *Utah History Encyclopedia*. https://www.uen.org/utah_history_encyclopedia/w/WWII.shtml (accessed January 10, 2024).

Leuchtenburg, William E. "Franklin D. Roosevelt: Life before the Presidency." Miller Center, University of Virginia. https://www.millercenter.org/president/fdroosevelt/life-before-the-presidency (accessed January 10, 2024).

Lipstadt, Deborah E. *Beyond Belief: The American Press & the Coming of the Holocaust 1933–1945*. New York: Free Press, 1986.

Makos, Adam. *Spearhead: An American Tank Gunner, His Enemy, and a Collision of Lives in World War II*. New York: Ballantine Books, 2019.

Midgley, Leslie. *How Many Words Do You Want? An Insider's Stories of Print and Television Journalism*. New York: Birch Lane Press, 1988.

Olson, Sidney. "The Defeated Land." In *Great Reading from Life: A Treasury of the Best Stories and Articles Chosen by the Editors*. New York: Harper & Brothers, 1960.

———. *Young Henry Ford: A Picture History of the First Forty Years*. Detroit: Wayne State University Press, 1963.

Patterson, William D., ed. *America: Miracle at Work: The Best Public Interest Advertising of 1952 Based on the First Saturday Annual Review Awards*. Englewood Cliffs, NJ: Prentice Hall, 1953.

Penrose, Antony, ed. *Lee Miller's War: Beyond D-Day*. London: Thames & Hudson, 2005.

Pogue, Forrest C. *United States Army in World War II: European Theater of Operations, The Supreme Command*. Washington, DC: Office of the Chief of Military History, Department of the Army, 1954.

Report of the Study for the Ford Foundation on Policy and Program. Detroit: Ford Foundation, 1950.

Rooney, Andy. *My War*. New York: PublicAffairs, 1995.

Sherwood, Robert E. *Roosevelt and Hopkins: An Intimate History*. New York: Harper & Brothers, 1948.

Stacey, C. P. *The Canadian Army, 1939–1945: An Official Historical Summary*. Ottawa: Edmond Cloutier, 1948.

Weber, Ronald. *Dateline—Liberated Paris: The Hotel Scribe and the Invasion of the Press*. Lanham, MD: Rowman & Littlefield, 2019.

Wertenbaker, Charles. *The Death of Kings*. New York: Random House, 1954.

Who's Who in America. Vol. 23, *1944–1945*. Chicago: A. N. Marquis Company, 1944.

Winfield, B. H. "Franklin D. Roosevelt's Efforts to Influence the News during His First Term Press Conferences." *Presidential Studies Quarterly* 11, no. 2 (Spring 1981): 191.

Zelizer, Barbie. *Remembering to Forget: Holocaust Memory through the Camera's Eye*. Chicago: University of Chicago Press, 1998.

MANUSCRIPTS AND PERSONAL PAPERS

Archives of Iowa Broadcasting, Wartburg College. WHO Radio Collection. WWII Broadcast Scripts from Front.

Beinecke Rare Book and Manuscript Library, Yale Collection of American Literature. Mary Welsh Hemingway Papers.

Benson Ford Research Center, The Henry Ford. Mills, Edmunds and Nevins and Hills Series. Benson Ford Research Center, The Henry Ford. Sidney Olson Research Notes on Henry Ford, 1952–1953.

David M. Rubenstein Rare Book and Manuscript Library, Duke University. J. Walter Thompson Company. Sidney A. Olson Papers, 1957.

Harry S. Truman Presidential Library. James T. Quirk Papers. Box 1: WWII, 1942–1946.

Houghton Library, Harvard University. Dispatches from *Time* Correspondents: First Series. Roy Larsen Papers.

New-York Historical Society. Henry R. Luce Papers, MS 3014.

New-York Historical Society. Time Inc. Bio Files, MS 3009.

Private Collection, Sidney A. Olson Papers.

South Caroliniana Library, University of South Carolina. John Shaw Billings Papers.

University of Nebraska–Lincoln Libraries, Records, Archives, and Special Collections. Rainbow Division Veterans Association (RDVA).

Index

357

Ford, Edsel, 354n7

Ford, Henry, 2, 317, 354n7

Ford, Henry, II, 317

Ford Motor Company, Willow Run bombers of, 2

Fortresses. *See* Flying Fortresses

Fortune: Crosby in, 297; Isbrandtsen in, 300; Manhattan Project and, 39; "Paramount" in, 297; Reader's Digest and, 312; "The Republicans" in, 297; senior editor at, 295, 296, 302–4

Fort Worth Star-Telegram, 43

42nd Infantry Division (Rainbow Division): at Dachau concentration camp, 250, 251, 252, 255–56, 259, 262; in Geldersheim, 223; Munich and, 272–73; in Nuremberg, 239–40; in Schweinfurt, 219, 222–24, 228; 242nd Regiment of, 223–24

45th Infantry Division (Thunderbird Division), 350n239; in Burkenbuhl, 236; at Dachau concentration camp, 252, 253; in Nuremberg, 239–40

400 Eight Air Force, 70

410th Regiment, 283

14th Armored Division, 239

Fourth Armored Division, 177, 181, 184, 190, 200; German

prisoners of war of, 185–86; in Germany, 204

France/French: at Dachau concentration camp, 257, 258–59, 260; in Germany, 214; in Munich, 272; as slave laborers, 214, 229, 233, 255. *See also specific locations and topics*

Frankfurt, 246

Frauenkirche., in Nuremberg, 240, 243

Fredericks, Robert T. (Maj. General), 239, 309, 349n209

Frederick the Great, 185

freedom of the press, 289

Freidin, Seymour, 288–90

Friedenthal, David, 249

Fries, Konrad, 348n216

Fuerbringer, Otto, 26, 303; beer and, 99

Fuerbringer, Winnie, 303

Furst, Peter, 264–65

Fussell, Paul, 35

Gaffey, Hugh J. (Maj. General), 181

Geilenkirchen, 86

Geldersheim, 218; 42nd Infantry Division in, 223

Gellhorn, Martha, 106, 343n107

Gemünd, 112

Genghis Khan, 246

German deserters, 77

German evacuees: Hitler and, 108; in Holland, 93, 108

McIntyre, Marvin H., 8
McLain, Raymond S.
(General), 153
McNair, Lesley (Lt. General), 96
Mein Kampf (Hitler), 351n256
Die Meistersinger (Wagner), 240
Men on Bataan (Hersey), 347n188
Merken, 137
Merman, Ethel, 317
Merrick, Colonel, 288
Meyer, Eugene, 6, 296, 336n20
Michailovich, 80
Middle East (Guedalla), 75–76
Midgley, Leslie, 152, 309–10,
345n143, 345n156, 345n160;
gin rummy with, 172
Miller, Lee, 350n244
Mills, Hillis, 26, 286, 303
minefields: at Cologne, 159–60;
at Dachau concentration camp,
257; Germany supply for, 138;
at Holland, 103, 129
Moller, Joseph A. (Col.), 57,
341n60
Monnet, Jean, 13
Montgomery, Bernarrd "Monty"
(General): at Aachen, 153; dim
view of, 59
Monuments Men, 348n211,
348n216
Moore, James (Brig. General), 130
Mormon, 2
Mosquito, of RAF, 68, 70, 76
"The Movie Hearings," in
Life, 298

Mulheim, Captain, 164, 272
Munchen-Gladbach, 345n142;
Eighth Air Force and, 148;
looting of, 151; RAF and, 148;
29th Division at, 142–44
Munich, 36, 206, 339n27; Dachau
concentration camp and, 274;
42nd Infantry Division and,
272–73; German prisoners
of war in, 270–71; Poles in,
272; Russians in, 272; SS in,
273; underground movements
in, 274
murals, at Dachau concentration
camp, 256–57
Murray, Lt., 295
Murrow, Edward R., 317
Myers, Bob, 197, 202

Nagaski, 39, 339n27
Namur, 90
National Conference on Crime, 6
National Recovery
Administration, 7–8
National Review, 337n54
Nazism, 77; ELAS and, 80;
German lack of motivation
for, 155; hatred for, 273;
indoctrination of, 274–75; in
Nuremberg, 241–42; political
clamps of, 199. *See also specific
individuals and topics*
Neckar River, 211, 212; beauty of,
213, 233
Nerin, Djun, 258

ABOUT THE AUTHOR

Margot Clark-Junkins attended Mount Holyoke College and received an MA in design and curatorial studies from the Cooper Hewitt, Smithsonian Design Museum. She writes a column called "Following the Front" for Substack and is currently working on a book of short stories.